ALSO BY JOHN B. "RED" CUMMINGS, JR.

*Murder, Manslaughter, and Mayhem on the SouthCoast,
Volume One: 1800 to 1969* (2017)

*Murder, Manslaughter, and Mayhem on the SouthCoast,
Volume Two: 1970 to 1999* (2017)

*Lobstah Tales: A History of the Moby Dick/Back Eddy
Restaurant in Westport, Massachusetts* (2016)

Cream of the Crop: Fall River's Best and Brightest (2014)

*The Last Fling: Hurricane Carol 1954,
Stories from Westport, Massachusetts* (2011)

MURDER, MANSLAUGHTER, AND MAYHEM
ON THE SOUTHCOAST
VOLUME THREE 2000 TO 2016

INCLUDES UPDATED CASES FROM 1800-1999

John B. "Red" Cummings, Jr.
with Stefani Koorey, PhD

Hillside Media

Westport, Massachusetts

Hillside Media
Westport, Massachusetts

© 2018 John B. "Red" Cummings Jr. All Rights Reserved.

Printed in the United States of America. No part of this book may be used or reproduced in any manner whatsoever without written permission from the publisher except in the case of brief quotations embodied in critical articles and reviews.

All inquires should be sent to:
John B. Cummings Jr.
Hillside Media
245 Old Harbor Road
Westport, MA 02790
Tel: 508.636.2831
or John@hillsidemedia.net

Printed in the United States of America on acid-free paper.

Book and cover design by Stefani Koorey, PearTree Press, Fall River, MA

MURDER, MANSLAUGHTER, AND MAYHEM ON THE SOUTHCOAST

Dedication

To the Survivors

This book and its prior two volumes highlights the atrocities of the times in the SouthCoast of Massachusetts and Rhode Island. From the mid 1800s until the start of the current century, murders and manslaughters have occurred in the area at an alarming rate.

Until the start of the twenty-first century, most deaths in the SouthCoast were at the hands of those born and raised in the area. The influx of new residents generated a higher crime rate and murder rate on the SouthCoast. In the following pages, like those that have come before, the reader will encounter mini-biographies of those who have been murdered. Most of the victims were somehow in conflict with the killers—but not all. All of the survivors suffered the same heartbreak of losing a loved one due to a horrible event.

Parents, grandparents, siblings, spouses, and children experienced the ultimate heartache. That there were arrests and convictions in these crimes is really no consolation to the victims' family members. Justice for a dead victim is hollow indeed to those left behind. And anyone who thinks that a guilty verdict brings some kind of "closure" is sadly mistaken.

We salute those still saddened by these terrible events and keep them in out hearts and prayers.

CONTENTS

Preface	xv
Foreword	xvii
Editor's Note	xix
1. 1800-1999: Volumes One and Two Revisited	**1**
1826 Daniel Charles	3
1843 Silas Williams	5
1851 Polly Barrows	7
1853 Ellen Murphy	9
1855 Valentine S. Almy	11
1856 David S. Hathaway Jr.	12
1859 Samuel B. Manchester	14
1871 Bruneau Berarde	15
1880 Charles H. Thomas	18
1881 Annie McMullen	21
1881 Exilda Charon	27
1881 Raymond P. Dennis	30
1884 John Schofield	34
1885 William D. Slocum	36
1901 John Mowbry	38
1902 Peleg Cornell	40
1903 Angelene and Amedee Chabot	43
1903 Tillinghast Kirby	45
1909 Hattie Carter	49
1914 Annie Walsh	50
1914 Alice Grace Faria	53
1914 Delvina Grenier Blanchard	54
1916 Diana Jeffrey	55
1924 Walenty Juszynski	57
1927 Ernest Pelletier	58

1931 Hope, Dwight, and Aveling Allinson	59
1938 Wilfred Bedard	61
1947 Samuel Genesky	63
1948 Joseph Bolay	64
1965 Helen Rogers, Napoleon Poisson	65
1965 Judith Ann Szatek, Raymond G. Frenette	66
1966 Charles Caton King Jr.	68
1966 Frank Duarte	69
1969 Anthony Tosca, Duane L. Blake	70
1984 Edward LeBlanc update	75
1992 Joseph Freitas	77
1994 Daniel Correia	79
1994 Jeffrey Rosanina	81
1995 Timothy Lamere	83
1996 Jane Doe	85
1997 Michael Barros	86
1997 Filipe Barros	87
1998 Demarco Traynum	89
2. 2000-2009: A New Century of Hope	**93**
2000 Athena Harvey	95
2000 John Duarte	97
2000 Joseph Canto	100
2000 Nancy Shonheinz	103
2001 Raymond Matos, Robert Hebert Jr.	107
2001 George Carpenter	108
2001 Rose Moniz	110
2001 Oranuch Sousa	111
2001 Lisandro Medina, Edward Negron	112
2001 Marcus Cruz	115
2001 Ivandro Correia	116
2002 Elijah Omar Bey	117
2002 Christopher Farrington	118
2002 Sheryl Gordon	119
2002 David Gasiar, Gary Fragoza	120
2002 Ryan Aguiar	121

2002	Marlene Rose	123
2002	Elizabeth Thomas, Kenneth Aubin	124
2002	Albert Lopes	125
2002	Edward J. Tolan Jr.	126
2003	David Silva	128
2003	Joshual Santos	132
2003	Robert Bernard	137
2003	Leonard Silviera	138
2003	Keone Mendes	140
2003	Patrick Murphy	141
2003	Brendon Camara	142
2003	Jose Torres	146
2003	Michael White	147
2003	William Cassavant	151
2003	Alberto Gonzalez	152
2003	Laurie Tavares	157
2004	Frank Pereira Jr.	159
2004	Rey Davila	160
2004	Jessica Corvelo	163
2005	Courtney Sau	164
2005	Tom Murray	166
2005	James Gauoette	169
2005	Susy Goulart	171
2005	Dana Haywood	174
2005	Suzanna M. Soares	177
2005	Anderson Rosa	179
2005	Christopher Barros	182
2005	Rudolph Santos	185
2006	Krista Lucianno	188
2006	Nathan Harrigan	190
2006	Justin Barry-Henderson	191
2006	Thomas Reynolds	192
2006	Antonio Semedo	193
2006	John Oliveira Jr.	194
2006	Valerie Oransky	197
2006	Esteban Tum Chach	199

2006	James Cadet	201
2006	Dwayne Lassiter	203
2006	Wayne Mendes	204
2006	Tory Marandos, Robert Carreiro, Scott Medeiros	205
2007	Shakeem Davis	206
2007	Jason Glover	208
2007	William Dupras	209
2007	Baby James Cerce	211
2007	Jerome Woodard	212
2007	Baby Joshua Pacheco	214
2007	Albon Wilson	215
2008	Edwin Medina	216
2008	Frederick Thompkins	218
2008	Veronica Rosales, Luis Moulds-Tiul	219
2008	Joshua Fitzgerald	220
2008	Derek Hogue	224
2008	David Walsh	225
2009	Robyn Mendes, Katherine Gomes	227
2009	Troy Pina	228
2009	John K. Martin	230
2009	Wayne Rice	232
2009	Bianco Rosado	233
2009	Charles Smith	234
2009	Nettie Becht, Luis Diaz	235
2009	Scott Monteiro	238
2009	Elizabeth Barrow	241
2009	Osvaldo Gonsalez Martinez	242

3. 2010-2016: It's Not Getting Better — 245

2010	Arthur Burton	247
2010	Andrew Taylor	249
2010	Jonathan Nieves	250
2010	David Arruda and Alfred Arruda Jr.	252
2010	Conrad Beaulieu	253

2010 Olivia Cruz	256
2010 Michael Correia	258
2010 Edward Platts	261
2011 Michael Duarte	263
2012 Reksmey Tieng	266
2012 Aja Pascual	267
2012 Lisa Mello	268
2013 Baby Ariel Eluziario	269
2013 Rebecca Felteau	270
2013 Tiffany Ann Durfee	271
2013 Mitchell Stevenson, Christian Wilson	272
2013 Joyce Howland	273
2013 Sharone Stafford	274
2014 David Rodriguez	275
2014 Conrad Roy	276
2014 Sophie Kostek	278
2014 Melissa White	279
2015 Kyle Brady	281
2015 Mabilia Maranhao, Sharif Goode	283
2015 Anthony Carvalho	284
2015 Brian Jones	285
2015 Marcel Francois	286
2015 Donald A. DePina	288
2016 Maria Branco	289
2016 John Cloud	290
2016 Sabrina DaSilva	291
2016 Jerrod Cohen	292
Unsolved Cases, 1800-2016	294
Acknowledgments & References	303
Index	307
About the Author	324

PREFACE

Our mission upon setting out to chronicle murder, manslaughter, and mayhem on the SouthCoast, was to call attention to the victims, those ordinary individuals who suffered at the hands of others.

The crimes highlighted in Volume One were primarily feuled by passion and alcohol; the murders in subsequent volumes appeared, more and more, to be connected to the purchase, sale, consumption, and distribution of illegal drugs. Prior to the opioid crisis of today—where prescription narcotics have caused a nationwide epidemic—back in the 1970s and 1990s, it was illegal street drugs that flooded our SouthCoast communities, leading to high murder rates and a larger than ever backlog of unsolved crimes. The current flow of heroin and fentanyl into our area has placed the city of New Bedford at the center of the national crisis. The US Drug Enforcement Administration (DEA) has selected the city to send a team of investigators to help battle drug trafficking—one of only six cities nationally. The high incidences of overdoes on the SouthCoast has created the need for this extra attention.

The murderers used guns, knives, axes, fists, fire, rope, and any other tools, including their bare hands, to commit their dastardly deeds. Mothers killed their children, husbands and wives killed each other, and children murdered their parents. Police officers were killed in cold blood while doing their jobs.

Murder does not discriminate. Victims and slayers came from all races, nationalities, gender, and age groups. Many used drugs or sold drugs. Some killers were just bad" people who did not regret their actions and had no qualms about how they killed their victims.

There have been quiet decades and during other times it seemed like murder was rampant. Every year in the new century saw multiple killings take place—primarily as a result of drugs and gangs who were introduced to the SouthCoast during prior decades.

The time is now to stop the hate. Stop the brutality. Stop the Murder, Manslaughter, and Mayhem in the SouthCoast.

John. B. Cummings, Jr.
October, 2018
Westport, MA

FOREWORD

John B. Cummings Jr., has again demonstrated his abiding interest in the history, personages, and mores of his beloved Fall River and its SouthCoast environs. This work involves the macabre subject of murder and mayhem, the tracing of over 399 cases from 1800 to 2016.

This overall work is divided into nine historical eras and each era is rendered in rich historical detail in a lucid style that illustrates the changing sociological background of the different periods of time. The author then capsulizes, in summary fashion, the ghastly and gruesome essence of each crime so that it can be easily grasped by the reader.

Some of the cases in the earlier volumes include the legendary Lizzie Borden double-ax murders that shocked Victorian Fall River and the world; the celebrated "Pinky" Hathaway case that scandalized the Depression Era southeast with its sexual overtones; the unsolved "roadside murders" of a series of young prostitutes in the 1980s; and the brutal drug and gang related assassinations of the gory 1990s.

The work is the result of exhaustive research, a two-year examination of the records of the Massachusetts Superior Court, the Fall River Historical Society, the Fall River Public Library, the *Fall River Herald News*, scholarly reference works on the history of the SouthCoast, and interviews with many authorities who are expert in law enforcement and in the history of Fall River and its changing social and economic patterns and customs.

The nineteenth century belief in moral progress was shattered by the catastrophic wars of the twentieth century. The horrendous killings endemic of twenty-first century urban life has established that our system of criminal law is inherently incapable of preventing murderous behavior or of successfully punishing it.

What is necessary for public peace is a return to traditional moral values, rooted in human nature and recognized by the light of conscience, which respect the sanctity and dignity of each human person. "Do unto others as you would have others do unto you" is the foundation of public order and the basis for the full and free exercise of personal rights. This work illustrates the disastrous social consequences when this precept is disdained and disregarded.

The underlying theme of this very instructive work is that virtuous behavior in conformity with deeply-held human values creates a society that is truly civil.

Edward F. Harrington
United States Senior District Judge

EDITOR'S NOTE

This book represents the third volume of murders on the SouthCoast. We were originally planning to compile enough murders to fill only two books, but as we delved deeper into the facts and circumstances of the communities in the SouthCoast region, sadly, more and more murders were uncovered.

In fact, the first section of this edition is essentially an addendum to the first two books, with 43 additional murders included. The reasons these cases were overlooked are many. In some instances, the sources for the new information were readers—they kindly emailed us and spoke with us at our various book signings and talks to let us know of them. In addition, a more painstakingly thorough search of news accounts uncovered many new cases, some of them quite tragic. Additionally, Fall River historian Phil Silvia gave us the heads up on two deaths by tragic means that he detailed in his series titled *Victorian Vistas* that helped immensely.

The eras represented in this volume include some of the most murderous ever. The violent crime rate, in which homicide is included, rose substantially in New Bedford in the years 2000-2009, prompting the resignation of the chief of police in 2003. Most of these murders were gang related, a complex back and forth of revenge killings. Because of the nature of the murders, New Bedford suffered from a "code of silence"—where witnesses were hesitant to come forward for fear of retribution. This means we have a larger than average number of unsolved cases from the late 1990s through the 2000s.

Deviating a bit from our regular format, we are including a list of unsolved crimes (as of 2015) in an effort to assist law enforcement in bringing the families of these victims some justice. But also, because so little is known about the details of these cases, a list format makes more sense than a full-page narrative.

A little explanation about legal procedure is in order to clear up any questions that might arise in the cases in this book. In Massachusetts, the order of events is as follows: Inquest, arrest (which may come before the inquest, depending on the case), arraignment and plea, Preliminary Hearing at the District Court, Grand Jury (to determine probable cause and to issue indictments), and then, if indictments are handed down, the court trial is held in the Superior Court, which for the SouthCoast region may be either New Bedford or Taunton. For murder cases in Rhode Island, called capital cases, there is no Preliminary Hearing. After probable cause if found and an indictment is issued by the Grand Jury, the case is tried in the Superior Court, which for the SouthCoast of Rhode Island (Tiverton, Little Compton) is in Newport.

You will find the arrangement in this volume similar to the other two—each of the cases are arranged in chronological order and a clearly delineated way, starting with the victim's name as the title, followed by vital information headings such as a statement of the crime, the victim, the accused, details of the murder, trial information, an afterword that brings us up to date on the story, and a further reading section that doubles as the case's bibliography.

Some of these cases have been widely covered in the press. Consequently, these stories are more fleshed out than others because there is more information from many sources to help tell the story of the crime and the victim. Because this is a location-centric book (the SouthCoast), in many cases the only source of information is one or two local newspaper stories. In these instances, the material may seem thin, but the drama of the event is important nonetheless and deserves to be told.

The SouthCoast encompasses a wide swath of cities, towns, and communities in two states. These include, in Massachusetts: Acushnet, Berkley, Dartmouth, Fairhaven, Fall River, Freetown, Marion, Mattapoisett, New Bedford, Rochester, Somerset, Swansea, Wareham, and Westport. In Rhode Island, the communities included are Little Compton and Tiverton, because of their close proximity to the other towns and cities in Massachusetts.

This book does not purport to be a comprehensive compendium but, rather, a detailed sampling of the crimes that occurred. There will be omissions—mostly due to a lack of publicly available information. In each case, however, care has been taken to insure that the facts presented are as they have been previously reported. It is the wish of the author and editor that this book is an accurate representation of the murder, manslaughter, and mayhem on the SouthCoast.

Stefani Koorey, PhD
October, 2018
Fall River, MA

CHAPTER I

1800-1999
VOLUMES I AND II REVISITED

In the first two volumes of our book, spanning the years 1800 to 1999, we detailed a total of 196 cases of murder, manslaughter and mayhem on the SouthCoast involving 219 deaths. In the interim, more murder cases were discovered and we deemed them worthy of inclusion, not only to provide a more thorough accounting of the events, but to honor the, before now, unknown victims of these heinous acts—a particularly important mission of this series.

The cases presented in this first chapter of volume three number 43, which include a total of 48 deaths. The actual number of victims is probably quite higher because we *know* we have not found *all* of the killings from this time frame. To do so with confidence would take a large team of researchers years to accomplish.

The cases in this section of our book are especially interesting, we think, as they span such a large number of years and include some "old fashioned" methods of murder. In this chapter, a mother drowned hre children by throwing them in the river and jumping in after them, committing suicide. A teenage boy killed two innocent people while they were in a car in a popular but secluded lovers' lane. Another teenager stabbed two adults to death in their apartment. And it is in this chapter that we discover someone who might just be our first serial killer—Angles Snell.

So what have we learned from the intense study of these murders in our three volumes? Husbands are more likely to murder wives than the other way around (although it does happen), women are much more likely to be victims of brutal violent and deadly attacks, and people kill people for every conceivable reason: jealousy, greed, lust, anger, financial reward, pride, and hatred. And some murders, oddly enough, seem to have no known motive other than opportunity, known as stranger killings. We discovered that thrill killers existed even in the nineteenth century, as evidenced by the senseless slaughter of men in their homes as they slept and women as they went about their daily routines.

Even though the crimes detailed in these volumes are horrific, they are nonetheless fascinating. The murders, the investigations, the trials, and the final end of the convicted all makes for a gripping examination of human nature, social norms, and governmental response. We hope you find it as engrossing to read as it was for us to write.

DANIEL CHARLES

The axe murder of "a vagrant colored man" who was living with the accused, in Tiverton, Rhode Island, on the evening of the 15th of January, 1826.

Victim: Daniel Charles, age unknown.

Accused: Sarah Howland ("a colored woman"), age unknown.

Details: The victim, Daniel Charles, was reported to have been living with Sarah Howland in Tiverton, RI. The New York *Evening Post* reports that the coroner concluded that on the evening of the 15th of January, 1826, "a quarrel took place between them at their residence, (supposed from intemperance) and in the scuffle, the light being extinguished, the prisoner seized an axe, and struck the deceased on the head, which immediately terminated his existence."

Trial: Sarah Howland was tried twice for the murder of Daniel Charles, the first trial earning her a verdict of guilty. The Supreme Court at Newport determined that this first conviction should be overturned because "Chief Justice Wilbour had, during the recess of the Court, sent to the Jury, at their request, and without the knowledge of the prisoner's counsel or the Attorney General, a written definition of the crime of murder, which was, in effect, that murder consists in willfully taking the life of a fellow being. Under this definition, the sheriff should hang a criminal by virtue of this precept, or he who should take the life of a robber or assassin, in his own defence [sic], would be equally guilty of murder, because he would do the act willfully, that is, intending to do it" (*Weekly Raleigh Register*).

Her second trial, held for three days that same March term in 1827, also returned a verdict of guilty. Sarah Howland was sentenced to death for her crime.

Afterword: Documents held in the Rhode Island State Archives and the Rhode Island Historical Society indicate that on three occasions, once in 1827 and twice in 1829, Sarah Howland petitioned the Rhode Island Assembly for a postponement of her sentence, then a continuation, and lastly commutation of her death sentence to a life sentence. All three of her petitions were granted.

Further Reading:

"Murder." *The Evening Post* (New York, New York), February 1, 1826.
"RI vs. Sarah Howland." Albert C. Green Papers, 1804-1863. Rhode Island Historical Society. Box 13, Folder 6, MSS 452, Item 6.
Weekly Raleigh Register (Raleigh, North Carolina), March 30, 1827.

Grave of Daniel Charles, horizontal marker, no carving, Town Cemetery, Common Burial Ground and Memorial Garden, Tiverton, RI. (rihistoriccemeteries.org)

SILAS WILLIAMS

―――∞∞∞―――

Murder in Freetown, Massachusetts, by beating, on August 4, 1843.

Victim: Silas Williams, 49 (born June 23, 1794).

Accused: John C. Clark (age unknown) and Calvin Thomas Jr., 18.

Details: According to the *New-York Tribune*, we learn that the *Taunton Whig* "gives the particulars of a murder in Freetown, at the house of a man named Silas Williams. It appears that two men, [John C.] Clark and [Calvin] Thomas [Jr.], went to Williams' house, where they met a third person by the name of [Alson G.] Ashley, to drink rum. The result, as might have been anticipated, was a drunken quarrel. Williams ordered Clark and Thomas out of doors. They resisted, from words proceeded to blows, and before the affray was ended, Williams was so badly beaten that he died within a day or two afterwards. Clark and Thomas have both been committed to take their trial next September."

The *Buffalo Courier* reported that "all of the murderers were arrested and taken to Taunton for examination…The precise object of this assembling together does not appear, yet it may be inferred, from a *jug of rum!*"

Ashely was discharged, reported *The Liberator*, "there being no evidence to convict him."

Trial: There are no details beyond the recording of this crime as to an indictment, trial, or conviction.

Afterword: Of note we find from genealogical records that Alson G. Ashley (1817-1845), age 26 at the time of the murder, was the brother of Silas Williams' wife Mehetible (1803-1848).

Calvin Thomas Jr. was born on February 1, 1825, and was 18 years old at the time of the murder. He joined the militia in 1846 and stayed until his death on November 28, 1863, at age 38, dying of "chronic diarrhea." He was married on June 4, 1848, at age 23, to Hope Ann Richardson (1830-1912), age 16. They had three children, Levicy Steele, Frank L., and Ellen Maxfield.

From this investigation into the life of Calvin Thomas Jr., it would not appear that he served any time for the murder of Silas Williams, and thus we might conclude he was either not brought to trial or was acquitted.

Because John C. Clark is such a common name, it was not possible to determine his outcome or if he alone was charged, convicted, and sentenced for the murder of Silas Williams.

Silas Williams left seven children when he died.

Further Reading:

"Murder." *New-York Tribune* (New York, New York), August 11, 1843.
"Murder in Freetown." *Buffalo Courier* (Buffalo, New York), August 14, 1843.
"Murder in Freetown." *Buffalo Daily Gazette* (Buffalo, New York), August 14, 1843.
"Murder in Freetown." *The Liberator* (Boston, Massachusetts), August 25, 1843.

Grave of Silas Williams, born June 22, 1795, died August 4, 1843. Rounsevell Cemetery, Freetown, Massachusetts. (Findagrave.com)

POLLY BARROWS

Husband accused of beating wife to death in Freetown, Massachusetts, on January 25, 1851.

Victim: Mary "Polly' Barrows, 46.

Accused: Isaac C. Barrows, 40.

Details: According to *The Brooklyn Daily Eagle*, "at an inquest held upon the body of Polly Barrows, of Freetown, Mass., on Saturday last, by Coroner E. W. Peirce [sic], the verdict of the jury was in substance—that the deceased came to her death in consequence of blows inflicted upon her person the evening previous, by the hands of Isaac Barrows, her husband, while in a state of intoxication. The poor woman, while passing him, accidentally knocked off his cap, whereupon, with brutal ferocity, he inflicted blows upon her that caused her death."

"We have received a communication from a respectable citizen of Freetown, containing some very severe strictures upon the decision of the Police Justice before whom Isaac Barrows was examined on the charge of murdering his wife Polly Barrows," reports the *New-York Tribune*. "A Coroner's jury, empaneled from among the citizens of Freetown, by Coroner Ebenezer W. Pierce, investigated the circumstances of the woman's death, and found upon their oaths, that it was 'caused by blows inflicted upon her person by Isaac Barrows, her husband.' Upon this verdict Barrows was committed to Taunton jail until Tuesday, when his examination took place, resulting in his discharge. No evidence was adduced for the defence whatever, and the prisoner's own counsel was willing to concede an aggravated assault and battery! Our correspondent says the decision has caused great astonishment and dissatisfaction in Freetown, and that petitions will be got up to have the Justice removed."

Afterword: The victim in this case, Mary (Goff) Barrows, sometimes known as "Polly," was born on December 24, 1804. She was married to Isaac C. Barrows about 1832. She had five children with Isaac: Elizabeth C. (April 20, 1832-1902); Isaac H. (May 1838-1930); Mary Melissa (April 1, 1840-March 20,

1890; George W. (April 10, 1845-1930); and Phebe A. (February 4, 1948-1861).

There is no death record for Isaac C. Barrows, but it is known he died sometime before 1855.

Mary (Goff) Barrows is buried in Oak Grove Cemetery in Pawtucket, Rhode Island.

Further Reading:

"The Alleged Murder at Freetown." *New-York Tribune* (New York, New York), February 3, 1851.
"Rum's Doing." *The Brooklyn Daily Eagle* (Brooklyn, New York), February 1, 1851.

Grave of Mary Goff Barrows, born December 24, 1804, died January 25, 1851, Oak Grove Cemetery, Pawtucket, Rhode Island. (Jo-Ann Croft, Findagrave.com)

ELLEN MURPHY

Wife murdered by her husband by forcing sulphuric acid down her throat in front of her five children at their home at 93 Bedford Street, in Fall River, Massachusetts, on April 10, 1853.

Victim: Ellen Murphy, 40.

Accused: John Murphy, unknown age.

Details: The "fiendlike barbarity" of the murder of Ellen Murphy by her husband, John Murphy, was detailed in the *Hannibal Journal* from an article in the *Fall River Evening News*. The murder, they relate, "exceeds anything of the kind that we ever heard of.—Both parties were addicted to habits of intemperance."

"Last Saturday [April 9, 1853], it appears, the wife being abroad on one of her drunken rambles, the husband went in pursuit of her, to bring her home, having a rope in his hand. Before setting out, however, he had procured half a pint of gin from a woman in the neighborhood, and drank it.—Having got his wife home, about one o'clock [sic—if you follow the story this would have to be around eleven p.m., not 1 a.m.], he threw her upon her bed; and, compelling the oldest daughter to hold her mother, he tied the hands and feet of the latter together with cords, then tied her to the back bed post with cords proceeding from the hands and the feet. He also passed a rope around her body, thus securing her more firmly. Meanwhile he quieted her by telling her that if she would let him tie her, he would give her some liquor. Having made her fast, he went out to into the shed, and returned, bringing in some vessel a quantity of some liquid, telling his wife that he would now give her a sup of liquor.

"He then attempted to get the oldest daughter to administer the liquor to her mother, but she, mistrusting wrong, firmly refused. Having stripped the woman of all her clothes, except her chemise, and having pulled that off from her neck and shoulders, and torn it open in front, he proceeded to turn the liquid which he had brought from the shed down her throat. It appears as though he was aware that this liquid would stain and discolor any article of clothing, but was ignorant of the fact that it would stain the skin.

"The liquid given the woman appears and is supposed to have been *sulphuric acid*.

"On having this stuff turned down her throat, the poor woman struggled and showed signs of nausea. She was too strongly confined with the cords, however, to free herself, or to do anything for her relief. The five children went to bed in another bed-room, while the savage husband staid about the coach of his agonized dying wife. The latter, by words or signs, called for water, telling her daughter that she was burning up inside. Some water was given her by one of the daughters. The daughters, it appears, lay in bed the most or all the time, but the eldest two kept note of their father's operations. About twelve o'clock, according to the account of the girls, he gave his wife another quantity of liquid in the cup. This he called tea. It is judged to have been a quantity of the acid diluted.

"The dying woman continued to moan until about 3 o'clock on Saturday [sic—Sunday] morning, when, as the eldest daughters state, the noise of her plaints ceased. It is probable that death occurred at this point in time. The husband unbound his wife, stripped the chemise off and put on a clean one. He then fled. The daughter went to the house [sic—business, 36 Bedford Street, grocer] of B.F. Winslow, Esq., and told him that their mother lay dead in the house, having been murdered by their father. This was early on Sunday morning. Mr. Winslow, on going to the house, found the woman dead and in the position already described. The spectacle presented was a horrid one. There was a column of froth from the mouth about an inch high; and the sides of the chin, neck and breast were furrowed with rills of the liquid, which had marked the course over those parts with crooked black lines."

Trial: John Murphy was found guilty and sentenced to be executed after one years' imprisonment. According to *The Burlington Free Press*, "He received his sentence of death without any emotion, and upon being remanded to jail, coolly inquired of the officers whether he would probably be hanged in Taunton or New Bedford."

Further Reading:

"The Fall River Murder." *Sunbury American* (Sunbury, Pennsylvania), April 23, 1853.
"A Hardened Wretch." *The Burlington Free Press* (Burlington, Vermont), January 5, 1854.
"A Horrible Murder." *Hannibal Journal* (Hannibal, Missouri), May 12, 1853.
"Horrible Murder." *The Liberator* (Boston, Massachusetts), April 29, 1853.
"John Murphy." *The Buffalo Commercial* (Buffalo, New York), December 27, 1853.

VALENTINE S. ALMY

Murder by gun in Little Compton, Rhode Island, on August 14, 1855.

Victim: Valentine S. Almy, 23.

Accused: Charles E. Almy, his cousin, 25.

Details: According to *The Brooklyn Eagle*, "We learn that an awful tragedy occurred at Little Compton, R.I., yesterday, which resulted in the death of a young man named Valentine S. Almy, son of Mr. Frederick Almy. It appears that the deceased was on his way to a fishing excursion, and stopped for a short time at the residence of his uncle, Mr. John E. Almy. While there, and standing near a fence, his cousin, Charles E. Almy, son of Mr. J.E. Almy, went into a corn house near by, and took a gun and shot Valentine, wounding him mortally. He lingered from 9 o'clock in the morning, when the fatal act occurred, until half-past 2 o'clock this morning, when he died. Charles immediately fled to his room, and declined answering any questions as to the cause of the murderous act—only stating that 'Valentine knew what it was for.' Valentine on being interrogated before he died, said that he knew nothing about it. The deceased was 23 years of age. He was at home on a visit, having been for some time employed in the apothecary establishment of Mr. Sylvester Almy, in Boston."

Trial: There is no information as to whether there was a trial.

Afterword: Charles Edward Almy died on February 5, 1874, at the age of forty-three, having gone insane, according the Almy family genealogy. He is buried at the Almy Cemetery in Little Compton, Rhode Island.

Further Reading:

"Awful Tragedy in Little Compton." *The Brooklyn Daily Eagle* (Brooklyn, New York), August 16, 1855.

DAVID S. HATHAWAY JR.

Murder by pistol in Freetown, Massachusetts, on September 22, 1856.

Victim: David Simmons Hathaway Jr., 44.

Accused: Adaline (Hathaway) Clark, 42.

Details: An unusual and incomplete tale of murder unfolded in Freetown, Massachusetts in 1856. David S. Hathaway Jr., widower and farmer, was living in the household of Seth and Adaline Clark. Adaline was a Hathaway by birth, and was David's first cousin, their fathers being siblings.

On September 22, for some unknowable reason, Adaline shot and killed David S. Hathaway with a pistol.

Trial: In April of 1857, Mrs. Adaline Clark was tried and convicted of manslaughter in the death of David S. Hathaway and was sentenced in October of 1858 in the Bristol County Court of Common Pleas to five years at hard labor in the House of Correction.

Afterword: Adaline must have served her time and then released, because we know from genealogical records that she lived until her 82nd year, dying of enteritis on September 5, 1896, in Freetown, Massachusetts. She is buried in the Assonet Burying Ground in Freetown.

Further Reading:

"Sentenced for Manslaughter." *Richmond Dispatch* (Richmond, Virginia), October 30, 1858.
"Trial of a Woman for Manslaughter." *Richmond Dispatch* (Richmond, Virginia), April 6, 1857.

Grave of Mrs. Adaline (Hathaway) Clark, born January, 1814, and died on September 5, 1896, Assonet Burying Ground, Freetown, Massachusetts. (Findagrave.com)

SAMUEL B. MANCHESTER

Murder of a man in Westport, Massachusetts, on July 19, 1859.

Victim: Samuel B. Manchester, 21.

Accused: Loring Palmer, age unknown.

Details: Loring Palmer, of Little Compton, Rhode Island, was arrested for the murder of Samuel B. Manchester (b. February 11, 1838), of Westport, Massachusetts, for a crime committed on the 19th of July while the two were on a "drunken spree." There are no details as to the manner or method of death of Mr. Manchester, however, the record indicates the cause as "fracture of the brain."

Trial: The trial of Loring Palmer for the murder of Samuel B. Manchester began on July 27, some eight days after the crime. According to the *Detroit Free Press*, "While the court was adjourned for dinner, Palmer was lodged at the station house.—When the officers went to bring him again before the court, it was found that he had attempted suicide by cutting his throat from ear to ear with a jack-knife. Surgical attendance was immediately procured, and the wound was dressed. The *Mercury* states that up to a late hour last evening Palmer survived, but little hope is entertained of his recovery."

Afterword: Loring Palmer's fate is not known. There have been no further records or reports located as to his disposition or if he died the day he attempted suicide during the trial. Samuel B. Manchester is buried in Adamsville Church Cemetery, in Little Compton, Rhode Island.

Further Reading:

"Murder Trial—Attempted Suicide of the Prisoner." *Detroit Free Press* (Detroit, Michigan), August 2, 1859.

BRUNEAU BERARDE

Beating of a man in Fall River, Massachusetts, on June 14, 1871, with his death occurring July 8, 1871.

Victim: Bruneau Berarde (aka Bruno Birard—per his probate records), 48.

Accused: John Riley, age unknown.

Details: The death of Bruno Birard is a sad story of suffering and most probably ethnic animosity. The story appeared only the *Fall River Daily News* and the quoted material is thus assumed to be from that source.

"Coroner Dillingham on Saturday summoned a jury to hold an inquest on the body of Bruneau Berarde, the Frenchman who was injured in an affray with John Riley at Mechanicsville, on the 14th of June, and who died on Saturday morning [July 8]… The inquest was commenced at the house of the deceased, No. 29 Lindsey street, Mechanicsville [a neighborhood section of Fall River], and adjourned till Monday, at the City Court House. A number of witnesses were examined, some of whom witnessed the affray. Drs. Contant, Smith and Hartley, who were called a different times during Berarde's illness, and Dr. Davis, who with Dr. Hartley made a post mortem examination of the body, also appeared and gave their testimony.

"Alexis Antaya testified that he was present at the shop of Thomas B. Lawton, near the Weetamoe mill, on the afternoon of June 14th, with the deceased and two or three other Frenchmen, when two Irishmen, John Riley and Daniel McCarty, came in and called for beer. The Frenchmen were in engaged in conversation among themselves, when McCarty, who was considerably intoxicated, commenced to mock them. This led to some high words, and Mr. Lawton ordered McCarty, and also Riley who was somewhat intoxicated, to leave his store. When going out, McCarty turned to the Frenchmen and swore that he would 'fix them yet.'

"A few minutes after the Irishmen left, the Frenchmen went out the back door of the store and went home. Soon after, Antaya says that while sitting at his window he saw two men a field near by, one of them prostrate on the ground, and the other down on his knees pounding him. He rushed to the spot and recognized the prostrate man as Berarde, and the other as Riley.

Berarde was bleeding profusely from his mouth and ears, and was very badly bruised on his face and head. He raised him up and asked Riley 'what he had done that for?' Riley replied 'because he made for me first.' Antaya then assisted Berarde to his home. He also testified that Berarde said to him that as he was walking out, he passed Riley, who was leaning upon the fence with is face buried in his hands, and that the latter came up behind him and struck him a terrible blow in the back with something heavy, which knocked him down.

"Reuben Peckham testified that he was passing on the opposite side of the street when the fracas occurred, and that he heard loud talking between the men and then saw Berarde take off his hat, throw it on the ground and make towards Riley. That Riley struck him in the face, knocked him down, then jumped upon him, seized him by the throat with one hand, and pounded him with the other. Peckham did not interfere between the two men, but passed on.

"Dr. Contant, who was the first physician called, testified to finding his patient bleeding from the mouth, and suffering great pain internally. He said 'he thought best to use the lancet, and took two pounds of blood from him to relieve his pain.' As he considered him 'at the point of death' he did not call again.

"Drs. Smith and Hartley, who were subsequently called, testified to finding very severe bruises about the face and eyes, and a bruise on the back of the right shoulder, as if made with a stone or club.

"Drs. Hartley and Davis testified that at the post mortem examination they found several ribs broken, a diseased condition of both lungs, and in the left lung gangrene and gray hepatization.

"The jury, last evening, returned the following verdict. 'That the said Bruneau Berarde came to his death of the eighth day of July 1871, from gangrene and gray hepatization of the left lung; and that the said condition of the left lung of the deceased, in their opinion, was induced, in connection with other causes, from injuries received at the hands of John Riley, on the 14th day of June, 1871.'

"Riley, it will be recollected, made his escape from prison on the 27th ult, and has not yet been found. The remains of Berarde have been forwarded to Canada for interment" (July 11, 1871).

John Riley was re-arrested at "Mooseup, Conn., by officer Mark P. Chace, brought back to the city this morning, and lodged in prison. The date of his trial has not yet been fixed.

"Riley told the officer, that from the lock-up, he went directly to Oak Grove Cemetery, thence to Mechanicsville, then along the railroad track to Taunton and Providence. Being eyed pretty sharply by the police of Providence, on his arrival the next morning, he concluded to travel farther, and took the track of the Hartford & Fishkill road, until he reached Mooseup, about 33 miles beyond Providence, where he found work at his business,—that of a mule spinner, in a cotton mill. He was arrested while at work" (July 12, 1871).

Afterword: There were no records found beyond these newspaper articles as to the outcome of this murder, the trial that was assumed, or the verdict of the jury. With John Riley being such a common name, further research would be necessary to determine his final state.

Bruno Birard left behind a wife, Aurelie (Peloqun) Birard, and fourteen children.

Further Reading:

"Coroner's Inquest." *Fall River Daily News* (Fall River, Massachusetts), July 11, 1871.
"Fatal Result." *Fall River Daily News* (Fall River, Massachusetts), July 8, 1871.
"Re-Arrested." *Fall River Daily News* (Fall River, Massachusetts), July 12, 1871.

CHARLES H. THOMAS

Murder by gun in dispute over a hencoop at Tiverton Four Corners, Rhode Island, on November 9, 1880.

Victim: Charles H. Thomas, 40.

Accused: Moses Grinnell, 70.

Details: According to the *Boston Post*, "Moses Grinnell, an old man between 69 and 70 years of age, shot Charles Thomas, age 40, killing him instantly. It is said that Grinnell and Thomas, the latter being a reputed son-in-law, have not been on very good terms; also that Grinnell has had considerable trouble with other members of his family. N. Hatheway [sic] of this city [Fall River, Massachusetts], who has been his counsel in previous cases, says that Grinnell is not a malicious man, but is rather one possessed of a quick, excitable temperament, which would lead him to do such a deed on the impulse of the moment.

"The affair caused intense excitement in the town, where the parties are all well known. Opinions differ as to who was most to blame in the matter. Some think that the old man has been so harassed by family troubles that he was driven to the deed. All parties concerned are people in the humbler walks of life. In the Justice Court at Newport last Monday, Ben. H. Grinnell and wife were fined for assault on Moses Grinnell, the father of Benjamin. Benjamin, who lived with his father, made arrangements to secure another dwelling. On his father's farm was a hen coop which he (Benjamin) had built, and he determined to take this to his new home.

"As he is crippled from paralysis he got Thomas, who lives as husband with is sister, Mrs. Almy, to assist him in removing the coop. Grinnell ordered both is son and Thomas to leave his premises, telling the latter if he did not he would shoot him. Thomas persisted in taking away the coop, and the elder Grinnell got his gun and shot Thomas dead, as before reported. The old man then told Benjamin to leave, or he would shoot him also, and Benjamin left. The old man was in the village store last evening smoking his pipe as if nothing had happened.

"The constable kept close watch of him, however, and to-day committed him to the Newport jail, where he is now confined. Thomas was about 40 years old and has a bad record, having served in the State Prison, having been convicted of an attempted house robbery in Dartmouth, Mass., some fifteen or twenty years ago."

Moses was arraigned on the charge of murder, to which he pleaded not guilty. He was committed for trial at the next term of the Supreme Court of Rhode Island. The *Williamsport Sun-Gazette* reported that at his arraignment, "The old man looked sad and care worn, and seems to feel keenly the position in which he has placed himself."

Trial: The trial of Moses Grinnell for the murder of Charles H. Thomas began on May 16, 1882, after having been postponed several times. The *New York Times* reported that the most severe punishment Grinnell could earn if found guilty was life in prison. Thomas, the victim, it is mentioned was Grinnell's son-in-law "without the sanction of law." Further, "The testimony offered by the State today substantiated the story given…An attempt of the defense to show that Grinnell acted in self-defense has received no confirmation from the testimony thus far offered. The attending physician's examination showed that Thomas received his wound as he was turning away from the murderer. The prisoner is nearly 75 years old [sic] and appears quite unconcerned over his situation. He is either slightly demented or else not of average intelligence" (May 17, 1882).

According to lengthy report in *The Sun*, Grinnell's "explanation of the affair, as told on the stand, was that on leaving the [village] store [where he met his grandson, who told him that Benjamin, his father, and Charley Thomas were going up the road to remove the hen houses] he made for the henhouse, and on his arrival there found the two men carrying out the boxes, and Benjamin's young son removing stones from the underpinning. He ordered them to desist, and told Thomas to clear off the premises. Thomas, he claims, took up a stone of several pounds weight and threatened to smash the old man's head. Grinnell, knowing the character of Thomas as he claims, went away to the house to avoid trouble. When he got into his house, he says, he laid down on the lounge, from which he could look down on the henhouse. Pretty soon he saw his chickens fly in every direction, and thinking the hawks were around again, he took up the gun and went out to shoot them. On getting down to the henhouse, not seeing any hawks, he looked in at the door and Thomas saw him. Thomas took up a heavy piece of wood, and with an oath said that he would send him (Moses) to —. and advanced toward the old man. The latter could not retreat, boxes being behind him, and acting, as he claimed, in self-defense, he fired the contents of his gun into Thomas, whose death was instantaneous.

"It was proved by the defense that Thomas was convicted in 1849 of highway robbery and burglary with deadly weapons and sentenced for life, but was pardoned out after serving sixteen years."

The following day, May 18, 1882, the *New York Times* reported that "at 8 o'clock this evening the jury…returned a verdict of murder in the first degree, thus imposing a life sentence on Grinnell, now 70 years old [sic]. The prisoner received the verdict with great composure, and sentence was deferred to enable his counsel to file exceptions for a new trial. It is probable, however, that this will not be done, and the murderer will be sentenced to-morrow. The defense showed that Grinnell's children were leagued against him to get his property from him, but failed to show that they had entered into a deliberate conspiracy to swear him into State prison for life. A startling bit of testimony was offered by Grinnell's daughter, who has been married, divorced, married again, and, while a widow, had lived 30 months with Thomas, the murdered man. She charged that 21 years ago her father, the prisoner, attempted criminal assault upon her, and that since then she has never spoken to him or entertained feeling toward him. She was the principal witness for the defense."

Afterword: Moses Grinnell appears again in the news when, in 1885, the *Newport Mercury* reported on Rhode Island government officials, including Governor George Wetmore, several members of the Governor's personal staff, some state officers, and the members of the General Assembly. They first visited the State Prison where they "came across poor old Moses Grinnell who took life some four or five years ago in Tiverton. He appeared to be pretty well broken down and is allowed to hobble about without any particular work."

Further Reading:

"An Aged Murderer Convicted." *New York Times* (New York, New York), May 18, 1882.
"Arraigned on the Charge of Murder." *Williamsport Sun-Gazette* (Williamsport, Pennsylvania), November 19, 1880.
"The Grinnell Trial." *Newport Mercury* (Newport, Rhode Island), May 20, 1882.
"Official Visit to the State Farm." *Newport Mercury* (Newport, Rhode Island), June 27, 1885.
"An Old Man's Crime." *Boston Post* (Boston, Massachusetts), November 11, 1880.
"A Rhode Island Tragedy." *The Sun* (New York, New York), May 18, 1882.
"A Rhode Island Trial." *New York Times* (New York, New York), May 17, 1882.
"Sentenced for Life at Seventy." *The Times* (Philadelphia, Pennsylvania), May 22, 1882.

ANNIE McMULLEN

Woman beaten to death by her husband at 26 Canal Street, Fall River, Massachusetts, on July 24, 1881.

Victim: Annie McMullen, 30.

Accused: Thomas Henry McMullen, 31.

Details: Annie McMullen, the 34 [sic] year old wife to John McMullen [sic—Thomas H. McMullen] was beaten to death by her husband when he was told she had been intimate with another man, whom he had suspected.

According to the *Boston Post*, "John McMullen [sic] is a teamster in the employ of a grain deal in this city [Fall River], and John L. Dwelley [sic], a blacksmith, has for some time been jealously watched by McMullen, because of Dwelley's [sic] intimacy with his wife. Yesterday morning, while McMullen was attending to his horses, Dwelley [sic] went to his house, and when McMullen returned his little daughter told him that Dwelley [sic] had been in the bedroom with her mother. McMullen's jealousy and ire was naturally aroused and immediately assaulted Dwelley [sic], pounding him severely, and subsequently he attacked his wife, and it is said that frequently during the day he pounded and beat her.

"About 5 o'clock this morning, McMullen went to Officer Daily [sic] and told him that he had found his wife dead in her bed. The officer went with McMullen to his home, and the unfortunate woman was found dead, and pounded and beaten in a most shocking manner. A broken bed slat was also found, covered with blood. McMullen was at once placed under arrest, and Dwelley [sic] was locked up as soon as yesterday's trouble was ascertained. The murdered woman is about 35 years of age [sic], and leaves two children. The body was cold when found, and she had undoubtedly been dead for some hours."

According the extensive reporting in the *Fall River Daily Herald*, there is much more the story. "It seems that McMullins [sic] and his wife have been in the habit of drinking to excess and indulged in frequent brawls. Yesterday morning, McMullens [sic], slightly intoxicated, entered his house in the rear of 26 Canal street, and found a man named John L. Dwelly seated in the kitchen.

After saluting him with 'How do you do,' he proceeded, it seems, to his wife's chamber and found her in bed. He caught hold of her, dragged her out upon the floor, and jumped upon her face and other parts of her body. He then went into out to fight Dwelly, and gave him a number of blows, cutting him badly about the head and face.

"Dwelly rushed from the tenement to the yard as soon as he could and was bleeding freely from his wounds. It is said that he received a stab from a knife, but it is only a rumor. Dwelly then left the premises and has not been seen about there since. McMullins [sic] remained in the house, and no one knows what happened after Dwelly's departure. Everything became quieted until the afternoon about 2 o'clock, when the row was begun again. The woman was heard to cry piteously in the room where her body was found. The second row lasted about an hour. Nothing was thought of this occurrence by the neighbors, as it had become a common thing for the parties to have family quarrels.

"McMullins [sic], it appears from his own story, left the house after beating his wife in the afternoon and remained out all night and until early this morning, when he claims that he found his wife dead at the bottom of the flight of stairs leading to his tenement and that he carried her corpse up stairs and laid it on the bed. He then started out and came across Officer Dailey. He informed the officer that he had found his wife dead at the bottom of the stairs and that he had carried her in his arms and put her in bed.

"Medical Examiner Dwelly found the body badly marked, as though it had been kicked and beaten. The left hand was all black and [the] back was swollen, as were also the fingers and arms, as though the deceased in her attempts to ward off the blows, received them on her hands till they became powerless. Her legs presented a fearful sight. Her back and sides were more or less injured and her face was dreadfully pummeled.

"Over the right eye was a flesh wound made not long before her death. On the right side of the head, back of the ear, was a deep gash, probably the place where the death blow was dealt. The Medical Examiner after making a thorough examination of the wounds thought that the deceased died of concussion of the brain, caused by the blow on the head.

"The room in which the body was found is on the south side of the building. The body lay in a pile on the bed bolsted with pillows and quilts. The bed clothes as well as the clothing on the woman's body, were saturated in blood and the walls of the room were covered with spots of it.

"The poor woman was about 30 years of age, was the mother of two children, a girl and a boy [Emma and Thomas]. The girl, the older, is but 3 years of age. The mother's maiden name was Annie Ennis and she resided in Taunton prior to her marriage to McMullins [sic] with the family of Mr. Terry Martin. She first met her husband in East Taunton and shortly after marriage took up housekeeping in this city. The brutal husband is about the same age as his wife. He is small in stature, and is known to be a very ugly man when in liquor. Formerly a fish-peddler, but of late he has been in the employ of Geo. F. Kingsley, grain dealer.

"When the body was found this morning the blood had become dried and a very unpleasant odor was issuing from the corpse. In the bedroom was a pail filled with water, some of which was spilled upon the floor. The woman's clothes and hair were filled with splinters as though she had been dragged on the floor and her hair was also tangled with bits of straw. The children were taken care of by their father's mother, who resides on Union street.

"A post mortem examination was held this afternoon, but the prisoner McMullins [sic] has demanded a re-examination with a surgeon of his own selection, Dr. Terry…From the examination this forenoon it was learned that the injuries are all external. The top of the head is beaten into a jelly. The skull was taken off and the interior vital parts of the body inspected but no injury was found in brain or heart. It appears that the injuries were sufficient to cause a suspension of the nervous system, which would result in death.

"Messrs. [Nicholas] Hatheway, [John W.] Cummings [the author's grandfather] and [David F.} Lingane were retained as counsel for the prisoner" (July 25, 1881).

At the preliminary hearing, Medical Examiner Dwelly testifed to some important facts. It is vital that the reader understand the extent of Annie's injuries—what one man could physically do to his own wife, the mother of his children.

When the Medical Examiner went into the 8x10 foot bedroom, he "noticed the bed was in disturbed condition; the foot of the bed was bare and two or three slats were taken out; these slats were missing from the foot of the bed; the woman lay on the bed on her back, inclined to the right side; the legs were drawn up by the side of her head; the clothing was very much disarranged; she had on a calico dress of dark patterns; it was torn in front and pulled off at the right side; the woman was dead; her hair losse [sic] and her back was bloody; the face was very dark; the eyes closed and the eyelids swollen; the left eyelid had a wound in it; under the brow was a contused wound not made by a sharp instrument; it was one inch in length from the outer corner of the orbit, extended towards the nose; the wound extended through the skin, but did not go into the eyeball or the bone; blood was oozing from the wound; the sides and fore part of the head were much swollen and discolored; the legs were bare partly to the knees; their hair hard [sic] some sticks, splinters of wood imbeded [sic] in them; made more extended examination afterwards; the bed clothes were stained with blood; the pillow under her head was saturated in blood and some clothes lying about looked as if they had been used in rubbing over the blood; …made an autopsy about 9 o'clock; the body was stripped at the undertakers and on examining it a large number of contusions were found; the head was very much swollen and there was an effusion of blood under the scalp, which was puffed up; that condition of the wounds was found all over the top of the head on the scalp; above the ear was a wound extending about one inch in length, cut to the bone; there was quite a flow of blood from that imprisoned under the scalp; it was not a very old wound; it was not made by blunt instrument or by a very sharp one. (He stated that it might be made by one of the bed slats.)

"On top of the head was another wound, one inch in length, extending partly through the skin; it might be made by the glancing of a blow; on the right brow, extending down over the temple was another; there was a large number of these contusions on the head, the result of repeated blows; the arms had a large number of contusions on the back of both hands and fingers, extending principally below the elbow; there was a great many on the body, especially on the breast and sides; the principal wound was on the left side near the region of the liver, covering several inches in extent and appeared like a cushion, caused by the application of force and a hard substance; there was another on the right arm below the elbow; the backs of the hands were black and blue, and swollen" (July 29, 1881).

McMullen claimed that his wife had received her blows as she fell down the stairs, however, when asked why there was no blood found at the foot of the stairs, he had no answer for it.

McMullen was judged "probably guilty" and was bound over for the Grand Jury at the September term of the Superior Court.

In December, the Grand Jury indicted Thomas H. McMullen for three counts for the murder of his wife: the first count that he killed her by kicking and striking her with his hands and feet and with a club; the second count that her with the same assault she died the next day; and the third count alleged that he killed her by some means to the jurors unknown.

Trial: The trial of Thomas McMullen began on April 18, 1882. It lasted until April 21, when he was convicted of murder in the second degree and sentenced to the State prison for life.

Outcome: On Thanksgiving Day, in 1891, Thomas H. McMullen was *pardoned* by the governor of Massachusetts, William E. Russell (1891-1894), as part of the custom of the Commonwealth. Thomas Henry McMullen lived another nine years, dying on March 1, 1900, at the age of fifty, in Fall River, Massachusetts.

Afterword: On November 28, 1891, an editorial appeared in *The Courier-Journal* (Louisville, Kentucky), that is worth reprinting here in full, as the use of the pardon in many cases in these volumes has flummoxed the authors no end. We agree with much of the sentiments expressed by the author.

"Murder is the crime which excites in the American mind the keenest sympathy 'for the unfortunate criminal.' It is dangerous: to violate almost any law except that against murder.

"Burglary, if we catch the burglar, is apt to be punished with some swiftness, for it touches the 'pocket nerve,' and no successful plea of self-defense has ever been made in behalf of a burglar. Horse-stealing, if not punished with death at the hands of a mob, opens wide the doors of the penitentiary.

"Forgery, too, if the forger is not too highly distinguished in financial circles, may involve the criminal in legal difficulties.

"Arson, assault, conspiracy and innumerable crimes of every degree of turpitude are punished with some severity; but it is rare that a murder is committed in such a bungling manner that the murderer is punished, except in so far as an expensive trial is a punishment. The laws are so drawn, the trials are so conducted, the sympathy of the people so worked on, that conviction for murder or manslaughter is almost impossible in America.

"When all the resources of the law fail, and the criminal by an accident finds himself in prison, he becomes a notable character, and the recipient of marked attention from State officers as well as from visitors, who aim to compensate him for his enforced retirement, by showering flowers and sweetmeats on him in abundance.

"The prisons of Massachusetts are said to be unusually attractive. So thoughtful, so considerate, so sentimental is society in the Bay State that the prisons have become much more inviting than many of the homes of the private and hard-worked citizen. Nothing there is allowed to offend the feelings of the most sensitive, with the result that the number of criminals has in the past twenty years increased far more rapidly than the population.

"But even these model establishments for the amelioration of the condition of the criminal classes are not good enough for the murderers. Something more must be done for them; so the Governor selects murderers as the beneficiaries of his Thanksgiving clemency.

"The story is told in a dispatch from Boston: 'Boston, Nov. 27.—According to custom the Governor pardoned two State prison convicts on Thanksgiving Day. The fortunate men are Charles Briggs, who was committed in 1881 on a life sentence for murder in the second degree, in killing Charles Slanson because of jealousy on account of Briggs' wife, and Thomas H. McMullen, who was sentenced for life in April 1882, for murder in the second degree, in killing his wife.'

"Here are two murderers, whose crimes must have been without reason or excuse, or else no jury would have been so heartless as to send them to the penitentiary. At their trials neither 'self-defense,' 'temporary or emotional insanity' or provocation availed. One man murdered another actuated by jealousy, while the other killed his wife.

"It is difficult to imagine any extenuating circumstances which cry for leniency in the case of man who kills his wife. Perhaps he was drunk. Perhaps his brutality and indifference to her happiness had so crushed her spirit as to make it impossible to oppose him. Or, as he was found guilty of murder in the second degree, the poor woman may have resisted his blows, and tried ineffectually to protect her own life, or that of her child.

"In all the prisons of Massachusetts it surely might have been possible to find some men more worthy than these two of executive clemency. Their victims have no one to plead for them. The dead are soon forgotten. Charles Slanson and the wife of McMullen had no one to plead for them with the Governor for justice on Thanksgiving Day.

"So the crime and the victim are forgotten, and a shallow sentimentalism chooses Thanksgiving Day for the pardon of these red-handed criminals without giving a thought to the family of Slanson as it kept its holiday with its specter in the house, and with no consideration for the children of the murdered woman, who are now restored, perhaps, to a devoted father, who unfortunately took the life of their mother and of his wife.

"Sentimental philanthropy by such displays as these in Boston on Thanksgiving Day, brings itself and the law into supreme contempt."

Further Reading:

"Alleged Wife Murderer." *Fall River Daily Herald* (Fall River, Massachusetts), July 25, 1881.
"Criminal Trials" *Fall River Daily News* (Fall River, Massachusetts), December 10, 1881.
"Jealousy and Murder." *Boston Post* (Boston, Massachusetts), July 26, 1881.
"McMullen in Court." *Fall River Daily Herald* (Fall River, Massachusetts), July 26, 1881.
"Murderers a Privileged Class." *The Courier-Journal* (Louisville, Kentucky), November 28, 1891.
"Tried for Alleged Murder." *Fall River Daily Herald* (Fall River, Massachusetts), July 29, 1881.

EXILDA CHARON

Woman shot to death by her husband as she slept at 2 Stewart Street in Fall River, Massachusetts, on December 7, 1881.

Victim: Exilda Charon, 28.

Accused: Frank Charon, 29.

Details: According to the *Boston Post*, on December 7, 1881, "Frank Sharon [sic], a young barber formerly doing business at Bowenville [a neighborhood section of Fall River, Massachusetts], but who lately has had a shop at Somerset, was arrested on Nov. 20 for assault on his wife. The case was continued until this morning by the district court. Yesterday, Sharon and his wife visited a law office in this city [Fall River] and made arrangements to have the case settled in court, the wife acknowledging satisfaction. Sharon and his wife retired as usual last night [at the home of Mrs. Sharon's parents in Fall River], but the former arose about 4 o'clock this morning, dressed, took a short walk, and, returning home, entered the chamber where his wife lay sleeping. He kissed her three times, he says, and, drawing a pistol, shot her as she lay asleep, in the left side of the neck.

"The woman died almost instantly. Sharon then came down town and delivered himself to the police. He says something crossed his mind and told him to do it. Mrs. Sharon leaves three children, the oldest 5 years of age [sic], and was soon to give birth to a fourth. Sharon appeared very calm and smoked a cigar as unconcernedly as if nothing had happened. He is 29 years of age. When arrested $21 and a flask half full of whiskey was found on his person. He was arraigned in court at 9 o'clock and committed to jail without bail."

The *Fall River Daily News* gives us this account: "About two weeks ago Frank Charon an inhabitant of Somerset was arrested for beating his wife and appeared in the District Court held in this city but had his case continued until to-day. His wife, it seems was *enceinte* [pregnant] and through the effects of the whipping which her inhuman husband gave her with a floor brush she was prostrated and unable to appear against him. The woman was brought to this city by her parents residing in Eagan's block, corner of North Main street and Ferry lane, where she has since lived [2 Stewart Street]. The husband, who evidently regretted his bad conduct, since his arrest besought her to settle their grievances and live a life of peace. His wife, a woman of amiable disposition, kindly granted his request and was willing to acknowledge satisfaction in court this morning. Frank, her husband, by kind consent of his wife's parents was allowed to live with them at their home. Since their union he did nothing in the line of work and loafed about without labor.

"Yesterday he was about a good deal and imbibed liquor quite freely. However, he returned to his home about 5 o'clock where he remained until 10 o'clock at night when he went out to do some shopping and shortly after returned. On his return he seated himself in a chair near the table and created a little curiosity by relating certain incidents in his life and finally wound up his tale by saying there is always a black sheep in the best of families. After finishing the history of himself he disposed of his children by giving one to one person and another to another.

"He and his wife shortly after retired, giving no rise to any suspicions of his contemplating any terrible crime. It is unknown whether he slept the entire night or whether he was laying awake in bed pondering over the fearful deed he had resolved to commit. However, he awoke his wife this morning at about 4 o'clock, and both arose and dressed. He afterwards went out. The woman, seeing that it was rather early to rise, returned to bed, in which were her two young children. Taking the youngest of these in her arms, she reclined and entered into a quiet slumber.

"The man returned and, after visiting the room and seeing that his wife was asleep, went into the attic and took his revolver from his coat pocket and returned to his wife's chamber. After entering the room he approached the bedside and, bending over the doomed woman, kissed her three times.

"Then stepping back he cocked his revolver and taking deliberate aim, fired sending one of the bullets through her neck. The woman awoke with a shriek and exclaimed, 'Oh my God!' Charon, who had to all appearances premeditated the murder and had formed plans of escape by leaving the room and kitchen door open after he entered the house, rushed out into the street and up to the central police station where he gave himself up to the authorities.

"The unhappy woman said nothing after making the exclamation but raised herself in the bed with her young child in her arms and bled profusely, covering her helpless children with her life's blood. The pistol shot awoke her relatives sleeping in adjoining apartments who in a half nude state rushed into the room and to their horror witnessed the result of a jealous husband's work. A sister of the dying woman took the babe from its mother's arms. The woman then fell back in the bed in an unconscious condition and in less than fifteen minutes after expired in great agony.

"Medical Examiner Dwelly held a post mortem examination this forenoon at 10 o'clock. The prisoner, after his arrival at the central police station, made known what he had done by saying he had killed his wife and desired to give himself up. His person was afterward searched and on it were found a small revolver, one chamber of which was empty, a silver watch, $21 in money, and a bottle half full of liquor. He was put in one of the cells until the opening of court at 9 o'clock.

"He lived in Somerset for the past two years, where he enjoyed a good reputation and attended to his business as a barber. Of late he has been addicted to drink, and has on several occasions beaten his wife. He was arrested on that charge Nov. 24. He is 29 years of age of about 5 feet 3 inches in height and weighs about 120 pounds. His complexion is dark and has two small piercing eyes. He wears a very think, dark moustache and a small imperial chin whisker, giving his face a very treacherous and vicious appearance.

"The deceased woman's name is Exilda Charon, her maiden name was Exilda Provencal. She was 27 years of age and was the mother of three children [Frank, 4, Charles, 2, and Mary, 1]. She had been married nearly seven years and was a most charming and faithful wife.

"The cause assigned for the crime by the prisoner is that she was too good looking for him and that all the neighborhood was after her. According to all reports there was no ground for this jealousy.

"An examination was made on the body this forenoon by Medical Examiner Dwelley [sic] assisted by two other doctors. It was learned that the ball entered the left breast and pierced the left lung, severing a large blood vessel causing a severe hemorrhage of which she died. The case goes before the grand jury at New Bedford this afternoon."

According the *The Burlington Free Press*, "the case of Frank Charon…the preliminary law measures were remarkably expeditious. The murderer was committed at five o'clock. He was brought before the police at nine o'clock and in the afternoon was indicted for murder by the grand jury in New Bedford and was committed to jail." He pleaded not guilty.

Trial: On April 18, Frank Charon retracted his former plea of not guilty and pleaded guilty of murder in the second degree. He was sentenced to State Prison for life.

Further Reading:

"Charon, the Wife Murderer." *The Burlington Free Press* (Burlington, Vermont), December 9, 1881.
Fitchburg Sentinel (Fitchburg, Massachusetts), April 18, 1882.
"Murder." *The Fitchburg Sentinel* (Fitchburg, Massachusetts), December 7, 1881.
"Murder at Fall River." *Boston Post* (Boston, Massachusetts), December 8, 1881.
"The Murderer in Court." *Fall River Daily Herald* (Fall River, Massachusetts), December 10, 1881.
"Taunton, Mass." *The New York Times* (New York, New York), April 19, 1882.
"Wife Murder." *Fall River Daily Herald* (Fall River, Massachusetts), December 7, 1881.

RAYMOND P. DENNIS

Murder by gun at 17 Almond Street, Fall River, Massachusetts, on December 8, 1881.

Victim: Raymond P. Dennis, 62.

Accused: Dennis Calden, age unknown, John Calden, 23, and Michael Sharkey, 25.

Details: The day after Mrs. Frank Charon was murdered by her husband, Fall River had another homicide on its hands. According to the *Boston Post* (December 9, 1881), "A murder was reported at the police station shortly after midnight. Raymond P. Dennis, age 62, being the victim. He was annoyed by some one breaking his windows. Seizing a gun, he went out to drive away a party of young men who were annoying him. They seized the gun from his hands and shot off the head of Mr. Dennis, the deed being witnessed by his family. This tragedy, coming within twenty-four hours of the wife murder, caused considerable excitement in the city, which is getting an unenviable reputation. The parties implicated were all recognized by the family of the murdered man.

"Dennis's house was a place of bad reputation, and the assailants were enraged at being unable to gain admission. The brains of the murdered man were blown all over the end of the house, and Medical Examiner Dwelley [sic] is of the opinion that Dennis must have been standing when he was shot. [John] Sullivan denies being at the place at all and the police to-night seem satisfied that he was not connected with the murder. The prisoner has not yet been released. He says he can prove an alibi and seems unconcerned. Two of the three men connected with the affair were arrested in this city this morning, but the man who did the shooting is, from the best information that can be obtained, still at large. The names of the two are Dennis Calden and Michael Sharkey. For the capture of the other man [John Calden, who police believe did the shooting], City Marshal [Sewell D.] Brigham has, to night, issued a circular offering $200 reward."

As luck would have it, the *Fall River Daily Herald* offered extensive and detailed coverage of this crime. "Early this morning, about 10:30 o'clock, three young men, slightly intoxicated, after carousing about in dens of iniquity the forepart of the night, wandered along by the shore and finally on to Almond street. As they approached the old brown block on the hight bank west of the Linen mill, a well-known landmark, they stopped.

"In this block there formerly lived a young woman named Rose Johnson, with whom the party was acquainted and upon whom the drunken roughs intended to call. They approached the front entrance to the building, but finding it locked, went around to the rear of the house, where there is another doorway facing the river. Access could not be obtained here and the men became angry. They began yelling, shouting and cursing and so disturbed the neighborhood that the inmates of the building were awakened from their slumbers.

"The man of the house, Raymond Perry Dennis, tried to tell the parties outside, as he heard the woman's name mentioned several times, that she did not live there and advised them to go about their business. Instead of complying with his request they turned upon him and used the most abusive and obscene language in their insults. The old man tried in vain to pacify the rascals from his bedroom window, but was finally forced to withdraw. The men outside became wild and one of the number said, 'stone the grey-headed old—head off,' and at the same time two stones much larger than a man's fist, were hurled through the open window.

"Mr. Dennis, seeing that the men intended to do some harm, dressed and taking his gun which was loaded with *four fingers of heavy shot*, went out by the rear entrance to frighten the disturbers off. His approach was heard and the murderers gathered at the door, and, as soon as it was opened seized him, and dragging him out into the yard, wrested the gun from him. One of the gang then placing the muzzle of the gun at the man's head and taking deliberate aim, fired, sending the full charge into the old man's head. The top of the skull was blown off, and part of the brains were scattered over the side of the building.

"The unfortunate man threw up his hands and fell lifeless to the ground.

"A young daughter of the deceased, who had been disturbed by the noise outside, had put her head out of an attic window and witnessed the scene as described above. The other inmates of the house were awakened by the report made by the discharge of the gun.

"The murderers then scampered off and in their haste the man who had fired the gun lost all presence of mind and carried the weapon a short distance with him, showing what direction the men took. The load being too much for him, and being intoxicated, and he finally concluded to drop it, which he did in the roadway.

"The report of the outrage was quickly spread among the residents in the immediate neighborhood. The son of the deceased notified the police of the murder and Medical Examiner Dwelly was also notified.

"The almost headless body was placed upon a door and carried into the house two hours after the sad event occurred. The scene of the tragedy is the yard northwest of the house and near the building, at the corner of which is a large pool of blood.

"The deceased was 61 years of age and wore a grey beard…He leaves a wife and four children, all of the latter having arrived at their maturity.

"A post mortem examination of the body was held at the residence of the deceased this forenoon by Medical Examiner Dwelly, assisted by Dr. [Seabury] Bowen, and it was decided that the man came to his death by being shot.

"Up to 1 o'clock three persons had been arrested on a complaint of being accomplices to the crime. One of them gives a good account of himself from 10 o'clock last night until this morning, which is corroborated by several witnesses. Another person arrested admitted being one of the party, and says that the person referred to above was not in his company. The last one arrested had nothing much to say, but according to the story of the second party is one of the gang. He is said to have been so close to the man at the time he was shot that part of the charge grazed his face and carried off part of his hat. Another, who claimed to be the third person, is still at large" (December 9, 1881).

The accused: Michael Sharkey "is about 25 years of age and is in delicate health. He has borne a very bad reputation and has contracted his bad health by his evil life. He admits being one of the three persons who murdered the old man. When asked if [John] Sullivan was one of the number he said 'no,' and then gave the names of the other parties, and told where one of them could be found. He said that John Calden is the man who fired the gun…and that his brother Dennis Calden was so close to the muzzle of the weapon that some of the shot grazed the side of his head and took off part of his hat. Upon this information the police secured the arrest of Dennis Calden and found the story of Sharkey to be correct in respect to the wounds and marks on Calden. The latter has nothing to say and will divulge nothing about the whereabouts of his brother John. The police are busily working the case up, and Marshal Brigham has issued the following:

"Two Hundred Dollars Reward. Wanted for manslaughter! John Calden, 23 years of age, height 5 ft. 10 in., light complexion, brown hair, blue eyes, large nose, slim build, has a very perceptible *scar* or *bunch* on the back of one hand, caused by a burn or other accident. He was dressed in a dark sack coat, badly worn, with faded yellowish stripes about one inch apart. The outside pockets had been torn down and sewed up. Vest and pants are alike, and made of cheap brown material. Round top soft hat, calico shirt, low shoes.

"The above reward will be paid for information that will lead to his arrest" (December 9, 1881).

Arraignment was held on December 10. The parents of each of the three men were present. Calden and Sharkey were represented by John W.

Cummings, Esq. [the grandfather of the author], and Sullivan by Milton Reed, Esq. Reed argued that there were good grounds for Sullivan to be released as he had an alibi for the time of the murder.

At the preliminary hearing on December 15, John Sullivan was discharged, having proved his whereabouts with an alibi. Dennis Calden and Michael Sharkey were held to await the action of the Grand Jury.

Trial: Very little information is available regarding the outcome of the legal case against Dennis Calden and Michael Sharkey. However, we learn from an article in 1884 that announced the capture of John Calden that the Dennis Calden and Michael Sharkey were both convicted of the crime, but to what extent or punishment, it is unclear.

Afterword: On June 9, 1884, a Chicago newspaper reported that "Officer Jones, of the Central Station, recently arrested a fugitive from justice name John Calden, alias James Courtney, alias 'Sailor Jack,' and locked him up at the Central Station until papers for his requisition arrive from Massachusetts. December 6, 1881 [sic]. Calden was released from prison in Fall River, where he had been serving time for some offense together with his brother. While there they planned a scheme to murder a man named Isaac Denny [sic], who they believed to have money. They attempted to rob his house, and when he appeared with a shotgun took it away from him and killed him with the weapon.

"John Calden was indicted for the offense, but succeeded in making his escape. He then came West and being concerned in some burglary in Wyoming was sent to the Territorial prison for eighteen months. He was released from there April 12 last, and came at once to Chicago. On May 27, together with four other thieves, he burglarized Varley's shoe store, at No. 264 Ogden avenue. His companions were arrested and two of them convicted, and the others held as accessories to the crime. Calden was shadowed by the police for his complicity in the affair, and his connection with the Fall River murder was discovered after his arrest."

Further Reading:

"Another Murder at Fall River." *Boston Post* (Boston, Massachusetts), December 9, 1881.
"The Fall River Tragedy." *Boston Post* (Boston, Massachusetts), December 16, 1881.
"Massachusetts." *Boston Post* (Boston, Massachusetts), December 10, 1881.
"A Murderer Captured." *The Inter Ocean* (Chicago, Illinois), June 9, 1884.
"Old Man Murdered." *Hartford Courant* (Hartford, Connecticut), December 9, 1881.
"A Peddler Killed." *Topeka Daily Capital* (Topeka, Kansas), December 11, 1881.

JOHN SCHOFIELD

Mill worker murdered in the yard of the Chace Mill in Fall River, Massachusetts, on March 22, 1884.

Victim: John Schofield, 58.

Accused: James E. Crann, age unknown.

Details: John Schofield, an "aged 'knobstick' spinner" employed in the spinning room of the Chace Mill in Fall River, Massachusetts, was assaulted and died of his injuries. Initially there were no suspects in the case. James E. Crann was later arrested and charged with the crime, based on sworn testimony of a witness to the attack.

According to the *Fall River Daily News*, the atmosphere around the Chace Mill was extremely tense as there was a labor strike in effect, ordered by the Spinners' Association. John Schofield, apparently, had crossed that strike line to work at the mill. "Schofield incurred the hatred of the strikers. They went out to watch when he came out from his work. Schofield started home one evening from his work, and on his way he was waylaid and killed. You talk to me about motives, from night till morning, but the men that killed Schofield were members of the Spinners' Association and you know it, every one of you, as well as you are sitting here. The strikers were engaged in a bitter and prolonged fight; these men were angry and ugly and hateful," argued Attorney [Hosea] Knowlton for the government, "because they thought he would work and they did not want him to. Men and women and children were coming home from work and he is struck down and killed and nobody was there to pick him up except a poor little knobstick spinner. Not one of these people knew anything about it."

An eyewitness, Ellen Foster, met with Alice Whally later in the evening after the assault on Schofield and said, "Alice, that man we saw at the steps was the man that struck Schofield." She repeated the same story to police officers [George] Seaver and Dexter and to Mr. George Robinson in the office of the Chace Mill one or two days before the arrest of Crann. But when it came to the trial, Ellen Foster had changed her narrative. Knowlton believed that she had been intimidated by the accused.

Trial: The trial was held in June of 1884, lasting only two days. After testimony had been presented, Judge Hamilton B. Staples charged the jury with this: "The defendant in this case is accused of manslaughter, it being alleged that he struck the second blow. Now, Mr. Foreman and gentlemen, suppose that he did just that for the sake of trying the rule of law; supposing that you should come to the conclusion that Crann did strike that blow, under what circumstances would you be justified in finding him guilty of manslaughter?

"In order to convict him of manslaughter, you must be satisfied that the death of Schofield would not have happened if he did not strike the additional blow. If you are left in doubt whether the death was caused by the wound or by the blow inflicted by the prisoner, you cannot convict the prisoner. You see the sound sense of that rule.

"It simply comes to this: if the blow inflicted by the prisoner shortened the dead man's life one hour, if it was the cause of his death when it happened, then, if he committed that assault he is liable to be convicted of manslaughter and if you are left in doubt upon the point, and if you think that Schofield's death was due to the original blow, then Crann cannot be convicted of manslaughter. It is competent for the jury to return a verdict of guilty on the whole, guilty of the assault which throws out the killing, or not guilty, which clears him altogether" (*Fall River Daily News*).

James E. Crann was acquitted of the murder of John Schofield.

Further Reading:

"News in Brief." *The Brooklyn Daily Eagle* (Brooklyn, New York), March 22, 1884.
"Not Guilty." *Fall River Daily News* (Fall River, Massachusetts), June 14, 1884.

PHILIP D. SLOCUM

Murder/Suicide at No. 18 South Water Street, New Bedford, Massachusetts, on June 6, 1885.

Victim: Philip D. Slocum, 45.

Accused: D.T. Sherburne (aka Charles Foss), 40.

Details: Philip D. Slocum was sitting at his desk in the counting room in his clothing store around noon time at 18 South Water Street in New Bedford, in the act of making an entry in the ledger, when a man names Charles Foss entered from the back room, leaned a moment against the railing dividing the counting room from the store, and, without speaking, drew a revolver and shot Slocum in the head, at the base of the skull. Slocum fell from his stool to the floor and probably died instantaneously. Foss then returned to the back room and pointed the muzzle to his right temple and fired—shooting himself, and thus committing suicide.

According to the *Harrisburg Telegraph*, "There were two men and a boy in the store at the time, but they did not at first realize what was done, so quickly had it passed. When they recovered from their astonishment and horror they at once sent for physicians, but Slocum was already dead when they arrived. Foss died within a few minutes after. Slocum is about 45 years old, married, and leaves a widow and six children. Foss is 40 years old, and has gone under the name of D.T. Sherburne. He belongs to New Hampshire, and has sailed from this post on a number of voyages. Slocum was trying to ship him as cooper and carpenter on the bark *Wave*. Foss was dissipated, and has been under the influence of liquor during most of the time he has been here. He asked Slocum when he came here to ship him to Hudson Bay, as he wanted to die if he could not be cured of the curse of drinking, and he had asked Slocum several times this forenoon if he was not going to ship him soon, but did not seem ill-natured. It is not known that they ever had any trouble."

The Brooklyn Daily Eagle reported that Slocum "for many years had been engaged in shipping men for whaling voyages. Several days ago a man known here as Charles Foss, but whose real name is D.T. Sherburn [sic], applied to him for a position as cook on the bark *Wave*, which sails in a few days for Hudson's Bay. Sherburn [sic] is well known among whaling men, and last sailed as a cooper of the bark *Sea Fox*. Mr. Slocum sent for Captain Benton, of the *Wave*, to come to his office this morning, and the latter agreed to ship Sherburn [sic]. Mr. Slocum told Benton that the man's failing was a love for liquor, and Sherburn [sic] himself said that he wanted to go to Hudson's Bay, to 'get the rum out of him.'…Sherburn [sic]…had attempted suicide once before by taking poison."

Outcome: As this was a murder/suicide, after the inquest there were no further legal matters in this case.

Further Reading:

"Killed at his Desk." *The Saint Paul Globe* (Saint Paul, Minnesota), June 7, 1885.
"New Bedford." *Green Bay Press-Gazette* (Green Bay, Wisconsin), June 8, 1885.
"A Shocking Tragedy." *The Brooklyn Daily Eagle* (Brooklyn, New York), June 6, 1885.
"Unexplained Murder." *Harrisburg Telegraph* (Harrisburg, Pennsylvania), June 6, 1885.

JOHN A. MOWBRY

Murder by stabbing at 6 Turner Court, New Bedford, Massachusetts, on December 11, 1901.

Victim: John A. Mowbry, 56.

Accused: Elizabeth Margaret Mowbry, 50.

Details: According the *Boston Post*, "John Mowbry, a ragpicker by occupation, 56 years of age, lived with his wife, the arrested woman, in that part of New Bedford called Holy Acre, so named because less righteousness is supposed to pervade that locality than elsewhere in the city. At 6 Turner court the two occupied a small tenement, two rooms of which they let to one Frank Bessey and his wife. Mowbry and his wife lived in two back rooms on the lower floor.

"Both husband and wife and been continually in trouble with the police in the 10 years they had lived in the city. Both had served terms innumerable in the House of Correction for drunkenness and disturbance of the peace.

"On the night of Dec. 11 Mowbry and his wife, Mr. and Mrs. Bessey, a Thomas J. Lovejoy and his wife, and an Italian, whose identity is fixed solely by the name 'Joe,' gathered in the Mowbry rooms for a night of revelry. According to the police, the supply of liquor ran short, and Joe, the Italian, sent Mowbry to purchase more, giving him a $5 bill. Mowbry returned with a quart of whiskey and $4 in change. Then the Italian handed Mrs. Lovejoy a dollar to buy food, and the sisters went out, leaving Mowbry, his wife and Joe, the Italian, in the room drinking.

"About an hour afterwards, Bessey, returning home, met Joe, the Italian, coming away from the Mowbry home, saying that the Mowbrys were in a row and he decided to get out. Bessey on going in saw Mowbry on the floor and Mrs. Mowbry bending over him. She saw Bessey, and appealed to him to help her husband to bed. Bessey refused and went out of the house and over to the Lovejoys, who lived across the street.

"He had not been there long when Mrs. Mowbry came running over and said her husband was dead. Lovejoy and Bessey rushed over and found Mowbry lying in a pool of blood on the floor just where Bessey saw them when he came in.

"They notified the police and found the man had been stabbed twice in the left side, evidently with a pocket knife. Suspecting Joe, the Italian, at once the officers started after him. He was not found, nor have the police succeeded in locating him to this day. Mrs. Mowbry, who was taken to the lockup on the charge of drunkenness and also held as a witness, claimed that in a row over money Joe had stabbed her husband.

"The next day, on being searched, a bloody 'jack knife,' identified afterwards as Mowbry's was found in the pocket of her underskirt. She denied all knowledge of it. The police then charged her with murder.

"Since her arrest she has told over half a dozen different stories of the murder, swearing each was true until the other was told. Her last story, induced by the police 'third degree,' is to the effect that her husband stabbed himself. This, from the nature and position of the wounds, is manifestly absurd.

"The police claim to be able to prove by Mrs. Lovejoy and Mrs. Bessey, who met the Italian leaving the house, that Mrs. Mowbry was heard in a violent quarrel with her husband after the Italian left.

"There occurs a discrepancy in Bessey's story, but the police claim to be able to clear that up. At present the evidence at best against Mrs. Mowbry is not exceedingly strong. It is for this reason the citizens are indignant over the action of the police.

"The woman does not realize her position. She is 50 years old, a wreck from drink and hardship. No one knows from whence she and her husband came. Frankly they were the lowest slums of the city. But her case has stirred up sentiment against the police which bids fair to crystallize into vigorous action" (December 23, 1901).

Trial: At the preliminary hearing, held on December 27, 1901, in New Bedford, Mrs. Margaret Mowbry was adjudged probably guilty and held over for the Superior Court trial. The *Boston Post* reported that Mrs. Mowbry stated this at her judgment: "'I would not dare to face my God and know that I had accused an innocent man. The Italian did not have a bit of trouble with my husband. All the trouble took place between my husband and myself, after everybody left the house.'"

On February 21, Elizabeth Margaret Mowbry was sentenced to five years in the House of Correction. She had pleaded guilty to manslaughter in the killing of her husband, John A. Mowbry, in a drunken row.

Further Reading:

"Mrs. Mowbry Clears Suspect." *Boston Post* (Boston, Massachusetts), December 28, 1901.

"Mrs. Mowbry Gets 5 Years." *Boston Post* (Boston, Massachusetts), February 22, 1902.

"New Bedford Aroused by 'Third Degree'." *Boston Post* (Boston, Massachusetts), December 23, 1901.

PELEG CORNELL

Murder by bludgeoning near Little Compton, Massachusetts, on February 11, 1902.

Victim: Peleg Cornell, 70.

Accused: Unsolved, until . . .

Details: The mystery surrounding the murder of Peleg Cornell baffled the police for years. They could not determine just who would want to kill an "aging hermit" in such a violent manner. In 1910, they finally had their answer, but it came to them purely by happenstance.

According to the *Newport Mercury* of February 14, 1902, "A dastardly murder was discovered yesterday in a lonely spot, two miles and a half from the village of Little Compton, on the Adamsville Road. The victim, Peleg Cornell, 80 years old [sic, other reports have him at age 70], lived alone, and when found was lying on the floor of his own house in a pool of blood, with his head battered in and almost severed from his body.

"The house where Cornell resided is a small one-story building with two rooms. It stands directly upon the roadway leading from Little Compton to Adamsville, about midway between the two places. All about the house are woods, while on the opposite side of the road is also a thick wood with a cart path leading back from the road nearly opposite the house. The nearest neighbor is only 500 feet away to the north, but trees intervene between the houses, cutting off the view even at this time of year, when the trees are stripped of their foliage. The only building within a mile on the south side is a schoolhouse, which stands on the crest of what is known as Simmons hill, a few hundred yards away. Peleg Cornell, then, was practically cut off from all neighbors as far as actual view of their premises goes.

"Tuesday night [Feb. 11] about 6 o'clock Cornell was last seen alive, and his neighbor, Davoll, who passed the place at 10:30 the same night, noticed that the house was dark and supposing that the old man had retired continued on his way to his own home, giving no further thought to the matter. Yesterday, as there continued to be no sign of life about the house, the coroner was notified, and, with the medical officer and town sergeant went to the house.

"When the officers broke into the house a horrible sight greeted them.

Lying on the floor of the inner room, with one arm stretched out and the other across his body, was the mutilated body of Peleg Cornell. A huge gash in the man's throat penetrated to the spinal column, almost severing the head from the body. At first sight it looked like suicide, for on the floor at one side and near the outstretched hand lay a bloody knife, without doubt the one which had inflicted the wound in the neck. Further examination showed that the head had been literally showered with blows dealt from some blunt instrument. A cut on top of the head, running back from the forehead, might have been made with a dull axe, while a blow that had crushed the frontal bone was evidently dealt with a blunt instrument, possibly the blunt side of an axehead. Another gash was found under the right eye, and a round bruise showed on the left side of the face near the ear.

"About the house everything was in perfect order, or at least as orderly as was ordinarily the case. From all appearances the old man had made all his usual preparations for retiring, and no signs of a scuffle were evident. In the oven of the stove was a little armful of wood, placed there as usual to dry for the morning fire. The oil in the lamp showed evidence of having burned but a comparatively short time, and a brick was found in the bed, wrapped in a cloth, having evidently been placed there by the unfortunate man for the purpose of warming the bed clothes. Two chairs were pulled up before the kitchen stove as though two persons had been seated there engaged in conversation, and, on a shelf near by was a glass halffull of cider.

"The autopsy, which took place yesterday afternoon, showed that death had probably been caused by the wound at the neck, but in the opinion of the doctors one or more of the wounds on the head were inflicted first, rendering the man unconscious. The murderer then, in the opinion of the doctors, after striking the old man on the head and felling him to the floor, had made his work more sure by going back and almost cutting off his victim's head. It was also decided by the autopsy that the man had been dead 36 hours or more when discovered, fixing the time of the murder as between the hours of 6 and 10:30 Tuesday evening.

"As to the murderer, there is at the present time no trace whatever, for after finishing his work he apparently left the house, locking it after him.

"In the cart path across the road from the house, and about 500 feet into the woods, school children found an axe, which was later identified as the property of Peleg Cornell, and turned over to Coroner Gifford.

"The dead man was born in Tiverton, and is thought to have a sister residing in that town at the present time. He had resided in Little Compton about three years having come here from Tiverton. Cornell, as was to be expected on account of his age, did not work and had no visible means of support. His house was known, however as a resort for rough characters, to whom it is said he sold cider, stronger liquor being rather difficult for him to obtain.

"He was known, however, to have small amount of money, some $25 or $30, just before his death, and this money together with the old leather wallet in which he carried it, was missing when the search was made by the town sergeant. There is little doubt in the minds of the authorities at Little Compton that robbery was the motive for the murder, and that for the paltry sum mentioned the old man was brutally murdered."

The Boston Post reported that, "In his younger days Cornell was convicted of arson in Portsmouth and served a long term in the State prison. He is said to have been apprehensive of bodily harm and had a huge club with which to protect himself.

"Cornell consulted a lawyer, it is said, with regard to the selling of cider, and learning that by refusing to sell by the glass, he kept within the law, conducted a business in that manner."

We also learn that rewards totaling $1000 had been offered by the state of Rhode Island and Little Compton for evidence that would lead to the arrest and conviction of the person who murdered Peleg Cornell.

Trial: In March of 1910, a man by the name of Angles Snell died in the Massachusetts State prison. He confessed to five murders before his death, one of them being Peleg Cornell. Snell will make another appearance in the book in the case of Tillinghast Kirby.

Afterword: Snell appears to be a man who murdered for money, and mostly complete strangers, making him an unlikely suspect in any unsolved crimes in the area that extended from Wareham, Massachusetts, to Little Compton, Rhode Island. Perhaps he was a true SouthCoast serial killer.

Further Reading:

"Aged Hermit Found Murdered." *Marshall County News* (Marysville, Kansas), February 21, 1902.
"Following the Death of Angles Snell." *Newport Mercury* (Newport, Rhode Island), March 19, 1910.
"Peleg Cornell, 80 Years Old, Found Dead and Mutilated." *Newport Daily News* (Newport, Rhode Island), February 14, 1902.
"Rewards." *Newport Mercury* (Newport, Rhode Island), February 22, 1902.
"Working on Cornell Case." *Boston Post* (Boston, Massachusetts), February 20, 1902.

ANGELINE & AMEDEE CHABOT

Murder/Suicide on Pleasant Street in Fall River, Massachusetts, on March 17, 1903.

Victim: Angeline Chabot (aka Angela, aka Angele Tremblay), 45.

Accused: Amedee D. Chabot, 44.

Details: Angeline Chabot was found murdered "in a space under a building in Pleasant street, used as a fish market. The head had been badly battered, apparently with a club. The police were informed that unkindly relations had existed between the woman and her husband, Amadeo [sic] Chabot, and are searching for the man.

"Mrs. Chabot was forty-five years old. Under the name of Angela Tremblay [city directories list her Angele] she carried on a restaurant [1809 Pleasant Street] not far from Beauregard's market, and she lived near by [at 1858 Pleasant Street]. It is believed that as she was going home from her restaurant she was attacked near the market and thrown down a bank by the side of the street and beaten to death by a person armed with a club. The body was hidden then under the building, where Omer Beauregard, the proprietor of the fish market [at 1807 Pleasant Street] found it.

"The Chabot family included the father, mother and two children. Cabot was about the vicinity during the forenoon, but he had disappeared before the arrival of the police. Save for the report of the unpleasant relations between the husband and wife the police are unable to fix upon any motive" (*Arizona Republic*, March 23, 1903).

A man who answered Amedee's description was reported to have presented a bloodstained bill in payment for a train ticket to Boston.

The *Fitchburg Sentinel* reports that on March 18, 1903, the day following the murder of Angeline Chabot, the body of her husband, Amedee, was discovered in the "North Watuppa pond by detectives Shea and Connelly, who had been searching the shores of the pond on a suicide theory. Chabot was believed by man to have gone to Canada and officers had been dispatched there to follow up a clue thought to have been furnished by a $2 bill covered with blood which was presented at the Fall River railroad station early Tuesday morning in payment for a ticket to Boston. The officers had proceeded as far as Nashua, N.H., yesterday, where they were pursuing their investigations.

"Detectives Shea and Connolly were searching the shores of the North Watuppa pond when their attention was attracted by an overcoat and sack coat hanging on the post of an unused sawdust bin. There were bloodstains on the coat, and in an open space in the bushes was found a package of paris green [toxic rodenticide]. Shea went down to the shore and about 20 feet away saw a piece of white cloth under the water and at once sent Connolly for assistance. While the latter was notifying police headquarters, two boys arrived with ice picks, taken from an ice house nearby, and the body was dislodged. It was in a crouching position with both hands grasping an old exhaust pipe which runs some distance out into the pond and which was formerly used by the Crystal Ice company. The man was in his shirt sleeves and was fully identified.

"The police believe the man committed suicide early Tuesday morning, the morning on which the body of his wife was discovered, and that before going out into the pond he took a large dose of paris green. Considerable poison was scattered about in the grass, which would indicated that Chabot had been in a hurry or was very nervous. No weapon with which the murder of his wife might have been committed was found upon his person."

Further Reading:

"Dead Woman Victim of Club." *Arizona Republic* (Phoenix, Arizona), March 23, 1903.
"The End of Chabot." *Fitchburg Sentinel* (Fitchburg, Massachusetts), March 19, 1903.
"Murder at Fall River, Mass." *Hartford Courant* (Hartford, Connecticut), March 18, 1903.

TILLINGHAST KIRBY

Man killed due to a fractured skull on boat near Westport, Massachusetts, on September 9, 1903.

Victim: Tillinghast Kirby, 87 years, 7 months.

Accused: Angles Snell, 62.

Details: The murder of Tillinghast Kirby occurred in a boat off Horse Neck, near Westport. Reports the *The Boston Daily Globe*, "Mr. Kirby was 87 years old, a resident of New Bedford, sportsman and hunter. He was on a fishing trip and was staying at Burden Head's cottage, Horse neck, according to his custom every summer. Though he was so old, he was a good swimmer and passionately fond of the water and of fishing.

"On the day of his death he went out in a white 'sharpie' to fish off the west side of Gooseberry neck, a small point of land at the end of Horse Neck beach. He failed to return that night and when F. Burden Head, with whom Angles Snell lived also, returned at 10 p.m. a search was started for Mr. Kirby.

"The next day Snell was hired by Edward A. Kirby, Tillinghast Kirby's son, to aid in the search. Snell went out with Gideon Butts and brought in the boat, which was anchored at the place where Snell said he last saw Kirby alive, and gave him some sea clams for bait.

"Kirby's rubber boots were found on the shore together; none of the fishermen believed they could possibly have washed ashore, but insisted that they must have been placed where they were found.

"Sept. 19, after heavy weather, which caused Mr. Kirby's body to break away from the pig iron with which it had been anchored to the bottom of the water, the remains of the old man came ashore on the eastern side of Gooseberry neck. The body was found by Frank Hitt and William Sylvester, two young men from New Bedford.

"Snell was arrested, primarily because he had no money, just before Sept. 9; he had plenty after Sept. 9 and Mr. Kirby's money, of which he was known to have a considerable sum on his person, was missing.

"After his arrest Philip Grinnell of Westport Point and Warren Gifford of Horseneck said they had seen the white sharpie—the one in which Mr. Kirby went fishing—with a green sharpie alongside. F. Burden Head said Snell went out in his green sharpie on the day of the murder.

"All the evidence brought out at the trial was circumstantial and showed more bad blood between Snell and Head than between Snell and Kirby."

The police later alleged that it was a quarrel over a woman that offered up the motive for the murder of Tillinghast Kirby by Angles Snell. According the *Fitchburg Sentinel* (September 21, 1903), "Snell is said to have been deeply in love with Mrs. Sarah Sherman, who was housekeeper for Snell, Kirby and one Burton Head. Snell and Head, who was also a fisherman, ran the house, while Kirby boarded with them.

"A year ago Snell brought Mrs. Sherman, a good looking woman of 40 years, to the house to act as housekeeper. Shortly after she came Head began to show her some attention, whereupon Snell became jealous. Snell and Head constantly quarreled over the woman.

"Mrs. Sherman aided with Head, and Snell endeavored to win back her affections. About a week before Kirby disappeared Snell came to Mrs. Sherman with an appeal to her to elope with him and get married.

"Mrs. Sherman twitted Snell about not having any money, and Snell declared that he would have money soon, enough to support both. He knew that Kirby had money in the bank, and asked the old man to lend him some. Kirby refused and the two had a quarrel.

"Snell anxious to take Mrs. Sherman away, believing that she would elope with him if he had any money, made a desperate attempt to obtain some. This, the police believe, explains the motive for a crime."

Trial: On October 17, 1903, Snell was adjudged probably guilty after a preliminary hearing and held for the Grand Jury. Snell was determined to be the last person to see have seen Kirby alive and he made conflicting statements about his whereabouts.

After a trial of nine days, on September 15, 1904, Angles Snell was found guilty of murder in the first degree. He was sentenced to death by electrocution. His death was to have occur during the week of December 10, 1905.

Afterword: On November 22, 1905, the Governor William L. Douglas of Massachusetts, on the advice of the Governor's Council, commuted the death sentence of Angles Snell to life imprisonment. Not only had one of the witnesses in his trial been more recently, in another case, charged with perjury, his council argued that there was doubt as to the mental soundness of Snell. Additionally, all twelve jurors in his original case had signed the petition supporting the commutation.

After his commutation, Snell was sent to Charlestown prison on November 24, 1905.

After Angles Snell "dropped dead" in State prison in Charlestown, Massachusetts on March 14, at the age of sixty-nine, of "sclerosis of coronary arteries," it was revealed that he had confessed to his jailer that he had committed five murders, with robbery as the sole motive. He admitted to killing Tillinghast Kirby and confessed to the murder of Philip Cornell [Peleg], an old hermit of Westport; two strangers who came to Westport on a vacation trip, and an unknown Portuguese who had paid Snell to guide him to an adjourning town. He also admitted to burning a barn for revenge.

Further Reading:

"Angles Snell Sentenced." *Fitchburg Sentinel* (Fitchburg, Massachusetts), October 14, 1905.
"Angles Snell in State Prison." *The Boston Daily Globe* (Boston, Massachusetts), November 25, 1905.
"Appeal for Commutation." *The Boston Daily Globe* (Boston, Massachusetts), November 1, 1905.
"Confessed Five Murders." *The Portsmouth Herald* (Portsmouth, New Hampshire), March 15, 1910.
"Death of Angles Snell." *The Portsmouth Herald* (Portsmouth, New Hampshire), March 15, 1910.
"Five-time Murderer." *Vicksburg Evening Post* (Vicksburg, Mississippi), March 18, 1910.
"Gives Life to Angles Snell." *The Boston Daily Globe* (Boston, Massachusetts), November 23, 1905.
"Held for Killing Aged Man." *The Brooklyn Daily Eagle* (Brooklyn, New York), October 18, 1903.
"Murder of an Aged Man." *The Boston Daily Globe* (Boston, Massachusetts), November 23, 1905.
"Prompted by Love." *Fitchburg Sentinel* (Fitchburg, Massachusetts), September 21, 1903.
"Snell Guilty of Murder." *Fitchburg Sentinel* (Fitchburg, Massachusetts), September 16, 1904.
"Snell is Saved by a Single Vote." *The Boston Daily Globe* (Boston, Massachusetts), November 23, 1905.

Angles Snell. *The Boston Daily Globe*, November 23, 1905.

Grave of Tillinghast Kirby, born February 9, 1816, and died on September 9, 1903, Oak Grove Cemetery, New Bedford, Massachusetts. (Findagrave.com)

HATTIE CARTER

"Colored" woman found murdered at 9 South Water Street in New Bedford, Massachusetts, on April 28, 1909. Probably died two weeks earlier.

Victim: Hattie Carter, 28.

Accused: Unsolved.

Details: The body of an unidentified black woman was found on April 28, 1909, in the upper room of a vacant tenement at 9 South Water Street in New Bedford, Massachusetts. Her body "was hidden beneath several bedticks that lay on a bed, the head covered with a sheet and apparently soaked in blood" (*Fall River Daily Evening News*, April 28, 1909).

The woman was later identified as Hattie V. Carter by her sister Louisa Johnson of Newport, Rhode Island. Hattie was the daughter of Joseph Johnson and Annie Stewart. No cause of death was officially determined because, according to her death record, her body was "in advanced putrification." Because of this condition, it was believed that Hattie's death occurred as long as two weeks prior to her discovery.

According to the *Fitchburg Sentinel*, Hattie "had recently paid a fine of $50 on a charge of keeping a disorderly house…The fact that the head was covered with a sheet tightly wrapped about it, that the body was between two mattresses and that the bed had been broken as if in a struggle, made it very improbable that the woman had taken her own life. Nothing was found in the room, however, to furnish a clue to the identity of her supposed murderer."

Of note is the fact that her death record lists her as being married but no husband's name is listed. Since most murders are committed by someone the victim knows, it would have been important for the police to pursue this line of reasoning. Unfortunately, and perhaps because of her race, there appears to have been minimal work done to determine who killer might be.

Further Reading:

"Body Found in Vacant House." *Norwich Bulletin* (Norwich, Connecticut), April 29, 1909.
"Indications of Murder." *Fitchburg Sentinel* (Fitchburg, Massachusetts), April 29, 1909.
"Murder in New Bedford." *Fall River Daily Evening News* (Fall River, Massachusetts), April 28, 1909.

ANNIE WALSH

Death and mutilation of a woman aboard coal barge docked in New Bedford, Massachusetts, on January 10, 1914.

Victim: Annie Walsh, 30.

Accused: Captain Charles Matrony, 25.

Details: The death of Annie Walsh and the subsequent murder investigation is a strange case, not only for the manner of her demise, but for the mixed signals the police gave to the press as to whether the case would be solved at all. The story was so gruesome as to be carried by the International News Service to newspapers across America.

Deemed in the newspapers as "a New Bedford woman of rather questionable character," Annie was thirty years old at the time of her death. The sensational details as reported in *The Buffalo Enquirer* are as follows:

"One of the most brutal murders in the history of New England was revealed early today [Jan. 10] when the headless and partially dismembered body of Annie Walsh, thirty years old, was found aboard the coal barge *Snipe* at its dock. The body was lying in a bunk.

"The clothing on the bunk was soaked with blood and the walls of the little cabin were spattered in many places.

"Captain Charles Matrony of Bristol, R.I., was arrested, charged with the slaying. The police claim they found the captain crouching in a dazed condition with a rope around his neck in a corner of the cabin.

"The police believe that Miss Walsh's slayer had planned to cut up the body, as Hans Schmidt dismembered that of Ann Aumuller, in New York, and that when he heard the police coming he tried to commit suicide.

"He admitted, they say, he had been drinking heavily, but declared he remembered nothing about the crime. Miss Walsh, the victim, was an orphan and without relatives so far as known. She lived at No. 338 Purchase street.

"The first information of the slaying came to the police when Louis Therrien, accompanied by his twenty-year-old daughter Flora, came to the police station shortly after midnight and reported that a woman had been killed aboard a Philadelphia & Reading coal barge lying at her dock on the water front.

"Therrien said he had been invited earlier in the evening to pass the night aboard the *Snipe*. He was horrified to see the woman's body, partly cut in pieces, lying before him when he entered the cabin.

"He went first to his home, roused his daughter and then went to the police station to tell what he had discovered. Therrien was held as a witness.

"After arresting Matrony, the police found a short-handled axe stained with blood, and a knife which evidently had been used in cutting up the body.

"Capt. Matrony came here in the *Snipe* with a cargo of coal from Perth Amboy, N.J. last Monday. He sailed from Perth Amboy just after Christmas. He told the police that he was the son of Anton Matrony of No. 55 Richmond street, Bristol, R.I. and that he had two brothers and three sisters there.

"The police first called the murder an 'open and shut case,' but the crime was clouded in mystery by further investigation. Although Matrony was formally charged with murder and his case continued till January 21, the police are not at all confident of his guilt.

"There are contradictions in the story told by Therrien, according to the police.

"First he said that he went to the barge, thinking to find work; that he looked in the lighted window of the cabin; that he saw nothing of the captain and that thereupon he notified the police.

"Then the police found that Therrien, Matrony, Miss Walsh and another woman were together late that night.

"Therrien later said that upon arriving at the barge he went into the west cabin. He said that he was very drunk, but that he locked the door to prevent anyone robbing him. Half an hour later, he declared, he awoke and called out to Capt. Matrony.

"Receiving no reply he opened his cabin door to investigate, saw the dead body in the bunk of the east cabin and bolted from the barge. But he did not go direct to the police, he admits instead he went to his home, told his daughter the story and they both went to the police station."

Trial: The preliminary hearing ended on January 22, 1914 and Charles Matrony was adjudged probably guilty. He was held without bail for the February term of the Superior Court.

At the trial on February 12, Charles Matrony withdrew his plea of not guilty of murder in the first degree and instead pleaded guilty to second degree murder in the killing of Annie Walsh. Matrony's council argued that he had been intoxicated at the time of the crime.

On February 21, 1914, Captain Charles Matrony was sentenced to life imprisonment in Massachusetts state prison for the murder of Annie Walsh.

Afterword: Census records for 1930 show that Charles Matrony, at age forty-one, was then an inmate at the Boston Massachusetts State Prison.

Further Reading:

"Axe Murder Puzzles Police." *The Allentown Leader* (Allentown, Pennsylvania), January 12, 1914.
"Life Sentence for Captain of Barge." *Norwich Bulletin* (Norwich, Connecticut), February 14, 1914.
"Matroni Held for Trial." *Fitchburg Sentinel* (Fitchburg, Massachusetts), January 22, 1914.
"Mutilated Body of Woman Found in Ship's Cabin." *The Buffalo Inquirer* (Buffalo, New York), January 10, 1914.
Newport Mercury (Newport, Rhode Island), February 21, 1914.

ALICE GRACE FARIA

Wife murdered by her husband in their home at 7 Margin Street in New Bedford, Massachusetts, on April 27, 1914.

Victim: Alice Grace Faria, 26.

Accused: Marcellino Faria (aka Charles Faria), 30.

Details: Alice Grace was born on May 2, 1884 in Portugal. She immigrated to America in 1891 and married Marcellino Faria on Marcy 18, 1905. They had one child, Louis, born in 1907 and died in 1991.

On April 27, 1914, her husband, for reasons unknown to us, slit his wife's throat with a razor in their home a 7 Margin Street in New Bedford. He then attempted to kill himself but was unsuccessful. He was arrested and adjudged probably guilty, and indicted for murder in the first degree.

Trial: Marcellino Faria waived his trial and pleaded guilty to murder in the second degree and on December 3, 1914, was sentenced to life imprisonment.

Afterword: Census records from 1920 place him in state prison in Charlestown, Massachusetts, working as a cook in the prison kitchen. Other genealogical sources show him as dying on February 25, 1955, in New Bedford, at age 61.

Further Reading:

"For Murder of Wife." *Fitchburg Sentinel* (Fitchburg, Massachusetts), December 8, 1914.
"Life Sentence for Murderer." *Norwich Bulletin* (Norwich, Connecticut), December 4, 1914.

DELVINA GRENIER BLANCHARD

Wife murdered by her husband in their home at 54½ Hathaway Avenue in New Bedford, Massachusetts, on October 30, 1914.

Victim: Delvina Grenier Blanchard, 51.

Accused: Cleophas Blanchard, 51.

Details: Cleophas Blanchard was a jealous man. He is alleged to have quarreled with his wife Delvina over her wanting to attend a wedding of a friend. Believing that his wife had affections for another, he slit her throat with a razor in the kitchen of their New Bedford home and then fled to New Hampshire. He eventually returned and turned himself into the police.

Trial: Cleophas Blanchard waived his trial and pleaded guilty to murder in the second degree and on February 15, 1915, was sentenced to life imprisonment. Sometime later he was removed to the State Hospital for the Insane in Bridgewater, Massachusetts.

Afterword: Census records for 1920 place Cleophas Blanchard in the State Hospital for the Insane in Bridgewater, Massachusetts, working as a bedmaker. Massachusetts death records show him dying in 1928 in Bridgewater, at age 65.

Further Reading:

"New Bedford Murderer Has Taftville Relatives." *Norwich Bulletin* (Norwich, Connecticut), October 31, 1914.
"To Life Imprisonment." *The Boston Daily Globe* (Boston, Massachusetts), February 16, 1915.

DIANA JEFFREY

Murder and attempted suicide on the fourth floor of the Stag Hotel, 83 Elm Street, New Bedford, Massachusetts, on April 1, 1916.

Victim: Diana Jeffrey, 21.

Accused: Peter J. Finirnov, age unknown.

Details: Mrs. Diana Jeffrey, formerly of Fall River, was estranged from her husband, Joseph. He had been refused a divorce from Diana the week before in the Bristol County Superior Court. He had alleged that she had been frequently seen drinking with men in the Stag Hotel and other cafes in the city. The Jeffreys had a three-year-old son.

On the evening of April 1, 1916, Mrs. Diana Jeffrey was shot three times on the fourth floor of the Stag Hotel and her body dragged down a flight of stairs and hidden in a bathroom. She was discovered about an hour later by Thomas Potter, the proprietor of the hotel, at 8 o'clock. He claimed that her body was still warm. Mrs. Jeffrey was shot behind the left shoulder, through the abdomen, and just below the heart.

The guests at the hotel were questioned and the police were left with no leads. Fourth floor occupants stated they heard a series of muffled sounds, like revolver shots at 7 p.m., but paid no heed to the noises.

In a strange turn of events, Peter J. Finirnov, recently arrived to New Bedford from Poland, confessed early the next morning to the crime. He said they had quarreled over money. After killing the woman he turned the gun on himself, shooting himself through his left lung. He then left the hotel, rode more than two miles in a street car, and collapsed.

Once arrested, Finirnov changed his story to say he had been shot under a railroad bridge by Walentz Katzmarick, a fellow Pole, who was at once taken into custody and charged with assault with intent to murder. Katzmarick denied the charges against him. Police brought in Miss Matilda Sullivan who positively identified Finirnov as the man she had seen with Mrs. Jeffrey the night before. At this, Finirnov again confessed that he had shot Mrs. Jeffrey twice through the body with a 38-caliber revolver and then fired a shot into himself.

At the time of the final article in this case, Finirnov was in extremely critical condition but expected to recover. Unknown still was how he dragged Mrs. Jeffrey's body down a flight of stairs when he was so wounded.

Outcome: No records could be located as to the outcome of this case. It is unknown if Finirnov died from his wounds or went to prison or the State Hospital for the insane (Bridgwater), a place where, at one time, many murderers in Massachusetts spent their final years.

Further Reading:

"Confesses to Killing Woman." *Boston Post* (Boston, Massachusetts), April 3, 1916.
"Woman is Murdered in Hotel." *Boston Post* (Boston, Massachusetts), April 2, 1916.

WALENTY JUSZYNSKI

Husband murdered by wife in New Bedford, Massachusetts, and then hidden underneath the floor of the living room at 651 South First Street, on or near August 24, 1924.

Victim: Walenty [aka Joseph] Juszynski, unknown age.

Accused: Mary Juszynski, unknown age.

Details: On September 24, 1924, according to *The Morning News*, the body of a man supposed to be Joseph Juszynski, who had been missing since August 24, was found concealed beneath the flooring of the living room of his home.

"Mrs. Mary Juszynski, the supposed wife of the dead man, has not been seen or heard from since about a week after her husband's disappearance. The police found that the body had been crowded through a trap door in the floor of the living-room, the feet doubled back over the head. The man's back was broken, and there was a large hole in the head. A note purporting to have been written by Mrs. Juszynski, found in the store, spoke of a dead man under the floor, and of drowning herself; and also that two knew about the body under the floor. The note was vaguely written and one translation was to the effect that there were two men under the floor. Dr. Shanks, medical examiner, consulted the district attorney, expressing the opinion that the entire floor should be ripped up to see if there is another body."

Another news report said that the note said that Juszynski had been killed because he was "cruel to women." Mary Juszynski was arrested in Cohoes, New York, and extradited back to New Bedford to stand trial.

Trial: After a five day trial, Mary Juszynski was sentenced to life imprisonment on February 25, 1925, by Judge Hugo A. Dubuque. It was reported that no witnesses were called for the defense.

Further Reading:

"Found Under Floor: Wife is Missing." *The Morning News* (Wilmington, Delaware), September 25, 1924.
"Life Term Given to Slayer of Husband." *The Bridgeport Telegram* (Bridgeport, Connecticut), February 25, 1925.

ERNEST PELLETIER

Man shot to death in the back as he sat on his porch at 94 East Main Street on the night of August 27, 1927, in Fall River, Massachusetts.

Victim: Ernest Pelletier, 46.

Accused: Napoleon Pelletier, 30.

Details: Ernest Pelletier, a bachelor, was killed by a single shot to the back as he sat on his front port at 94 East Main Street in Fall River. The police began with two theories—one that a relative had killed him, as Ernest was heavily insured, and the other was that Ernest's recent threats to inform the police of illegal liquor sales in Fall River and Tiverton if he were not furnished free liquor inspired the killing.

On September 19, 1927, brother Napoleon, a 30-year-old city employee, who had been out of work for three months, was arrested and charged with the murder.

Ballistic experts declared that the bullet that was taken from Pelletier's body came from a Spanish automatic that had been found at the bottom of Cook Pond four days later by a group of boys. Records of a mail order firearm linked the gun to Napoleon. Police also learned that Ernest was an alcoholic who had quite a bit of life insurance, "for a man of his class."

Trial: At the preliminary hearing, Judge Edward F. Hafiny adjudged Napoleon probably guilty and found that the State had established that Napoleon had been near the scene of the shooting and admitted that at one time he had owned a weapon like the one used. Napoleon was held without bail to await the Grand Jury. After a trial that lasted one week, Napoleon Pelletier was acquitted by a jury in Superior Court on April 16, 1928.

Further Reading:

"Charged with Slaying Heavily Insured Brother." Reading Times (Reading, Pennsylvania), September 20, 1927.
"Pelletier is Acquitted." *The Scranton Republican* (Scranton, Pennsylvania), April 17, 1928.

HOPE, DWIGHT, & AVELING ALLINSON

Mother drowned two of her three children in Buzzards Bay, then committed suicide, at Barstow's Wharf in Mattapoisett, Massachusetts, on March 13, 1931.

Victims: Hope, 6, Dwight, 3.

Accused: Aveling Hopewell Allinson, 33.

Details: Known for being despondent, but never suicidal, Mrs. William Chester Allinson (Aveling Hopewell), 33, of Saylesville, Rhode Island, hurled her three children (Wayne, 8, Hope, 6, and Dwight, 3) from a wharf in Mattapoisett and then jumped in after them to apparently kill herself. Wayne had learned to swim the previous summer and survived to tell the story of the horrific event.

Constable Sylvester Savage was informed by telephone a small boy was seen walking on Water street, his clothes wringing wet. Savage found the boy who told him he was Wayne Allinson and his mother had tried to drown him.

According to the *Delphos Daily Herald*, "the boy told the police how his mother had taken him and his sister and brother on a 'picnic' to see the New York boat pass through Cape Cod canal. They drove from Saylesville in an automobile he said, and parked it near Barstow's landing, a long-unused pier. Then the walked down the pier.

"At the end of the pier Mrs. Allinson pushed the two small children into the water and then tried to throw Wayne in, but he struggled with her. She finally picked him up in her arms and jumped off the pier."

State police were called to drag the water for the bodies of the victims.

Further Reading:

"Child Escapes from Chilling Ocean Waters." *Delphos Daily Herald* (Delphos, Ohio), March 14, 1931.
"Mother Flings Two to Death; Takes Own Life." *The Sandusky Register* (Sandusky, Ohio), March 14, 1931.

Demented, She Drowns Children and Self

"Standing on a pier at Mattapoisett, Mass., with her three children—shown with her in the picture on the right—Mrs. William C. Allison [sic] of Saylesville, R.I., pushed them one by one into the icy water and then leaped in herself. Her 9-year-old boy Wayne (right) swam to safety. The body of 6-year-old Hope (left) was recovered, but an initial search of Buzzards Bay by grappling crews failed to reveal the bodies of Mrs. Allison and her baby, Dwight (center). Mrs. Allison, who was prominent in Massachusetts and Rhode Island society, is shown at left in a seated portrait. She recently had suffered a nervous breakdown. *The Post-Crescent* (Appleton, Wisconsin), March 18, 1931.

WILFRED BEDARD

Husband murdered by wife with a knife at 112 Lowell Street in Fall River, Massachusetts, on February 28, 1938.

Victim: Wilfred Bedard, 30.

Accused: Alma E. Bedard, 23.

Details: After a day-long argument, Alma Bedard, 23, plunged a butcher knife into the side of her husband, Wilfred, above the heart, moved him to the bed, and left him to die. The quarrel was over Wilfred's demand for 25 cents which she said he wanted to use to buy liquor.

Alma admitted to the stabbing after six hours of interrogation by the police, after first asserting that she had found him in that condition on the floor and had moved him to the bed.

According to the *Fitchburg Sentinel*, "An installment collector brought the first news of the tragedy, to Bedard's mother, telling her there was 'something wrong' at her son's home. The mother encountered her daughter-in-law in the yard of the latter's home and told her to call a physician after the younger woman said she could not afford to do so."

Wilfred and Alma were married in 1936 and had no children.

Trial: On July 2, 1938, Alma Bedard was convicted of manslaughter in the stabbing death of her husband, Wilfred. Judge Joseph L. Hurley sentenced her to twelve years in the Massachusetts Reformatory for Women in New Bedford.

Afterword: Census records from 1940 show that Alma was still in jail two years later and working as a mill operator. Genealogical records indicate that by 1948, Alma had been released and was working at the New Bedford YMCA, living at 310 Pleasant Street in New Bedford.

Further Reading:

"Fall River." *Fitchburg Sentinel* (Fitchburg, Massachusetts), July 2, 1938.
"Held in 25 Cent Stabbing." *The Gaffney Ledger* (Gaffney, South Carolina), March 8, 1938.
"Man Stabbed to Death; His Wife Arrested." *Fitchburg Sentinel* (Fitchburg, Massachusetts), March 1, 1938.
"Woman Arrested on Murder Charge." *North Adams Transcript* (North Adams, Massachusetts), March 1, 1938.

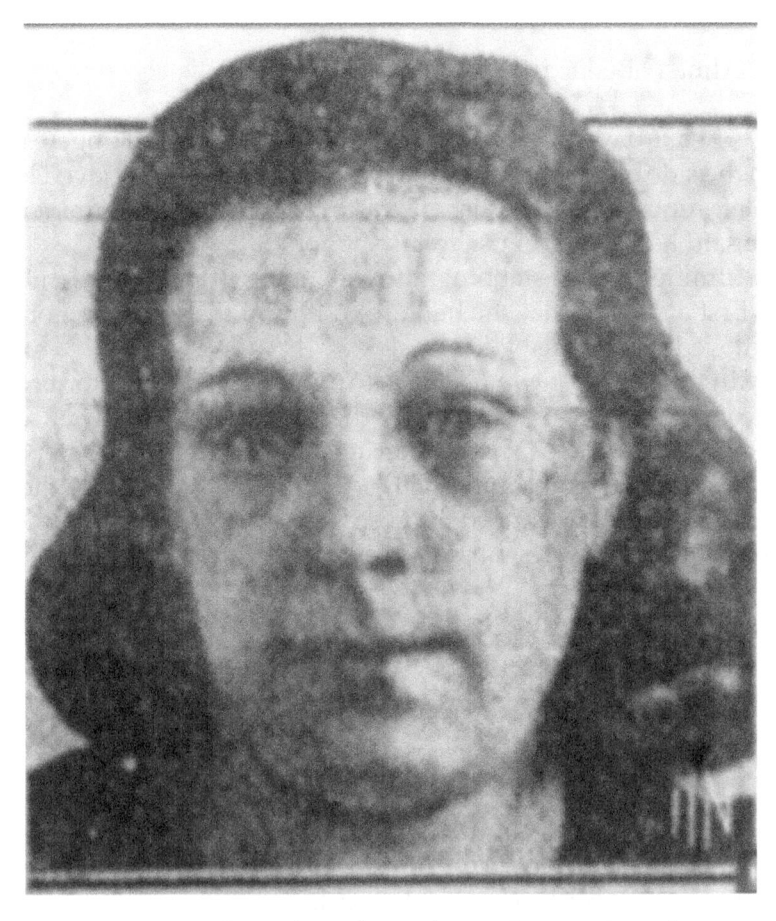

Alma E. Bedard, the 25 Cent Murderer. *The Gaffney Ledger* (Gaffney, South Carolina), March 8, 1938.

SAMUEL GENESKY

Man killed during a robbery of his pawnbroking establishment, located at 856 Acushnet Avenue, New Bedford, Massachusetts, in 1947.

Victim: Samuel Genesky, 72.

Accused: Antonio Francisco, 30.

Details: Antonio Francisco committed larceny when he robbed New Bedford pawnbroker Samuel Genesky. During the robbery, shots were fired. Francisco was arrested and convicted for the holdup in 1947 and was serving a prison sentence in state prison. While serving that sentence, and several weeks after the robbery, Genesky died from his injuries, thereby raising the charges of murder against Francisco.

Trial: Antonio Francisco waived his trial and pleaded guilty to murder in the second degree. On February 28, 1949, was sentenced to life imprisonment.

Further Reading:

"Held on Murder Charge." *Fitchburg Sentinel* (Fitchburg Sentinel), November 17, 1948.
"New Bedford Man Gets Life Term." *The Berkshire Eagle* (Pittsfield, Massachusetts), March 1, 1949.

JOSEPH BOLAY

Shotgun killing of man in his home in Somerset, Massachusetts, on September 24, 1948.

Victim: Joseph Bolay, 58.

Accused: Russell Bolay, 16.

Details: Russell Bolay, 16 years old, shot and killed his father with a shotgun in their home in Somerset, Massachusetts. Mrs. Bolay said her son had come home and found her husband, Joseph, drunk and arguing with her. The boy pleaded with his father to stop. When he refused, Russell grabbed the shotgun and fired at his father when he made a threatening gesture toward his mother.

Other reports state that Joseph Bolay had advanced toward Russell when he was shot. The police had been called to the house and had arrived just before the shot was fired. Russell is quoted as saying, "I was trying to protect my mother."

Outcome: No other information has been located.

Further Reading:

"Boy, 16, Is Held As Father Slayer." *Press and Sun-Bulletin* (Binghamton, New York), September 25, 1949.
"Kills Father as Police Come; Defending Mother, Son Says." *St. Louis Post-Dispatch* (St. Louis, Missouri), September 25, 1948.

NAPOLEON POISSON & HELEN ROGERS

Stabbing death of a man and woman at 19½ Nye Street in New Bedford, Massachusetts, on February 12, 1965.

Victims: Napoleon Poisson, 74, and Helen Rogers, 50.

Accused: Unnamed boy, 16.

Details: The bodies of Napoleon Poisson and Helen Rogers were found in Poisson's home at 19½ Nye Street in New Bedford. Rogers lived at 11 Nye Street. When discovered, the officials said they had been dead about ten to twelve hours. The kitchen of the house was splattered with blood and a knife was found near the bodies.

Eight hours after the bodies were discovered, a 16-year-old boy, whom the police refused to identify by name, was arrested for the fatal stabbing.

A neighbor who lived below Napoleon Poisson said that she heard a "little scuffle" about 1 a.m. and woman's voice call out, "Stop it, stop it, Jackie, please, please, no more."

Outcome: No other information has been located.

Further Details:

"New Bedford Boy Accused of Two Slayings." *Nashua Telegraph* (Nashua, New Hampshire), February 13, 1965.
"Pair Found Dead of Stab Wounds." *Hartford Courant* (Hartford, Connecticut), February 13, 1965.

JUDITH ANN SZATEK & RAYMOND G. FRENETTE

Engaged couple killed by gunshots as they sat in their parked car in a lane off Bullock Road in Freetown, Massachusetts, on May 1, 1965.

Victims: Judith Ann Szatek and Raymond G. Frenette, both 21.

Accused: Robert Garron, 16.

Details: On May 1, 1965, in a lover's lane in Freetown, Massachusetts, Judith Szatek (nursing) and Raymond Frenette (engineering) were parked in Frenette's car. For no apparent reason, someone shot Miss Szatek three times in the chest and Mr. Frenette four times in the head. Seven .22-caliber casings were found at the scene. The police found Frenette's wallet contained $6 and Szatek had $20 in her purse, ruing out robbery as a motive for the murders.

The pair had been last seen driving into the lane by a resident at 7 p.m. Their bodies were discovered sixteen hours later at 12:30 p.m. The medical examiner determined they had been died for approximately ten hours, putting their time of death at around 10:30 p.m. The couple was found by Charles Westgate of Freetown while out horseback riding. The windshield and a door window on the right side of the car were riddled with bullet holes. When the police arrived, the driver's door was open.

Szatek and Frenette had been engaged for three years and were planning an August wedding.

According to the *Fitchburg Sentinel*, "a reconstruction of the crime indicated Miss Szatek was first struck in the chest from a distance by a bullet that went through the windshield…Frenette was then shot three times in the head and chest as he started to get out of the car. Then the killer fired two more shots into Miss Szatek."

Robert Garron was arrested on May 6, 1965, based on information given to the Taunton police department by an unidentified citizen, at his place of employment, F.B. Rogers Silver Col, in Taunton. Garron's car, a station wagon, was impounded and was said to have matched the description of a vehicle seen near the scene of the crime.

Trial: Robert Garron, charged with the murder of Judith Ann Szatek and Raymond G. Frenette, was ordered committed to Bridgewater State Mental Hospital for thirty-five days for mental evaluation. Deemed a "violent" youth, District Attorney Edmund Dinis said he was determined that this was in the best interests of the health of the defendant.

Afterword: Oddly, no other details were found regarding this case. It is not known if Garron was permanently committed, what he pleaded in his case, whether there was an indictment, or a trial. It is entirely possible that Mr. Garron is still alive, as he would be only in his mid 60s today.

Further Reading:

"Cartridge Cases Only Clues in Slaying of Engaged Couple." *Bennington Banner* (Bennington, Vermont), May 3, 1965.
"Couple Slain in Parked Auto." Chicago Tribune (Chicago, Illinois), May 3, 1965.
"Search Pushed in Slaying of 2." *The Pittsburgh Press* (Pittsburgh, Pennsylvania), May 4, 1965.
"Slaying Reward Offered." *Fitchburg Sentinel* (Fitchburg, Massachusetts), May 4, 1965.
"'Violent Youth' Undergoes Mental Tests in Bay State Lover's Lane Killing." *Bennington Banner* (Bennington, Vermont), May 7, 1965.
"Youth Charged with Murder of Couple in Car." *The Bridgeport Telegram* (Bridgeport, Connecticut), May 7, 1965.

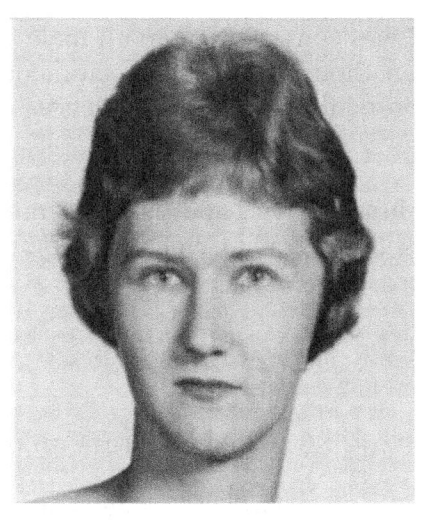

Judith Ann Szatek. Fitchburg State University year book, 1965.

Raymond G. Frenette. SMTI year book, 1965.

CHARLES CATON KING JR.

Fatal shooting of man trying to break up a bar fight in New Bedford, Massachusetts, on May 14, 1966.

Victim: Charles Caton King Jr., 43.

Accused: Delpha D. Ricard, 63.

Details: Charles C. King Jr. was in the proverbial wrong place at the wrong time. He was at a cafe (bar) in New Bedford late Saturday night, May 14, 1966, when a fight broke out. In the melee, King was shot three times with a .32-caliber pistol and died on the scene. The shooter, Delpha D. Ricard, 63, father of five, escaped the location and was later apprehended after a six-state alarm had been issued. He was returned to New Bedford for arraignment and indicted for the murder. He was committed to the Bridgewater State Hospital after his arrest in November until he was adjudged competent to stand trial.

Trial: On May 3, 1968, Delpha D. Ricard was convicted by an all male jury of the first degree murder of King. Even though the jury recommended clemency, Judge Robert H. Beaudreau imposed the mandatory sentence—life imprisonment.

Afterword: Delpha D. Ricard died on June 6, 1984, and as a veteran of World War II, is buried in the Massachusetts National Cemetery in Bourne, Massachusetts.

Further Reading:

"Man Gets Life in Gun Death." *Newport Daily News* (Newport, Rhode Island), May 3, 1968.
"Suspect Charged in Fatal Shooting." *Hartford Courant* (Hartford, Connecticut), May 16, 1966.

FRANK DUARTE

Fatal shooting of man outside of a bar on Purchase Street in New Bedford, Massachusetts, on October 23, 1966.

Victim: Frank Duarte, 52.

Accused: Frederick Rollins, 48.

Details: Frank Duarte of New Bedford was killed from a gunshot wound in the stomach suffered outside a Purchase Street Bar in the city. Police arrested Frederick Rollins, also of New Bedford, soon after and charged him with murder. The crime was the result of an argument.

Trial: Frederick Rollins was convicted of second degree murder and sentenced to life in prison. In 1968, Rollins won a new trial but the outcome was the same.

Afterword: In 1974, in honor of Christmas, the Governor's Council of Massachusetts voted unanimously to commute the sentence of Frederick Rollins, after two and a half hours of hearings and a passionate plea from councilor Patrick F. "Sonny" McDonough for granting the traditional Christmas commutations. He termed the two commutations "a candle of hope." "If a man feels there is a body that can put him back on the street it gives him a ray of hope to remain a human being and not become a mad, wild animal in jail."

The other man who had his sentenced commuted was Vincent Delle Chiaie, 48, convicted in 1947 for murdering a 7-year-old Lawrence, Massachusetts, girl after trying to rape her.

Further Reading:

"Commuted Terms Give Ray of Hope." *Tampa Tribune* (Tampa, Florida), December 25, 1974.
"New Bedford Killing." *Newport Daily News* (Newport, Rhode Island), October 23, 1966.
"Second Trial was Wasted." *Newport Daily News* (Newport, Rhode Island), January 31, 1968.

ANTHONY TOSCA & DUANE L. BLAKE

Fatal shooting and then burning of two men on Lake Road, in Tiverton, Rhode Island, on August 1, 1969.

Victim: Anthony Tosca, age unknown, and Duane L. Blake, 25.

Accused: Robert O. Lewis, and later, Maurice Charest, ages unknown.

Details: The facts of the case are as follows: "On the morning of August 2, 1969, one Clifford Hancock discovered two charred, dead bodies in the woods adjacent to Lake Road in the town of Tiverton. He called the police, who identified the dead bodies, and subsequent autopsies disclosed that the victims had been shot before being set afire.

"Hancock had gone into the woods that morning because while driving along Lake Road early the previous evening he had noticed a fire burning in the nearby woods and had also seen a man, later identified as defendant, run out of the lane leading from the woods and get into the passenger seat of a station wagon backing out of the lane. The station wagon was proceeding in the same direction Hancock was headed, and as he followed it he could see the left profile of the passenger. He also noted that the wagon had New Jersey license plates and a loud exhaust.

"During the ensuing police investigation, a list of names and addresses, including defendant's [Robert Lewis], was found on the body of one of the murdered men. The police then attempted to locate defendant for questioning, and on the afternoon of August 3, two officers cruising in a section of town to which he had reportedly moved saw a station wagon that generally fit Hancock's description of the one he had seen leaving the scene of the crime, except that it had Rhode Island plates fastened with what appeared to be new nuts and bolts. It was parked in a driveway, and the names on the mailbox in front of the adjoining cottage were 'Lewis' and 'Richard.'

"The police then approached the residence, knocked on the door, and a Mrs. Carol Richard answered. She told them that defendant was living with her, that they both knew the victim on whose body defendant's name had been found, and that defendant was expected home later that day. She also informed them that the station wagon was hers, a fact confirmed by a later examination of the registration, and that it had not been out of the yard on the evening of August 1.

"Earlier in their investigation the police had discovered paint scrapings on some embedded rocks at the murder scene, and in order to ascertain whether they had come from the parked station wagon the officers asked Mrs. Richard if they could examine the wagon. She gave her permission, and the police then inspected its underside and observed dents and scratches on the splashpan and a cross member. Because Mrs. Richard told them that defendant would be returning at about 5:30 p.m., they left and returned at that hour. When they learned that he had not yet come home, they departed and stationed themselves a block or two down the street.

"About an hour later Mrs. Richard, accompanied by her sister and several children, left the house, entered the station wagon, and drove toward the officers. As she passed them, they heard a loud exhaust noise similar to that attributed by Hancock to the station wagon he had seen on Lake Road. The officers thereupon apprehended Mrs. Richard and took her and the station wagon to the Portsmouth State Police barracks. During the interrogation that followed she signed a written consent form authorizing the police to search the station wagon. The police then took the wagon to a lift, elevated it, photographed its underside, and took paint scrapings for comparison with those previously taken from the rocks at the murder scene. Later that evening Mrs. Richard signed another consent form authorizing the police to search her home for firearms, nonresident registration plates, and articles of clothing deemed to be of value to the investigation.

"During and following the Richard investigation the search for defendant continued, and on Monday, August 4, the eyewitness Hancock was shown more than 100 'mug shots' from the state police files in the Portsmouth barracks. He was unable to identify any of the photographs as being of the man he saw run from the woods and get into the station wagon. He did, however, select pictures of two men he thought had similar characteristics. That evening he was shown the station wagon which the police had seized the previous day, and after he had heard its exhaust noise he positively identified it as the vehicle he had seen at the murder site.

"Two days later a Fall River attorney who had represented defendant on a prior occasion; and had seen him only a few days before, received a telephone call from a Sergeant Donley of the Fall River Police Department asking him to bring defendant to his office on the second floor of the Fall River police station at 10 a.m. the following morning, August 7. Although the attorney was not told why the police were interested in defendant, he agreed to comply with the request. The police then notified Hancock that they would pick him up about 9 a.m. on August 7, to take him to the station. They did so, and en route to the station one of the two accompanying detectives told him they 'were going to the Fall River [D]epartment and an attorney was going to surrender a suspect in this case * * * and there was a possibility he might submit him to a lineup.'

"When they arrived at the station shortly before 10 a.m., Hancock and one of the detectives sat on a bench in the hallway of the second floor while the other detective went to search for Sergeant Donley. Soon thereafter Hancock saw defendant, his attorney, and Mrs. Richard approaching him as they walked toward Sergeant Donley's office. He recognized defendant as the man he had seen run from the woods onto Lake Road and get into the station wagon, and he so advised the detective seated next to him. The defendant was then arrested on a fugitive warrant for murder. Later that day, Hancock was shown a photograph of defendant and made a formal statement concerning the identification. Eight days later, on August 15, the police prepared and showed Hancock a rendition warrant, which was accompanied by the same photograph of defendant that Hancock had seen on August 7 after his initial 'hallway' identification" ("State v. Robert Lewis").

Trial: Robert O. Lewis was charged with two counts of first degree murder and stood trial in 1971. In his defense, Lewis said he "had returned July 31, 1969, from the Bangor Fair and New Brunswick and had driven his Cadillac into Fall River the next day. He described meeting Anthony Tosca in Fall River. Tosca asked him if he knew where he could get a moving van, and Lewis offered him the use of a station wagon. Lewis said Toasca was accompanied at the time by another man, whom he doesn't remember. The men agreed to meet at The Coachmen, a Tiverton restaurant, where Lewis promised to deliver the station wagon to Tosca.

"Lewis said he left his Cadillac at South Park in Fall River and a salesman friend drove him home to Portsmouth. He then drove the station wagon to The Coachmen. Tosca was in the company of a third man whom the defendant described as 'tall with sandy hair and a light complexion.' He doesn't remember meeting him, Lewis said he had known Tosca for about a year, but he hadn't seen him for three or four months before this meeting.

"Lewis drove the station wagon with the men to Wordell's Service Station. He told them to leave it there when they were finished with it, and he would pick it up. The men drove him to South Park where he picked up his Cadillac, and they drove off.

"The defendant said he drove home then and around 7 p.m. left again to go to his wife's house to escort his daughter to Lincoln Park.

"The next day he drove to Wordell's Service Station, where he found the station wagon and had snow tires changed on it. Later that day Carol Richard told him she had heard on television that Tony Tosca was killed. She asked if their station wagon was a Country Squire, and when she learned that it was, she said police were looking for one like it that was at the scene of the murder.

"Lewis said Wright asked him why he had not notified police when he had learned they were looking for the station wagon. 'I said I guess you'd say I panicked, Mr. Wright,' Lewis testified.

"Asked what he had done Sunday when he learned Carol Richard and the station wagon had been taken to the State Police barracks in Portsmouth, Lewis said he had sent an attorney there.

"The defendant told of going to the Fall River police station accompanied by Carol Richard and an attorney, James Seilgman, where he was first identified by Clifford Hancock as the man running from the murder scene. Lewis said he was arrested at that time, but he didn't know until much later that Hancock had made the identification" ("Surprise Witness").

At the trial in 1971, a surprise witness, Louis D. Melone, of Providence, told the jury that he was with Robert Lewis at Lincoln Park at the time the murders were alleged to have occurred. Melone said they met at Lincoln Park around 7:30 p.m. on August 1, the time Clifford Hancock saw Lewis run from the scene on Lake Road.

On March 10, 1971, Robert O. Lewis was found guilty of two counts of murder and sentenced to two concurrent life sentences.

Afterword: Robert Lewis applied for and was denied a motion for a new trial. Pending a hearing, Lewis escaped from custody. He was later captured (after 1973).

In 1976, Lewis turned states evidence, named an accomplice, and began testifying against him. He alleged that Maurice Charest had killed and burned the bodies of Tosca and Blake in 1969. He said that Charest agreed to kill Tosca because he was asked to do so by a fence, Russell Goldstein [*see Russell Goldstein murder, 1969, Volume One*]. Lewis said he disliked Tosca but didn't know Blake.

According to Lewis at Charest's trial, "Tosca approached Lewis and asked if he knew where he could sell a stolen Cadillac. Lewis said he made up some story and agreed to meet Tosca later that night at the Dedley Drug Store in Tiverton. He had Charest then drove around for a while and decided what they would do later if Blake was still with Tosca, when they were going to kill him.

"Lewis said he previously purchased a .33-caliber and a .45-caliber gun. He said he gave the latter gun to Charest.

"Cass [Frederick Cass, state prosecutor] asked if they had ammunition for the guns, and Lewis said they hadn't. He said that they told Goldstein that when they were going to kill Tosca, the fence got them ammunition.

"Lewis said he dropped Charest off in Fall River and drove to his home on Gormley Street in Portsmouth, which he shared with Carol Richards. He said he ate his dinner, stuffed the gun in his waistband and drove off to meet Charest again in Carol's white station wagon.

"He said Tosca still had Black with him. They parked their car in the

Coachman Restaurant parking lot, and the four men drove off to the area off Lake Road. They then drew their pistols and ordered the victims out of the car.

"Charest shot Blake and he shot Tosca, Lewis testified. They then poured gasoline on the men and set them afire. Charest started to drive out of the clearing but the undercarriage of the car got 'hung up' on rocks. Eventually Charest got it free and drove out to Lake Road. Lewis got in the car and the men drove off" ("Killer Names Accomplice").

Lewis' deal with the attorney general for his testimony here was a vacated sentence for his escape from the court house after his trial. Before he had escaped, Lewis was eligible for parole within ten years. Afterwards, that was increased to twenty-five years. The attorney general's office also agreed to write favorable letters to federal authorities in Virginia and his parole board.

After the seven-day trial, the jury took 42 minutes to acquit Maurice Charest of the murder of Tosca and Blake. The jury did not believe the testimony of Lewis. At his own trial for the murders, Lewis admitted that he knew Maurice Charest and that he had been to his house after he bought the station wagon for Carol Richard to put the license plates on the car for him.

Further Reading:

"Jury Acquits in Slaying." *Newport Mercury* (Newport, Rhode Island), April 2, 1976.
"Killer Names Accomplice." *Newport Mercury* (Newport, Rhode Island), March 26, 1976.
"Man Acquitted in 2 Slayings." *Hartford Courant* (Hartford, Connecticut), March 26, 1976.
"State v. Robert O. Lewis." 341 A.2d 744 (1975). No. 1785-Ex. Supreme Court of Rhode Island, July 28, 1975. law.justia.com/cases/rhode-island/supreme-court/1975/341-a-2d-744-0.html
"Surprise Witness Alibis Defendant at Murder Trial." *Newport Mercury* (Newport, Rhode Island), March 12, 1976.

EDWARD LEBLANC

Man shot and killed in his third floor apartment on Smith Street in Fall River, Massachusetts, on January 12, 1984.

Victim: Edward LeBlanc, 30.

Accused: Daniel Lapointe, 32.

Details: According to the facts presented to the jury as stated in his appeal in 1988, on January 12, 1984, Daniel Lapointe "telephoned the home of his ex-wife, Susan, to inquire about the delivery of Christmas presents to their daughter, Jamie. Susan and Jamie were living with, and Susan was engaged to be married to, Edward LeBlanc. LeBlanc answered the telephone and spoke to the defendant. LeBlanc was 'a little angry,' 'upset,' and 'sick of the situation' when he left Susan to go to the defendant's house to talk with him."

Lapointe was, at the time, "living with Linda Canuel and her daughter, Melissa, in the third-floor apartment of a three-family dwelling. Following his telephone conversation with LeBlanc, the defendant took a tranquilizer or 'stomach' pill and lay down on the sofa. Canuel and the defendant anticipated that LeBlanc was coming to the house. Canuel was watching from a window for his arrival. She saw LeBlanc park his automobile about two houses away and heard some glass being broken. Canuel heard LeBlanc come into the house and ascend the stairs. She told [Lapointe] that LeBlanc was coming. He got his loaded Walther 380 automatic gun and placed it in the waistband of his pants. Canuel went with her daughter to the daughter's bedroom.

"LeBlanc pounded on the front door of the [Lapointe]'s apartment. Canuel left the bedroom and urged the defendant to open the door. Canuel never saw a gun. When [Lapointe] unlocked the deadbolt and opened the door, an 'enraged' LeBlanc rushed in, his arms in the air. LeBlanc said, 'You die, - - -,' and advanced on the defendant. Canuel fled into the bathroom. She heard shots fired. When she emerged from the bathroom, [Lapointe] told her to call the police.

"The police arrived at the apartment and found LeBlanc's body on the floor of the living room, covered by a blanket. A knife was in LeBlanc's right hand. There were not signs of a struggle in the apartment. [Lapointe] showed the officers a badge, said he was a constable, and had just shot the man on the floor. [Lapointe] said that LeBlanc had come 'charging in with the knife,' and that he had shot him a few times and then shot 'some more to make sure he was dead…because that's what they taught him in 'Nam.'

"[Lapointe] told the police about the problems he had been having with his ex-wife and her boy friend, about the telephone call preceding LeBlanc's arrival, that he had been afraid of LeBlanc, and that, when LeBlanc burst into the apartment, the defendant 'saw the flash of something shiny.' When interrupted by the police and told that the police could determine whether the knife had been placed in LeBlanc's hand, [Lapointe] admitted putting the knife in LeBlanc's hand. [Lapointe] also said that he was heavily medicated and was being treated at the Veteran's Administration Hospital for post-traumatic stress disorder (PTSD). [Lapointe] indicated that, when Canuel told him that LeBlanc had parked his automobile, he had gotten his weapon. After LeBlanc came through the door, [Lapointe] shot him, first in the arm and then in the chest."

Trial: At trial, Daniel Lapointe's defense to the charge of murder was self-defense. The jury returned a verdict finding Lapointe guilty of manslaughter. He was sentenced to not less than 15 and not more than 18 years at the Massachusetts Correctional Institution, Cedar Junction.

Afterword: Daniel Lapointe appealed his conviction in 1988 on the grounds that the judge erred in permitting prosecution witnesses to testify as to the victim's reputation for peacefulness and in his instructions to the jury. The appeals court upheld the original conviction and found the sentence proper.

Further Reading:

"Commonwealth vs. Daniel L. Lapointe." 402 Mass. 321, February 1, 1988-May 9, 1988. Bristol County. masscases.com/cases/sjc/402/402mass321.html

JOSEPH FREITAS

Fatal shooting of man in front of a Dunkin' Donuts in New Bedford, Massachusetts, on January 2, 1992.

Victim: Joseph Freitas, 36.

Accused: Antonio Ferrer, 14.

Details: On January 2, 1992, Antonio Ferrer (age 14) shot and killed Joseph Freitas (age 36) in front of a Dunkin' Donuts in New Bedford. "On January 2, 1992, the defendant Ferrer, together with Andre Cortes, walked into a Dunkin' Donuts shop in New Bedford and ordered coffee, hot chocolate, sandwiches, and two donuts. While Donna Bertozzi, the server, filled the order, Cortes accosted her, thus: 'You're cute...I'd like to lick you from head to toe.' Cortes followed up with a question about when Bertozzi went off shift and added, 'Well, we'll be back.' The two paid for their food and took it into a red Chevrolet automobile in the parking lot, Cortes getting in on the driver's side and Ferrer on the other. Bertozzi, because she 'was scared,' told two regular customers, one of whom was Joseph Freitas, the eventual victim, what Cortes had said.

"Eight minutes later, Ferrer returned and ordered two more croissants. Freitas and Ferrer exchanged stares, which led to words (Ferrer: 'Do you have an eye problem?' Freitas: 'No, do you?') and a fight. Ferrer said, 'Let's take this outside'; they did. Outside Freitas shoved Ferrer to the ground. Ferrer got up and ran to the passenger side of the red Chevrolet. The car backed up about one hundred feet, the dome light on. Cortes was at the wheel; Ferrer looking down and to his right.

"After about two minutes, the dome light went off and the Chevrolet approached the entrance to the shop, where Freitas stood. As the car slowed to a stop, the passenger side faced the entrance. One shot rang out and Freitas fell, fatally wounded. After the shot, the defendant leaned back in the passenger seat; Cortes had a hand on the wheel and was looking to his right. The Chevrolet sped off. At the scene, police found a .22-caliber shell casing and a sandwich box with Ferrer's fingerprints on it. Freitas's mortal wound had been inflicted by a .22-caliber bullet" (Ferrer's appeal).

Trial: On May 10, 1995, Antonio Ferrer was convicted by a jury of second degree murder. He was sentenced to life in prison with the possibility of parole.

Afterword: Antonio Ferrer appealed his sentence in 1999 on the grounds that the trial judge erred in denying a motion for a required finding of not guilty and in ruling that the prosecutor could impeach the fourteen year old defendant with statements that the trial judge had ordered suppressed as to the government's case-in-chief. The appeals court ruled that there was no judicial error and affirmed his conviction.

Antonio Ferrer was paroled in March of 2008 to a residential program, but that parole was revoked on March 10, 2009, "for a drug arrest, association with a person known to have a criminal history, and failure to pursue employment. He was re-paroled in May 2009. Revocation proceedings were again initiated in August 2010 for violations that included drug transactions with a police confidential informant and association with a person known to have a criminal history. Mr. Ferrer's parole revocation was affirmed on November 23, 2010, and he was returned to custody. He was denied parole after a review hearing in September 2011, with a review schedule in five years from the date of the hearing" (parole report).

At age 39, Antonio Ferrer again applied for parole on September 27, 2016. He expressed sorrow for the death of Joseph Freitas and accepted responsibility for his actions. He claimed he had allowed his anger to assume control of him and made the worst decision in his life when he killed Freitas.

In a story that has become all to familiar to anyone who reads parole reports, Antonio Ferrer told how as a child he had grown up in a chaotic household with an alcoholic mother and a father who was in and out of prison. He claimed that he spent most of his youth "on the street" associating with the wrong crowd—including older, criminally minded people. On the day of the murder, Ferrer told the parole board that he had wanted to leave after his encounter with Freitas, but the friend who was driving the car handed him the gun and encouraged him to shoot Mr. Freitas.

The parole board denied his request for release saying that he had not as of yet demonstrated a level of "rehabilitative progress that would make his re-release compatible with the welfare of society." He is allowed to apply again for parole in 2020.

Further Reading:

"Commonwealth vs. Antonio Ferrer." 47 Mass. App. Ct. 645, February 9, 1999-August 30, 1999. Bristol County. masscases.com/cases/app/47/47massappct645.html
"Decision in the Matter of Antonio Ferrer, W58563." Review Hearing, The Commonwealth of Massachusetts Executive Office of Public Safety, Parole Board. March 9, 2017. mass.gov/files/documents/2018/02/08/Ferrer%2C%20Antonio.pdf

DANIEL CORREIA

Fatal drive by shooting of man in Magnet Park in New Bedford, Massachusetts, on April 15, 1994.

Victim: Daniel Correia, 14.

Accused: Richard Hazard, 28.

Details: According the Richard Hazard's parole hearing, the facts of the crime are these: "On April 15, 1994, at about 3:00 p.m., Scott Rose, Richard Hazard (then 28-years-old), Timothy Reaves, and Michael Coull went to Magnet Park (outside a New Bedford housing project) in Mr. Rose's Lincoln Town Car. Mr. Hazard went up to an 18-year-old man and asked if he had any dope (heroin) for sale. Mr. Hazard and the 18-year-old man then walked toward Mr. Rose, Mr. Reaves, and Mr. Coull, all of whom were waiting near the Lincoln. An altercation ensued, and a witness heard Mr. Rose say, 'We'll be back.'

"Two hours later, at about 5:00 p.m., the four men appeared at a house in Taunton, where Mr. Rose asked one of his friends to borrow a gun. The friend handed the gun and some green shells to Mr. Rose. At about 7:00 p.m., the 18-year-old man was in Magnet Park with his 14-year-old brother Daniel and some other friends. The brothers were leaning on a white car, talking. The 18-year-old man heard tires screeching and, when he looked up, saw the Lincoln driving past. The driver's side faced toward him. He saw a big pistol coming out of the rear driver side window, heard shots, and saw flashes from both driver side windows. He saw Mr. Rose, the driver, leaning back in his seat as he drove. The 18-year-old man and Daniel started to run when they heard the shots. As they took off, the 18-year-old man was struck in the leg and Daniel was struck in the heart.

"After an extensive chase, Mr. Hazard and the others were apprehended in Taunton. At the time of the shooting, Mr. Hazard was the front seat passenger in the Lincoln and was observed with a shotgun in his hand. Daniel had been shot with a .9mm gun, which had been in Mr. Reaves' possession."

Trial: Richard Hazard was found guilty by a jury of second degree murder and sentenced to life in prison with the possibility of parole. That same day,

Hazard was also convicted of unlawful possession of a firearm and assault and battery by means of a dangerous weapon and sentenced to serve a concurrent 3 to 5 years for the firearm offence and a consecutive 3 to 5 years for the assault.

Afterword: Richard Hazard first applied for parole in 2013 and it was denied because he did not accept responsibility for his actions.

Richard Hazard appeared before the parole board again on April 20, 2017, and his fate was decided on April 12, 2018. At the time of his hearing, Hazard was 53 years old. He apologized to the family of the victims and expressed remorse for the murder of Daniel Correia. He stated that what he did was "no less than despicable and reckless" and that the depth of his shame was "beyond words."

His story about his early upbringing sounds familiar in that many who appear before the board seem to have similar experiences as children. Hazard said his mother was an alcoholic and his father's job as a cross-country truck driver kept him away from home. Since he had no guidance, he was influenced by peer pressure. At the time of the killing he had merely wished to "scare people" and did not mean to kill anyone, although he acknowledged that this made him in no way less culpable.

Richard Hazard was granted parole with special circumstances.

Further Reading:

"Decision in the Matter of Richard Hazard, W59221." Review Hearing, The Commonwealth of Massachusetts Executive Office of Public Safety, Parole Board. April 12, 2018. mass.gov/files/documents/2018/04/12/hazard%20rod%202018.pdf

JEFFREY ROSANINA

Fatal shooting of man in the parking lot of the Shark Club on Coggeshall Street in New Bedford, Massachusetts, on April 29, 1994. The victim died on May 5, 1994.

Victim: Jeffrey Rosanina, 21.

Accused: Paul E. Solomonsen, age unknown.

Details: According to Paul Solomonsen's appeal transcript, the facts of the case are as follows: "On April 28, 1994, Paul Solomonsen awoke at about 11:00 a.m. and consumed some beer, some cocaine, and a prescription medication. Dinner later that day was followed by more cocaine, beer, rum, and—for entertainment—'scratch' lottery tickets. As the evening wore on, [Solomonsen] and a friend, Jose Buitrago, headed to the Shark Club, located on Coggeshall Street in New Bedford's North End, and, once there, consumed more beer. They soon ran out of money and left in search of additional funds. The pair returned a short while later, armed with financial means and three handguns.

"As closing time approached (it was now the small hours of the 29th), patrons of the Shark Club began to leave, [Solomonsen] and Buitrago included. Outside, [Solomonsen] had words with Thomas Branquino (with whom he had tussled earlier in the evening), the bar manager, and some of the bouncers. He then produced and brandished a handgun, and invited Branquino to 'fuck with [him) now.' The situation was defused when Buitrago escorted [Solomonsen] across the street to where their car was parked.

"After [Solomonsen] and Buitrago reached the car, however, Jeffrey Rosanina, not previously involved in the conflict with the defendant, left the Shark Club and walked toward them. When Rosanina reached the car, [Solomonsen] was seated in the passenger seat and the passenger-side door was open. Rosanina walked up next to the seated Solomonsen, leaned his right elbow on the car's roof, and appeared to converse with [Solomonsen]. Others, including Rosanina's brother, set off after him, but before they reached the car, two shots rang out: one bullet struck Rosanina in the chest; the other, in the head.

"Witnesses flagged down a State trooper patrolling Coggeshall Street, who quickly apprehended [Solomonsen]. The victim was rushed to the hospital, where he died several days later. At the scene, [Solomonsen] told the trooper that Rosanina had a knife and was going to kill him. [Solomonsen] said that he had been sitting in the car when a punch, delivered by an unseen assailant, landed on his mouth and he fell out of the car. There, [Solomonsen] saw a gun that he believed had dropped out of Rosanina's pants. Looking up, he saw Rosanina standing above him with a knife and shot twice. [Solomonsen] repeated this story later that morning at the police station. No knife was recovered from the scene."

Trial: "At trial, [Solomonsen] presented a self-defense theory of the case consistent with the version of events he told the State troopers at the scene and during his subsequent interrogation. He admitted, however, that the gun used against Rosanina was part of the arsenal that he and Buitrago had assembled that evening. [Solomonsen] also testified that, just before he was punched in the mouth, he saw someone advancing on the car with a baseball bat. The jury convicted [Solomonsen] after seven days of evidence of second degree murder and the unlawful possession of a firearm."

Afterword: "[Solomonsen] appealed his convictions and then moved for a new trial based on newly discovered evidence and on the ineffectiveness of trial counsel. With the appeal from his convictions stayed, the motion for a new trial was denied. [Solomonsen]'s appeal of that denial has been consolidated with the appeal of his convictions."

Further Reading:

"Commonwealth vs. Paul E. Solomonsen." 50 Mass. App. Ct. 122, April 12, 2000-September 26, 2000. Bristol County. masscases.com/cases/app/50/50massappct122.html.

TIMOTHY LAMERE

Fatal hit and run on Ashley Street in New Bedford, Massachusetts, on October 23, 1966.

Victim: Timothy Lamere, 21.

Accused: Steven Mattos, 37.

Details: In the early morning hours of August 1, 1995, Mattos, then age 37, intentionally drove a 1979 Dodge pickup truck and struck Mr. Lamere, age 21. Mr. Lamere suffered severe, and ultimately fatal, injuries. Mr. Lamere was taken to an area hospital and then flown to Brigham and Women's Hospital in Boston, where he died as a result of his injuries.

Mattos had spent the evening drinking beer at several locations in the New Bedford area. He and a friend then left a bar in search of cocaine. Mattos, while driving his business partner's truck, engaged in a heated argument with a group of people he had never met before, including Mr. Lamere. The argument was about Mattos being unable to drive his truck around a car that was double parked. Mattos yelled at the woman in the car, and Mr. Lamere was among the group of men who came to defend the woman sitting in the double parked car. After Mattos managed to drive past the group of people, he then turned the truck around, cut off a small car, and drove into a nearby gas station lot, traveling at an estimated speed of 40 to 50 miles per hour. At this point, Mr. Lamere was standing on the sidewalk next to the gas station. After turning into the lot, Mattos gunned his engine and deliberately ran over Mr. Lamere. Upon impact, Mr. Lamere was thrown approximately 40 feet into the air and landed on an adjacent road. Witnesses in the truck with Mattos stated that while this ordeal was occurring, Mattos said, "I'm going to get these [expletive]." After hitting Mr. Lamere, Mattos fled the scene.

Trial: On April 12, 1996, Steven Mattos was convicted of murder in the second degree and sentenced to life in prison. He was also convicted of leaving the scene of an accident, resulting in death, and received a concurrent one year sentence.

Afterword: Mattos appealed for parole three times. His initial hearing was in 2011, after which the Board denied parole with a review hearing in 3 years. At his 2014 hearing, Mattos was much more forthcoming and insightful than in his initial hearing. He characterized his performance in the first hearing as "terrible," observing that he minimized his actions and his role and that he assigned much of the responsibility to the people that he was with, rather than taking responsibility for his anger and the resulting violence.

In his 2014 hearing, he attributed his problems to alcohol abuse and anger and acknowledged that he was to blame for what he did. Four Board Members voted in favor of granting Mattos a parole to a long term residential treatment program, after one year in lower security. However, by statute, he needed five votes to be granted parole. Two of the Board Members who voted against granting him parole urged him to complete programming designed to address his anger issues, including two programs for which Mattos was wait-listed at the time of the hearing. The other Board Member suggested that Mattos participate further in programming that enabled him to offer insight in a more forthright manner. The 2014 split-vote resulted in a denial with a one year setback, thus requiring a hearing in 2015.

In 2015, the parole board voted six to one that Steven Mattos be granted parole to a long term residential program, with special considerations, after successful adjustment to one year in lower security.

Further Reading:

"Decision in the Matter of Steven Mattos, W60443." Review Hearing, The Commonwealth of Massachusetts Executive Office of Public Safety, Parole Board. June 3, 2015. mass.gov/files/documents/2018/02/15/Mattos%2C%20Steven.pdf

JANE DOE

Body of woman discovered floating off Popes Island Marina in New Bedford, Massachusetts, on October 30, 1996.

Victim: Jane Doe, approximately 30-45 years of age.

Accused: Unknown.

Details: The body of a still-unnamed white woman was found wrapped in two green garbage bags and a white and teal woolen blanket was found on October 30, 1996, by a maintenance worker at the Popes Island Marina in New Bedford. According to medical experts, she was found within 24 hours of being dumped in the water and within 48 hours of being killed. Police believe that the woman may have been put in the water elsewhere and the current pushed her body toward the docks.

The woman, known as Jane Doe, probably did not have children and there is not evidence of drug use or sexual assault.

The cause of death was ruled homicide as the woman had been hit in the face and shot a dozen times.

She wore a Belarusian ring, had unshaven legs and armpits, and poor dental work—which investigators believe may point to her being eastern European. When found, she was wearing a mustard colored long-sleeve turtleneck, size medium, made by Licorice, a white pullover sweater with multicolored rectangular designs, size medium, brand name Oakbrook, blue Levi's 521 jeans, pantyhose, underwear, and cotton socks.

She is known as "Popes Island Jane Doe."

Further Reading:

"Popes Island Jane Doe." CrimeWatchers.net. crimewatchers.net/forum/index.php?threads/popes-island-jane-doe-wf-30-45-found-in-the-harbor-at-new-bedford-ma-30-october-1996-graphic.6926/

MICHAEL BARROS

Fatal accidental shooting of teenager at 122 Rivet Street in New Bedford, Massachusetts, on April 19, 1997.

Victim: Michael Barros, 16.

Accused: Filipe Barros, 18.

Details: On April 19, 1997, Felipe Barros killed his friend Michael Barros as they played with guns. Felipe was not related the victim even though they shared a last name. Michael Barros had been living with Felipe and his family at the time of his death. Police charged Filipe with manslaughter, assault and battery, with a dangerous weapon and ammunition possession, and possession of heroin. Officers reported that they were treating the shooting as an accident.

Michael was shot once in the chest and was taken to St. Luke's Hospital in New Bedford and pronounced dead a short time later.

Filipe remained at the scene and cooperated with investigators. He maintained that the shooting was an accident. "A search of the teenagers' shared bedroom yielded two handguns, ammunition and two packets of heroin" (*Boston Globe*).

Outcome: Before resolution of this case, Filipe Barros was gunned down in August of the same year—see the next case in this book.

Further Reading:

"Teenager Held Without Bail in Roommate's Death." *Boston Globe* (Boston, Massachusetts), 21 April 1997.

FILIPE BARROS

Fatal shooting of man in front of Luso Assembly of God Church on Blackmer Street (one block south and one block east of his home) in New Bedford, Massachusetts, on August 9, 1997.

Victim: Filipe Barros, 18.

Accused: Nelson Rodriguez, 33.

Details: According to appeal records, on August 9, 1997, "witnesses saw Nelson Rodriguez leave his car with (what appeared to be) a black revolver and approach Felipe [sic] Barros and 2 other men, who were standing on the sidewalk. He pointed the weapon and shot Mr. Barros in the head. Mr. Barros went to the ground and was then shot in the chest by Mr. Rodriguez. One of the men was not shot, but also went to the ground. The other man fled the scene, but had heard Mr. Rodriguez say, "Do you remember the time you jumped me?" Mr. Rodriguez walked away and got into his vehicle, but then, returned to Mr. Barros on the sidewalk. He shot him two more times, killing him. Mr. Rodriguez then left the scene. About an hour later, police received information that Mr. Rodriguez was seen running toward the area of a sewer. A black .38-caliber Rossi revolver was subsequently retrieved from the sewer. Ballistics testing showed that the gun from the sewer was the same gun used in the shooting of Mr. Barros. In addition, a witness (who had not seen the shooting, but ran towards the shots after hearing them) saw Mr. Rodriguez get into his car and drive away."

Trial: "On November 18, 1998, in Bristol Superior Court, a jury convicted Nelson Rodriguez of first degree murder in the death of Felipe Barros. He was sentenced to life in prison without the possibility of parole. Mr. Rodriguez was also found guilty of possession of a firearm and sentenced to a concurrent sentence of 2 1/2-4 years. In 2010, Mr. Rodriguez filed a Rule 30 motion for a new trial on the grounds that it was a violation of his constitutional rights to have the courtroom closed during jury selection. He was granted a new trial and, on February 11, 2014, pleaded guilty in Bristol Superior Court to second degree murder, which resulted in a life sentence with parole eligibility at 15 years. Because he had already served over 16 years, Mr. Rodriguez became eligible for parole after sentencing."

Afterword: In 2014, Rodriguez was denied parole at his initial hearing. At the age of 53, Rodriguez again appeared before the parole board in May of 2017. He expressed his remorse to Filipe Barros' mother and explained his upbringing to help shed light on his actions. Rodriguez said his father had been incarcerated for trafficking when he was 5-years-old and he began experimenting with drugs at the age of eight. By the time he was 14, he was addicted and spent the next ten years "caught in a vicious cycle of addiction, criminal behavior, and incarceration."

"In 1989, at age 26 (and through the support of his brother), Mr. Rodriguez re-engaged in a methadone treatment program and was hired to work at the Boys and Girls Club. He lived, predominately, as a pro-social member of the community until 1997, when he relapsed. He was severely beaten after a confrontation with a drug dealer, resulting in a period of hospitalization and continued use of methadone and opioids. Approximately four months later, while in possession of a firearm, Mr. Rodriguez returned to the same area to purchase drugs with the hope of retaliation. In describing the situation, Mr. Rodriquez expressed his hatred toward the victim for the horrible and despicable things that had been done to him, stating, 'I had to pay for mine; he had to pay for his.'"

The parole board determined that "Nelson Rodriguez had not demonstrated a level of rehabilitative progress that would make his release compatible with the welfare of society. Mr. Rodriguez has served 20 years for the murder…yet his presentment was concerning, as it was devoid of empathy and indicative of rehabilitation." His parole was denied, with his next appearance to take place in four years.

Further Reading:

"Decision in the Matter of Nelson Rodriguez, W65587." Review Hearing, The Commonwealth of Massachusetts Executive Office of Public Safety, Parole Board. June 6, 2018. mass.gov/files/documents/2018/06/14/Nelson%20Rodriguez%20 2018%20ROD.pdf

DEMARCO TRAYNUM

Fatal shooting in the Hathaway Road McDonald's restaurant in New Bedford, Massachusetts, on April 26, 1998.

Victim: Demarco Traynum, 22.

Accused: Kevin E. Jackmon, 30.

Details: According to his appeal records, "on April 26, 1998, Jackmon and his accomplice, Demarco Traynum, entered a McDonald's restaurant in New Bedford and forced more than a dozen employees and customers, at gunpoint, into a small back office of the restaurant. They directed one McDonald's employee to bind the hands of some of the individuals held in the office and forced the assistant manager and another employee to empty the contents of the safe and the cash registers into a canvas sack.

"The robbery was interrupted by the arrival of two police officers, and a shootout ensued. In the course of the confrontation, Jackmon accidentally shot and killed Traynum. Subsequently, Jackmon seized two women, one of whom was six months pregnant, and escaped from the scene of the crime while holding the two women in headlocks and firing at the police. Jackmon later left the two women in a hotel in New York City and fled to North Carolina, where he was arrested nearly two months later after his photograph was aired on the television program *America's Most Wanted*."

Trial: Kevin Jackmon argued at his trial in 1999 that Traynum had committed suicide during the siege with police.

Jackmon was convicted by a jury of murder in the second degree, two counts of assault by means of a dangerous weapon, unlawful possession of a firearm, two counts of kidnapping, armed robbery while masked, use of a firearm while committing a felony, and fourteen counts of stealing by confining or putting in fear.

Jackmon was sentenced to three terms of life in prison—one for the murder; one for the taking of 15 hostages; and one for the armed robbery.

Afterword: Jackmon appealed his conviction claiming that there were errors in instruction to the jury and that he was sentenced for crimes of which he was not convicted.

His motion for a new trial was denied.

Further Reading:

"Commonwealth vs. Kevin E. Jackmon." 63 Mass. App. Ct. 47, June 1, 2004-February 23, 2005. Bristol County. masscases.com/cases/app/63/63massappct47.html.

Rising, David. "Jackmon pleads innocent to 44 counts; bail denied." *SouthCoastToday.com*, 7 July 1998. southcoasttoday.com/article/19980707/ news/307079999

CHAPTER 2

2000-2009
A NEW CENTURY OF HOPE

In the years 2000-2009, there were 1,640 murders in Massachusetts; approximately 20 of which were in Fall River and 60 in New Bedford—many of which remain unsolved. We use the word *approximately* because we don't have homicide figures for these two cities for the years 2000-2002.

The huge number of murders in New Bedford, a crime wave by definition, was largely due to gang related deaths, as retribution killings were on the rise and law enforcement was at a loss to stem the tide. This rash of murders led to New Bedford's chief of police, Arthur J. Kelly III, to resign in 2003 after the city's ninth homicide. There would be a total of 11 murders in that city in 2003, up from 7 the year before—the highest ever.

The high homicide rate caused other issues in New Bedford—a culture of silence by witnesses, which then led to an increase in unsolved cases. People were simply too afraid to speak up for fear that they would be next. In one extremely sad case, the mother of an indicted gang member (charged with murder of a rival gang member) was senselessly murdered—her case remains unsolved, now 12 years later.

In order to counteract the rampage, New Bedford instituted aggressive anti-crime efforts, including enforcing federal gun and drug charges against gang leaders and hoping that the efforts would cut into the illegal gun sales in the city. Then mayor Frederick Kalisz (1998-2006) believed that the rise in violent crime, of which homicide is statistically included, was due to the city undergoing a "demographic transition." Newly arrived immigrants, he felt, were clashing with longtime residents, leading to violent misunderstandings and mistrust between citizens and city officials.

One resident reported keeping her police scanner on at all times and each time she heard her street mentioned she ordered her children inside.

As the SouthCoast pushed into a new century, there was a hope that killings would decrease from the highs of the decade before, but, sadly, that was not to be. By 2010, Fall River ranked the 88th most dangerous city in the nation, partly due to the heroin epidemic with ties to the neighboring shipping port of New Bedford. Nearly 100,000 pounds of marijuana, cocaine, and heroin landed each year through the port and a large amount of this ended up in nearby Fall River.

The population of Fall River had dropped by the year 2000 to 91,000, down .8%—continuing its downward spiral since its high of 120,000 in 1920 when the cotton manufacturing mill system finally collapsed under its own weight.

The population of New Bedford, the other large city in the SouthCoast, boasts similar numbers and similar statistics. In 2000, the number of residents had fallen to 93,768, down from 99,922 the decade before.

As you read of the murders that took place in the area in the new century, it will become apparent that gangs and drugs had a dramatic influence on the local environment. Gangs from Boston and as near as Providence infiltrated the Fall River and New Bedford communities. They cut, shot, and tortured drug users and dealers. Heavy drugs caused outlandish behavior by both victims and the accused. In 2006, law enforcement swept the city of Fall River for guns, drugs, and gangs. It was estimated that between 300 and 500 people were selling drugs on Fall River streets in 2006.

It was a time when unsolved murders increased dramatically. The area had accumulated its share of cold cases but for the new century, even with the newest technology, there never seemed to be a solution to the most severe crimes. We know you will agree: EVERY crimes deserves to be solved to give some small sense of peace to the parents or family members of these victims.

So who killed Sarah Cornell, Andrew and Abby Borden, Russell Goldstein, Ray Raimondi, Joe Pemberton, Joe Medeiros, and Oranuch Sousa? How about Eric "Roz" Sullivan, Vin Wadlington, Antonio Simoes, Bernadette DePina, and Maria Mendez? Will these cold cases *ever* warm up? There are federal grants available to the police to help in solving old murders. Bristol County District Attorney Sam Sutter started a cold case unit and invested resources to the victims that time forgot. And he had some very good success. Sadly, the current DA, Thomas Quinn, has closed that shop and seems to no longer consider cold cases a priority.

ATHENA HARVEY

Man violently kills wife of 40 years in their home in Wareham, Massachusetts, on June 21, 2000.

Victim: Athena Harvey, 66.

Accused: Earl H. Harvey Jr., 68.

Details: On June 21, 2000, Earl Harvey, for reasons never revealed, murdered his wife Athena Harvey of 40 years in their home in Wareham. Her death was concealed until June 28, when her daughter, concerned about her welfare, visited the home and discovered her body.

Mrs. Harvey died from multiple stab wounds to her chest and blunt trauma to the head and neck. "Her body was found wrapped in sheets and located in a small room between the living room and the bedroom area, authorities said in court papers. Her head was wrapped in dark plastic with a white rope around her neck. There were large blood stains on the bed" ("Murder Suspect Tried to Distract Suspicion from Violent Killing").

With no signs of forced entry or robbery of their property or Athena's jewelry, police believed that her husband was a suspect and a warrant was issued.

In order to avoid suspicion regarding his wife's disappearance, after the murder on the 21st, Earl Harvey called a daughter to tell her that they were going to Maine on vacation and canceled his own birthday party for the coming weekend. He phoned Athena's hair salon to cancel her appointment for the next three weeks, and called the Wareham Council on Aging to say that the couple would be away for at least a month. In addition, he went to the post office and had the mail held and withdrew $600 in three separate withdrawals from the bank.

Earl Harvey was apprehended on July 4, 2000, while looking for a book at Savers, a thrift store in New Bedford's north end. He and his wife frequented the store weekly and the staff knew them both well. The couple would shop for Athena's clothes, buying a large quantity, as many as 20 items at a time. They would take the clothes home so Athena could try them on there and return the items that she didn't want or didn't fit.

Athena suffered from multiple sclerosis and was disabled.

Earl was arrested without incident.

The store's staff was completely surprised by the murder, describing Earl Harvey as a "jovial man" and the married duo "were a pleasant couple growing old together" ("Police Arrest Husband in Wareham Slay Case").

Outcome: On March 25, 2002, while awaiting trial at the Lemuel Shattuck Hospital Correctional Unit in Jamaica Plain, where he had been a patient since January, Earl Harvey passed away from natural causes. His health issues included diabetes, glaucoma, and heart problems.

Further Reading:

Augstums, Ieva. "Police Arrest Husband in Wareham Slay Case." *The Boston Globe* (Boston, Massachusetts), July 5, 2000.

Brown, Curt. "Murder Suspect Tried to Distract Suspicion from Violent Killing." *SouthCoastToday.com*. July 4, 2000.

"Elderly Murder Suspect Dies in Custody." *SouthCoastToday.com*. March 28, 2000.

Emery, Theo. "Wareham Murder Suspect Arrested." *SeaCoastOnline.com*. July 5, 2000.

JOHN DUARTE

Man beaten to death on Purchase Street in New Bedford, Massachusetts, on the evening of August 21, 2000.

Victim: John Duarte, 29.

Accused: Mario Barros, 17, Jao Gomes, age unknown.

Details: The details of the events of the murder are summarized in the Barros appeal of 2002: "Near midnight on the evening of August 21, 2000, there was a homicide on Purchase Street in New Bedford. A man had been kicked and beaten to death. The police saw evidence of the remains of paint balls, blood, and empty beer bottles at the scene. Detective Dean Fredericks of the New Bedford police department observed the victim's body at the hospital and saw trauma to his head and blood over his face. An eyewitness told the police that two young men had beaten the victim and fled the scene. One of them had yelled 'Mario' to the other as they fled.

"At about 6:00 A.M., Detective Fredericks met with State Trooper Ronald Blais and New Bedford police Detective Charles Perry. Detective Perry mentioned that he knew a young man named Mario Barros who lived in the neighborhood where the homicide had occurred. They checked and found an outstanding default warrant for [Barros]. They decided to use the warrant to gain entry to [Barros]'s home and to interview him about the incident. The underlying charge on which [Barros] had defaulted was for disturbing the peace. The police did not intend to take [Barros] into custody on the warrant unless their interview with him on the murder investigation proved fruitful.

"Police knocked on the door of [Barros]'s home a short time later, announced they had a warrant for his arrest, and were admitted without incident. [Barros] was dressed only in a T-shirt and boxer shorts, and was barefoot; it appeared as though he had been sleeping. He was seventeen years old. The three officers had an imposing and professional appearance and manner. They immediately began to question [Barros] in a small room in [Barros]'s home.

"Without giving [Barros] Miranda warnings, the police proceeded to ask him questions about the incident on Purchase Street. He told them that he and friends had been drinking and shooting paint balls. When asked if he owned a paint ball gun, he told them that he had sold his paint ball gun but still had the box. He asked the officers if they wanted to see the box, and they said they did. [Barros] then led the officers to his bedroom for the purpose of retrieving the box. When the officers followed [Barros] into his bedroom, they observed in plain view in the middle of the floor sneakers that appeared to have dried blood on them. [Barros], upon request, produced the clothing he had worn the previous night. The officers placed [Barros] under arrest, allowed him to get dressed, handcuffed him and took him to the police station.

"At the police station [Barros] was handcuffed by one wrist to the wall in the detectives room. He was given Miranda warnings at about 7:50 A.M. He stated that he understood his rights and signed a waiver, consenting to questioning. He made a phone call to his uncle stating that he would be unable to report for work. He was then interviewed for about twenty minutes. Toward the end of the interview, one of the detectives said that he did not think [Barros] was telling the truth. [Barros] then said he did not think he wanted to continue to talk to the detectives without an attorney. The detectives told him to think about it, and left the room.

"The detectives then learned that a witness had identified [Barros] from a photograph as one of the assailants. They returned to the room and informed [Barros] that he was being charged with murder. [Barros] thereupon became visibly upset, began breathing heavily with tears in his eyes, and asked rhetorically, 'He died?' He said he might faint. His handcuffs were removed. The detectives asked him if he wanted to talk to them. He said yes, and agreed to memorialize the interview on videotape. He was given Miranda warnings again and executed a second waiver form. He then gave an inculpatory statement" ("Commonwealth vs. Mario Barros").

Trial: Two men were accused in the killing of John Duarte. Joao Gomes, 25, was found not guilty of murder and assault with a dangerous weapon after a four day trial in 2003. He was, however, found guilty of assault charges in the beating. He was sentenced to 2 years in jail but freed from custody on time served.

Mario Barros was changed with murder in the first degree. Before his trial he appealed the manner in which his rights were violated. Barros had plainly asked for a lawyer but the interrogation proceeded without representation. The appeals court found that the testimony should be suppressed based on a clear violation.

No details regarding the outcome of this case could be located.

Further Reading:

"Commonwealth vs. Mario Barros." 56 Mass. App. Ct. 675, September 19, 2002-December 6, 2002. Bristol County. masscases.com/cases/app/56/56massappct675.html.
Doherty, John. "Man Acquitted of 2000 Murder." *SouthCoastToday.com*, April 4, 2003.
"One Held in N. Bedford Killing." *The Boston Globe* (Boston, Massachusetts), August 23, 2000.

JOSEPH CANTO

Man shot in the head and killed outside the L&P Lounge, 1746 Acushnet Avenue, in New Bedford, Massachusetts, on October 14, 2000.

Victim: Joseph Canto, 31.

Accused: Jason J. Almeida, 29, and Russell Andrews, 18.

Details: According to Jason Almeda's appeal in 2008, the facts of the case are as follows: "Responding police officers found the victim's body lying between a car and a truck in the rear parking lot of a lounge in New Bedford at 1:45 A.M. on October 14, 2000. The cause of death was a single bullet to the skull from a weapon that had been pressed tightly against the victim's left earlobe when the shot was fired. Two bullets were retrieved from the back of a nearby parked vehicle and a third was recovered from the wall of a building across the street.

"No physical evidence connected [Almeida] to the shooting, but three eyewitnesses testified to relevant events. The testimony of each of these witnesses, however, was not consistent with that of the others or with their prior testimony. Moreover, two of the eyewitnesses, David Grace and John Todman, testified while under indictment for perjury. Each had an agreement with the Commonwealth that the perjury charge would be dismissed in return for truthful testimony. The third witness, Olivia Pires Lara, was awaiting sentencing on drug charges in Federal District Court and had a cooperation agreement with Federal authorities relating to the Federal charges (although not to the present case). Each of these witnesses was 'scared,' but the cause of their fear was not identified.

"David Grace was twenty-one years old at the time of the shooting and had known both [Almeida] and Russell Andrews (the codefendant) for several years. He saw the two of them in the lounge during the evening of October 13, 2000. When last call was announced (now the morning of October 14), he 'saw everybody leaving from [a] pool table,' [Almeida] and Andrews among them. Grace left the lounge as well. In the rear parking lot, he approached a group of men which included Andrews and [Almeida]. When Grace was about twenty feet from the group, he 'saw a kid walking down the street . . . heading towards where they was at.' Grace heard gunshots and saw the 'kid' run past him. Grace ran in back of the 'kid,' seeing gun flashes behind him and to the side. He also saw [Almeida] with a gun in his hand, shooting. Grace heard a total of six or seven shots and finally saw the 'kid' fall between a truck and a car.

"John Todman was twenty-one years old at the time of trial and had known Andrews most of his life. He had known [Almeida] 'from when [he] was younger.' Todman came to the lounge on October 13, with Andrews and two other friends in a Ford Taurus automobile driven by Andrews. They parked on a side street near the lounge, and the four of them walked into the lounge together. Todman saw [Almeida] at the lounge. After last call was announced, Todman left through the back door, following Andrews and two other friends. While he was in the parking lot in a group of eight to twelve young people with [Almeida] standing about twenty-five or thirty feet from him, Todman saw 'some guy [the victim]…walk out…from the corner' of the street toward [Almeida]. When the victim was about ten feet from [Almeida], [Almeida] backed away. The victim walked 'closer and closer.' No one else was standing near either of them, and Todman heard no words exchanged, but he saw [Almeida] reach for his waist and pull out a gun. He saw a gun 'in the air' with 'fire' 'coming…up in the air' from [Almeida]'s hand, and Todman ducked behind a car. He heard a total of five or six shots.

"Olivia Pires Lara was twenty-six at the time of trial, was David Grace's cousin, and knew both Andrews and [Almeida]. She also knew the victim, who 'used to hang with [her] brother sometimes.' She too was at the lounge on the night of October 13. At some point that night, she looked out the rear door and saw [Almeida], Andrews, and 'quite a few' others arriving in a 'big car' (a Cadillac). The men all entered the lounge, and at a later time, she spoke to Andrews there. As she observed an argument between [Almeida], Andrews, and the victim on the dance floor, a 'bouncer' told them, 'Take that outside.' The victim left through the rear door, with the rest of the group following him. Lara looked out the door and saw the group gathered around the victim, arguing with him. Shortly thereafter, Lara went to the front door and then heard a shot. She ran down the street to the back of the lounge. There she saw the victim, [Almeida], Andrews, and others standing '[b]etween cars.' The victim and [Almeida] were standing within one foot of each other, arguing. Andrews was also standing at the victim's side. She heard yelling and swearing and saw [Almeida] run to the Cadillac, take something from it, and return. When Andrews pointed a gun at the victim's head, [Almeida] said, 'Give me that,' grabbed the gun from Andrews' hand, and shot the victim in the head behind the right ear. The gun was not visible in the darkness, but Lara heard the shot and saw the victim fall to the ground."

At the time of his death, Joseph Canto left behind a 16-year-old daughter and had just celebrated the birth of a son two days earlier.

Trial: Russell Andrews, Almeida's co-defendant was found guilty of unlawful possession of a firearm and assault with a dangerous weapon. Prosecutors asserted that Andrews helped chase down Mr. Canto and held a gun over him until Jason Almeida reached them and fired the bullet that killed Canto. Russell Andrews was sentenced to 10 years in prison.

Jason Almeida was convicted by a jury of murder in the first degree and unlawful possession of a firearm. He was sentenced to life in prison.

Afterword: Jason Almeida appealed his conviction in 2008 on the claim that he was denied the right to confront and examine a spectator to his trial and was denied meaningful cross-examination of a key identification witness. The court found there was no merit to his claims and his conviction was upheld.

Further Reading:

"Commonwealth vs. Jason J. Almeida." 452 Mass. 601, September 5, 2008-November 21, 2008. Bristol County. masscases.com/cases/sjc/452/452mass601.html.

Doherty, John. "City Man Sentenced to Life in Slaying." *SouthCoastToday.com*, May 21, 2002.

NANCY SHONHEINZ

Woman stabbed to death in Long Road home in Fairhaven, Massachusetts, on November 12, 2000.

Victim: Nancy Shonheinz, 36.

Accused: Robert J. Oliveira, 36.

Details: According the appeal filed by Robert Oliveira in 2006, the facts of the case are as follows: "The victim was a thirty-six year old physical therapist employed by St. Luke's Hospital. She and [Oliveira] had known each other since high school and had an 'on and off' relationship for many years. [Oliveira] worked on Cape Cod during the week and often spent the weekends at the victim's house in Fairhaven, where he kept some of his possessions, including exercise equipment.

"The relationship between [Oliveira] and the victim, however, had been deteriorating, and the victim was seeing other men. In early November, 2000, the victim confided in her coworkers that she was 'finished' with [Oliveira] and had begun dating someone who she felt was the 'right man.' On her birthday, November 9, the victim and this man had dinner together. On that same night, [Oliveira] called the victim's sister and asked her to speak to the victim for him. He told her that their relationship was not going well, that he did not want to lose the victim, and that he could not live without her.

"At approximately 6 P.M. on Saturday, November 11, the victim arrived at her parents' home, where she spent the next hour. At some point she telephoned her own home to see if [Oliveira] was still there. He answered the telephone, and they argued. The victim's mother overheard her accusing [Oliveira] of going through her pocketbook. [Oliveira]'s voice was very loud and the victim held the telephone away from her ear, repeatedly calling him a wacko. When she finished the telephone call, the victim told her mother that she did not want anything more to do with [Oliveira] and wished him 'out of her life forever.' The victim left for home at approximately 7 P.M., and her father telephoned and spoke to her there at 9:30 P.M. Sometime after 2 A.M., the victim was beaten with a blunt object, stabbed more than forty times in the chest and back, and died on the floor of one of the bedrooms in her home.

"Just before 8 A.M. the following morning, the victim's neighbor, while walking his dog in the nearby woods, saw the silhouette of a person he recognized to be [Oliveira] at the kitchen sink in the victim's house. At about 8:10 A.M., one of the victim's friends placed a telephone call to her. [Oliveira] answered the telephone and told her that the victim was busy. When the friend insisted on speaking to the victim, [Oliveira] told the friend that she was doing laundry and would call her later.

"At 8:58 A.M., that same morning, [Oliveira] telephoned his brother, 'Teddy' Oliveira, from the victim's home. He told Teddy that something had happened to the victim and that she was '[l]ying in a puddle of blood.' He asked Teddy to contact their father because 'I think I'm in trouble over here.' When Teddy asked what happened to the victim, [Oliveira] repeatedly said, 'I don't know.' He then screamed, 'I think I'm trying to hang myself for the second time.' There was a bang, some gurgling, choking sounds, and more screaming. Teddy urged [Oliveira] to pick up the telephone, to talk to him, and to contact the police. At 9:16 A.M., [Oliveira] dialed 911 and told the Fairhaven police department dispatcher, 'There's a death here,' and 'My girlfriend's dead.' He also stated, '[T]his is fucking crazy. Somebody get over here,' and when asked what had happened, said, 'I don't know. I was drinking, we were drinking. This went on since like four o'clock in the morning.'

"Officers Peter Joseph and Christopher Kershaw were the first to arrive at the victim's home. [Oliveira] appeared nervous and frantic, and pointed them to a door at the end of the hallway on the first floor. When the officers opened the door, they found the victim's body on the floor covered with a blanket. There was some blood on a nearby bed and a pool of blood around the victim's head. She had no pulse and her skin was very cold. When the blanket was removed, a number of stab wounds on her chest were apparent. Officer Kershaw escorted [Oliveira] out of the room and down the hall into the living room. [Oliveira] kept asking whether the victim was 'okay,' even though he had repeatedly told the dispatcher that the victim was dead. The officer noticed that [Oliveira] had abrasions all around his neck, as well as dried blood on his chin.

"The police obtained and executed a search warrant for the house. The house had a working burglar alarm, and there were no signs of forced entry. There was a groove in the stairway banister with a fiber affixed to it matching a bloodstained rope, found in the basement, which [Oliveira] had apparently used in attempting to hang himself. There was evidence of an effort to clean up and dispose of some of the victim's blood in the kitchen sink. In an upstairs bathroom, bloodstains were found in the sinks and on the faucet of one sink. The first-floor bathroom tested positive for blood in the sink, on the faucets, and on the shower floor. Subsequently, at the police station, [Oliveira] tested positive for blood on his left and right hands, his neck area, the inner elbow area of his right arm, his right and left upper arms, his right calf area, and his lower back. His underwear, jeans, T-shirt, and socks also tested positively for blood.

"In the kitchen, the police found six empty twelve-ounce 'hard lemonade' bottles, two empty beer bottles, a one-gallon Peach Tree Schnapps bottle that was three-quarters full, and one empty Rumplemintz 'shot' bottle. Another hard lemonade bottle was found half full on the kitchen table. Testing conducted during the autopsy revealed that the victim did not have any alcohol in her system at the time of her death.

"At several points at the house and later at the police station, [Oliveira] gave varying accounts of how much he had had to drink that night, ranging from 'two beers' to whatever was found 'downstairs' (in the kitchen). Officers who spoke to [Oliveira] testified that they had no trouble understanding him and that he did not appear to be intoxicated, although he did smell of alcohol.

"When [Oliveira] was asked about the dark purplish ring around his neck, he responded, 'Never mind me. What the fuck happened to Nancy?' When asked if he had tried to take his own life, he stated that he did not know. When asked why his jaw was twitching, he answered, 'Well, wouldn't you be nervous? This is fucked up.' He eventually told the officers that he and the victim were supposed to go to the movies the night before but they had had an argument so they went back into the house and he had a couple of beers. When asked what the argument was about, [Oliveira] replied, 'You don't know the half of it.' When asked whether they fought over a boy friend, [Oliveira] answered that he was not sure whether she was dating anyone at the time. He later admitted that the victim told him that he could be replaced and that he knew she was seeing other men.

"[Oliveira] also told the police that he and the victim were the only two people in the house, that the victim slept upstairs with him, and that he remembered waking up because the victim was no longer in bed. He looked for the victim and found her lying injured in the downstairs bedroom and telephoned 911. He denied knowing what happened to the victim and claimed that it was a 'blank,' or 'blurry.' He did not mention speaking by telephone to either his brother or the victim's friend.

"The medical examiner testified that the victim suffered forty-four stab wounds, all inflicted while she was alive. He also testified that there were two lacerations to the back of her head, a 'semi-sharp blunt object' having caused the larger one, resulting in a triangular piece of the victim's skull being pushed about one inch into her brain. The victim also had scattered abrasions on her chest and face as well as defensive lacerations on her hands. Multiple sharp and blunt force injuries were the cause of death."

Trial: "At trial, the Commonwealth proceeded on two theories of murder in the first degree: deliberate premeditation and extreme atrocity or cruelty. Defense counsel did not concede that [Oliveira] was the person who killed the victim. However, he developed evidence of [Oliveira]'s intoxication throughout the trial. In closing, defense counsel argued that if the jury should find that [Oliveira] stabbed the victim, intoxication would be a mitigating factor bearing on premeditation, intent, knowledge, and whether the killing was committed with extreme atrocity or cruelty, and that they should find him guilty only of murder in the second degree. The jury found [Oliveira] guilty of murder in the first degree on the theory of extreme atrocity or cruelty."

Robert J. Oliveira was convicted of murder in the first degree.

Afterword: Robert Oliveira appealed his conviction in 2006 on the grounds that judge's instruction to the jury with respect to the element of malice in murder committed with extreme atrocity or cruelty was erroneous. Oliveira asked for a new trial or a reduced sentence. The appeals court found the judge properly instructed the jury and the appeal was denied.

Further Reading:

"Commonwealth vs. Robert J. Oliveira." 445 Mass. 837, October 7, 2005-January 23, 2006. Bristol County. masscases.com/cases/sjc/445/445mass837.html.

RAYMOND MATOS & ROBERT HERBERT JR.

Murder by arson on Covel Street in Fall River, Massachusetts, on December 1, 2000.

Victims: Raymond Matos, 26, and Robert Herbert Jr., 28.

Accused: Joseph Megna, 71.

Details: A multifamily home was set on fire by the victims who were paid to do so by the accused. Both bodies of the trapped victims were found in the basement of the burned out building on Covel Street where gasoline was used to set the building on fire. Joseph Megna had a long criminal history of drug charges, filing a false insurance claim in connection with a fire that destroyed his business, Joe's Snack Shack, located on East Main Street in Fall River, and possession of stolen goods.

Megna was arrested in St. Petersburg, Florida, on January 26, 2001, and was indicted on two counts second degree murder, arson, and conspiracy for the fire that killed the two men he hired to burn down his own home.

Trial: Joseph Megna was convicted of second degree murder and sentenced to life in prison.

Further Reading:

"Arson Deaths Lead to Murder Charges." *The Tampa Tribune* (Tampa, Florida), 26 January 2002.
"Families Identify 2 Men in Fall River Tenement." *Boston Globe* (Boston, Massachusetts), 9 December 2001.
"Man Charged with Murder Arson Plot." *Boston Globe* (Boston, Massachusetts), 27 January 2002.

GEORGE CARPENTER

Fatal beating death of a man outside 86 Bluefield Street, New Bedford, Massachusetts, on February 16, 2001.

Victim: George Carpenter, age unknown.

Accused: Lionel Rodriguez, 24, Robert Tirado, and Ryan Marshall, ages unknown.

Details: The facts of the case, as detailed in the appeal record of Lionel Rodriguez are as follows: "In the early morning hours of February 16, 2001, George Carpenter was socializing and drinking at the home of Donna Medeiros, Ryan Marshall's mother. At some point, Ryan Marshall arrived home with his girlfriend and three additional friends, Robert Tirado, Jonathan Torres, and Heather Lawrence. An argument broke out between Mr. Carpenter, Mr. Marshall, and Mr. Tirado. Mr. Carpenter attempted to leave the gathering, but was prevented from doing so by Mr. Tirado, who slashed the tires of Mr. Carpenter's car. Lionel Rodriguez, Orlando Badillo, and Dennis Smith then arrived on the scene. Mr. Marshall, Mr. Tirado, Mr. Rodriguez, Mr. Badillo, and Mr. Smith attacked Mr. Carpenter. During the attack, Mr. Carpenter was struck with a tire iron, kicked multiple times, and beaten. Mr. Carpenter eventually lost consciousness, and died later that day as a result of internal bleeding caused by blunt force trauma."

Trial: In 2006, Lionel Rodriguez was convicted by a jury of first degree murder, on a theory of extreme atrocity and cruelty. He was sentenced to life in prison with the possibility of parole. Ryan Marshall was convicted of being an accessory before the fact to the murder and also on the theory of extreme atrocity or cruelty. A jury convicted Robert Tirado of murder in the second degree.

Afterword: In 2010, Lionel Rodriguez appealed his conviction on the grounds that there were errors in the admission of autopsy photographs and testimony of the medical examiner. The appeals court agreed and reduced his conviction to murder in the second degree. Again a sentence of life in prison with the possibility of parole was imposed.

Rodriguez applied for parole in 2016 and it was denied, with a review scheduled in 2 years.

Robert Tirado appealed his conviction in 2005, contending the judge erred in denying his request for a self-defense instruction. His appeal was denied.

Ryan Marshall appealed his conviction in 2012 on the grounds of double jeopardy. His appeal was denied.

Further Reading:

"Commonwealth vs. Lionel Rodriguez." 457 Mass. 461, March 5, 2010-August 9, 2010. Bristol County. masscases.com/cases/sjc/457/457mass461.html.

"Commonwealth vs. Robert Tirado." 65 Mass. App. Ct. 571, October 6, 2005-February 24, 2006. Bristol County. masscases.com/cases/app/65/65massappct571.html.

"Commonwealth vs. Ryan Marshall." 463 Mass. 529, March 8, 2012-October 15, 2012. Bristol County. masscases.com/cases/sjc/463/463mass529.html.

"Decision in the Matter of Lionel Rodriguez, W87065." Review Hearing, The Commonwealth of Massachusetts Executive Office of Public Safety, Parole Board. June 20, 2016. mass.gov/files/documents/2018/02/12/Rodriguez%2C%20Lionel.pdf

ROSE MARIE MONIZ

Woman bludgeoned to death in her home at 3448 Acushnet Avenue in New Bedford, Massachusetts, on March 23, 2001.

Victim: Rose Marie Moniz, 41.

Accused: Unknown.

Details: Rose Marie Moniz was found murdered in the bathroom inside her home on Acushnet Avenue in New Bedford. She has been bludgeoned to death. Alfred Cunha II, her father was going about his daily routine of waking her and having coffee with his daughter when he discovered her body.

Rose's case remains unsolved.

If you have any information regarding this cold case, please contact the New Bedford Police Department's Unsolved Homicide Tip Line at 1-866-SOLVE-07.

Further Reading:

Brown, Curt. "Pain Goes Beyond Slaying." *SouthCoastToday.com*, 19 April 2001. south-coasttoday.com/article/20010819/news/308199999.

ORANUCH SOUSA

Woman bludgeoned to death in Fall River, Massachusetts, on June 16, 2001.

Victim: Oranuch Sousa, 48.

Accused: Unknown.

Details: Oranuch Sousa was found dead in a grassy field behind Save-A-Lot supermarket in the South End of Fall River with multiple blunt force injuries to her head. Her body was discovered by a man and his son walking in the area.

Divorced some six years, Oranuch had recently requested that her former husband give her more money. Joseph Sousa, 40, went to meet "Suzy" on his motorcycle. The day after the murder, Joseph was seen burning and burying a pair of jeans that appeared to be blood stained in his back yard. In May of 2002, Police recovered multiple motorcycle related objects when they did their investigation of the his home. They also found "miscellaneous fabric, fibers, and dirt samples." Joseph Sousa has not been charged with any crimes related to Oranuch's death.

On August 15, 2002, Joseph Sousa was arrested on a separate case of rape allegedly committed against his live-in girlfriend of 6 years. He was arraigned in Newport Superior Court on three charges of assault. He had been a member of Tiverton's Zoning Board of Review since 1998.

Further Reading:

"Tiverton Official Denies Rape Charges." *SouthCoastToday.com*, 16 August 2002. southcoasttoday.com/article/20020816/news/308169964.

LISANDRO MEDINA & EDWARD NEGRON

Two men shot to death on Bell Rock Road in the Southeastern Massachusetts Bioreserve in Fall River, Massachusetts, on July 13, 2001.

Victims: Lisandro Medina, 26, and Edward Negron, 32.

Accused: Jarin Perez, 19.

Details: According to Perez's appeal records, the facts of the case are as follows: "Just before 4 P.M. on July 13, 2001, a driver returning home from work noticed a motor vehicle parked sideways in the middle of Bell Rock Road in Fall River. Its engine was still running. A bullet had pierced a hole through the driver's side window, the passenger side door was ajar, and a body lay on the ground fifty yards north of the vehicle. In response to a 911 call, the police arrived shortly thereafter. Lisandro Medina, also known as 'Choko,' was found dead, slumped over in the driver's seat. He had suffered two gunshot wounds to his forehead and a single gunshot wound to the back of his left shoulder. The victim found lying on the ground, Edward Negron (also known as 'Ti-Ti'), had suffered a fatal gunshot wound to the back of his head and four gunshot wounds to his back.

"Four discharged cartridge casings and four spent bullets were recovered from the crime scene. The Commonwealth's ballistics expert testified that all of the casings were fired from a weapon designed for .30-caliber class ammunition (such as an M-1 rifle), and that the rifle markings on the spent bullets were "almost exclusively unique" to having been fired from an M-1 carbine rifle.

"A week before the shootings, Perez bought an M-1 carbine rifle, a clip, .30-caliber ammunition, and a camouflage carrying case from Jerome Moton for approximately $400 in cash. On July 11, Perez showed the rifle to Reny Gonzalez, a friend and neighbor. Perez asked Gonzalez to store the rifle in his basement 'for a little while.' The following day, Perez returned to Gonzalez's house to pick it up.

"On July 13, at approximately 3:10 P.M., Medina drove to the home of Jeffrey Rutkowski. Negron was a passenger in Medina's vehicle. Medina asked Rutkowski if he could get one-half pound of marijuana for his friends, who were in a white Chevrolet automobile parked behind him. This automobile was driven by Perez's cousin, Julio Quinones. Rutkowski told Medina he would try, and Medina responded that he would telephone him in one hour. Medina drove away at approximately 3:25 P.M., followed by the white automobile. The shootings occurred shortly thereafter.

"At approximately 4:45 P.M. that same day, Perez went to Gonzalez's house and asked him to come outside. Perez told Gonzalez that he had gone to the 'reservation' (near Bell Rock Road) and 'murdered' two people, one of whom was named 'Choko.' Perez stated that the two individuals were talking about some people that he did not get along with in Puerto Rico, that he became scared, and that 'he killed them before they tried to do anything to him.' Perez also told Gonzalez that he fired a bullet through the window of the vehicle and that when the man in the passenger seat got out and started running, he shot him as well.

"A few days later, Perez told Gonzalez that he felt like the police were watching him, and asked if he could again store his rifle and its carrying case in Gonzalez's basement. Gonzalez agreed. A few days after that, Perez asked Gonzalez to help him dispose of the rifle. Gonzalez and Perez took the rifle, which was now in pieces, out of its case, wrapped it in a pair of jeans, and placed it in a backpack. Gonzalez then walked to a 'swamp type' body of water in Fall River and threw the rifle into the water. Two pieces of a rifle were later recovered, but no fingerprints were detected.

"The police first interviewed Perez on July 16, 2001. He told them that he had known Medina for approximately two months and that on the day of the shootings he telephoned Medina sometime between 11 A.M. and noon from Quinones's house. He then recalled that in fact he was in the Watuppa Heights section of Fall River at 11 A.M., where he had an in-person conversation with Medina and several other men. Perez also told the police that the last time he was in Quinones's white Chevrolet automobile was on July 6, 2001. On July 25, 2001, when the police questioned Perez a second time, he gave a different version of the events of July 13. He told them that on that morning he went to Quinones's house after breakfast and telephoned Medina at approximately noon. He and Quinones then went in Quinones's white Chevrolet automobile to Watuppa Heights, where they met with Medina and some other persons and discussed purchasing marijuana. Medina made a telephone call and, at approximately 1:30 P.M., Perez and Quinones followed Medina by automobile out of the Watuppa Heights housing development to Rutkowski's house for the purpose of completing a purchase. According to Perez, he and Quinones arrived home at around 1:45 P.M. Perez denied ever having been on Bell Rock Road and denied going to Gonzalez's house later that day. He also initially denied owning a camouflage rifle case, but later, after viewing a photograph of the rifle case seized from Gonzalez's house, stated that it was possibly his and that he used it to carry his BB gun."

Medina left behind a 4-year-old daughter. Negron left two daughters, ages 4 and 6.

Trial: Jarin Perez was charged with two counts first degree murder. He was convicted and sentenced to life without parole by Judge Richard Chin on both charges. Perez began his term at MCI Walpole Cedar Junction.

Afterword: Jarin Perez appealed his convictions in 2005 on the grounds that the judge erred in admitting evidence that the defendant and two others had assaulted one of the Commonwealth's key witnesses, that the judge improperly limited the defendant's cross-examination of a Commonwealth witness, and that the prosecution had made two misstatements during closing arguments. The appeal was denied.

Further Reading:

"Commonwealth vs. Jarin Perez." 444 Mass. 143, February 11, 2005-April 27, 2005. Bristol County. masscases.com/cases/sjc/444/444mass143.html.

Vaishnav, Anand. "Fall River Man, 19, Held in Slaying of 2." *The Boston Globe* (Boston, Massachusetts), 1 October 2001.

MARCUS CRUZ

Young man shot to death outside 187 Chancery Street in New Bedford, Massachusetts, on September 9, 2001.

Victim: Marcus Cruz, 17.

Accused: Jonathan Butler, 18.

Details: Marcus Cruz was gunned down on Chancery Street in New Bedford, across from the United Front housing development.

Cruz was one of the victims in a series of shooting incidents, mostly involving young Cape Verdean men. The crimes are believed to be gang-related.

The case remained unsolved until another young man, Jonathan Butler, a 22-year-old New Bedford man, was gunned down and killed on January 29, 2005, at the Westlawn housing development. Butler was an alleged member of the Monte Park gang. Ballistics tests on one of the guns taken from Butler 16 months previously (he had been released from jail on October 2, 2004, after serving a year for illegal possession of a firearm)—a .38-caliber pistol—was proven to have killed Marcus Cruz.

Further Reading:

Brown, Curt. "City Man, 22, Shot in Year's First Killing." *SouthCoastToday.com*, 31 January 2005. southcoasttoday.com/article/20050131/news/301319996.

Ferreira, Joao. "Justice Sought for Slain 17-Year-Old." *SouthCoastToday.com*, 10 March 2002. southcoasttoday.com/article/20020310/news/303109996.

IVANDRO CORREIA

Young man shot to death by a rival gang on Ruth Street in New Bedford, Massachusetts, on December 5, 2001.

Victim: Ivandro Correia, 17.

Accused: Unknown.

Details: The night Ivandro Correia was killed, he was riding in a car with Justin Cromwell and Charles and Dwayne Crowder. All three men are members in the Monte Park gang. According to a videotaped interview with his brother, Manuel "Manu" Silva, Manuel learned from one of the three men that the car carrying his younger brother pulled into a South End gas station shortly before the shooting. At that time, the men noticed they were been watched and followed by members of the rival Ruth Street gang, including Chad "Ears" Dargis, 25. Correia and his friends then drove onto Cove Street and then Ruth Street with Dargis and his friends following.

"Before long Mr. Dargis supposedly steered his car alongside the vehicle carrying Mr. Correia and someone opened fire. The teenager was fatally wounded. Mr. Cromwell and Dwayne Crowder were treated at St. Luke's Hospital for injuries authorities said. Mr. Dargis has never been charged in connection with Mr. Correia's death."

There is an earlier account that implicated Brandin Gonsalves, 24, the reputed leader of the Ruth Street gang. In 2002, an informant told investigators that Gonsalves fired a handgun at a car the night of Correia's death. Gonsalves has denied that he is a gang member or involved in the shooting.

Further Reading:

Henry, Ray. "Street Justice Weaves its Way Through City's Crime Troubles." *SouthCoastToday.com*, 28 February 2005. southcoasttoday.com/article/20050228/news/302289997.

ELIJAH OMAR BEY

Man shot to death on Acushnet Avenue and Wing Street in New Bedford, Massachusetts, on February 16, 2002.

Victim: Elijah Omar Bey, 35.

Accused: William J. Hector, 25, and Tyrone Fennicks, age unknown.

Details: Elijah Omar Bey was shot once in the throat as he and his brother approached a group of men on Acushnet Avenue and Wing Street looking to buy marijuana.

Arrested in the killing were William Hector and Tyrone Fennicks, associates of the Monte Park gang, a group that had been implicated in much of the retribution violence with other gangs in New Bedford.

Trial: William Hector was indicted for murder in the first degree. In 2003, he was acquitted of the crime, after several witnesses called by the state refused to show up at trial. Three witnesses were arrested and forced to attend the trial but much of their testimony contradicted earlier statements to police.

Afterword: In 2004, hours after his codefendant in the murder of Elijah Omar Bey, Tyrone Fennicks, was acquitted of first degree murder, William Hector was shot twice in the abdomen at his girlfriend's home at 35 New Plainville Road in New Bedford. His injuries were not life threatening.

Further Reading:

Doherty, John. "Former Murder Defendant Shot in New Bedford." *SouthCoastToday.com*, 25 January 2004. southcoasttoday.com/article/20040125/news/301259990.

"Neighborhood Again Asks for Patrols." *The Boston Globe* (Boston, Massachusetts), 25 February 2002.

CHRISTOPHER FARRINGTON

Man shot to death in front of the Atlantic Bar & Grill, near City Hall, in Fall River, Massachusetts, on April 2, 2002.

Victim: Christopher Farrington, 25.

Accused: Jerome Jaime White, 26.

Details: Christopher Farrington and Jerome White encountered each other in the Atlantic Bar & Grill near City Hall and immediately got into an argument over drugs. They left the barroom and walked to the street where White discharged four shots at Farrington.

Farrington was found on the ground near a black building on Sullivan Drive with a gunshot wound to the head.

Trial: Jerome White was indicted and convicted of manslaughter and sentenced to 9 to 10 years in prison.

SHERYL GORDON

Woman strangled to death and found buried in a shallow grave behind the Industrial Park in New Bedford, Massachusetts, on April 11, 2002. Her body was discovered on May 23, 2002.

Victim: Sheryl Gordon, 43.

Accused: Peter Tangherlini, age unknown.

Details: Peter Tangherlini confessed to strangling Sheryl Gordon, his former girlfriend, soon after leaving a class on the seven deadly sins in Dante's *Inferno*. He later told investigators that he killed her after midnight in an argument over her drug use. He said he lay in bed with the dead woman for one full day before getting rid of her corpse.

After her killing, Tangherlini filed a missing persons report. He appeared suspicious to the police when he would not look the detectives in the eye or say when he last saw Ms. Gordon alive.

Trial: Peter Tangherlini was found guilty of involuntary manslaughter in December 2003.

Further Reading:

Henry, Ray. "Lawyer Argues Strangling Death was an Accident." *SouthCoastToday.com*, 16 December 2003. southcoasttoday.com/article/20031216/news/312069987.

Henry, Ray. "Murder Confession Called into Question." *SouthCoastToday.com*, 6 December 2003. southcoasttoday.com/article/20031206/news/312069988.

Henry, Ray. "Unsolved Murders Haunt Families." *SouthCoastToday.com*, 11 January 2004. southcoasttoday.com/article/20040111/news/301119999.

DAVID GASIAR & GARY FRAGOZA

Two men killed by arson fire at 47 Manton Street in Fall River, Massachusetts, on May 5, 2002.

Victims: David Gasiar, 38, and Gary Fragoza, 43.

Accused: William Brophy, 45.

Details: David Gasiar and Gary Fragoza died in a fire started by William Brophy, after the two had been beaten by Brophy.

At one time, Fragoza and Brophy lived together.

After his arrest, Brophy was sent to Bridgewater State Hospital for a competency evaluation.

Brophy had been treated by a psychiatrist and had a long history of mental illness. He had been in and out of mental hospitals since the age of 10. It was reported that he had consumed three pints of 100 proof vodka and two six-packs of beer before the incident. Brophy had also stopped taking his medication about four weeks previously and had relapsed into alcohol dependency.

Brophy admitted to the police that he had started the fire around 11:30 p.m. by using a cigarette and a book of matches. He lit the cigarette and then placed it in the book of matches, leaving it on top of a mattress in one of the bedrooms of the triple-decker home.

When the fire broke out about 12:50 a.m., Gasiar and Fragoza were found unresponsive and pronounced dead at St. Anne's Hospital in Fall River.

Trial: William Brophy was convicted of two counts of manslaughter and sentenced to 19-20 years in prison.

Further Reading:

"Ferreira, Joao. "Fire Suspect to be Evaluated at State Hospital." *SouthCoastToday.com*, 7 May 2002. southcoasttoday.com/article/20020507/news/305079993.

"Murder Case Pending After Fire Kills 2." *The Boston Globe* (Boston, Massachusetts), 6 May 2002.

RYAN AGUIAR

Man shot to death while siting in his car in New Bedford, Massachusetts, on June 24, 2002.

Victim: Ryan Aguiar, 24.

Accused: Attim Almeida, 27, and Manuel Silvia, 19.

Details: Ryan Aguiar was sitting in his Nissan Maxima in front of his apartment in New Bedford when two men ran up and shot several times into the vehicle. Aguiar was struck three times.

Aguiar was a reputed Ruth Street gang member and police believe that his death was a retaliation killing for the December 2001 killing of Manuel Silvia's teenage brother, Ivandro Correia.

Attim Almeida was one of New Bedford's most wanted fugitive. The year before this killing police wanted to question Almeida about a series of shootings that has left two dead and four injured. He was apprehended in 2001 after Almeida crashed his vehicle to the parish hall of St. Martin's Episcopal Church in New Bedford's South End and punched a police officer. A clerk magistrate reportedly released him on personal recognizance despite his warrants and the note "do not bail" on his file. After his release, Almeida went underground.

In the days prior to Aguair's murder, Fall River police arrested Almeida on drug charges, but because he gave them a false name, he was again released on personal recognizance.

Trial: Manuel Silvia was charged with first-degree murder in the shooting of Ryan Aguiar, a man he held responsible for the death of his younger brother, Ivando Correia in 2001. Silvia was acquitted in 2005.

Attim Almeida was found guilty of manslaughter and served eight years in prison for the killing of Ryan Aguiar.

Afterword: Attim Almeida was arrested on August 7, 2018, and charged with assault and battery with a dangerous weapon, two counts of armed assault, discharge of a firearm within 500 feet of a building, carrying a loaded firearm, malicious damage to a motor vehicle, felony possession of a firearm, and subsequent offense and firearm violation with three previous violent crimes.

It is reported that Almeida has an extensive criminal record, with approximately 80 arraignments since 1994. He served eight years in prison for the manslaughter of Ryan Aguiar, and two years in prison in 1999 for possession of a firearm without a permit.

Further Reading:

"Ferreira, Joao. "Fire Suspect to be Evaluated at State Hospital." *SouthCoastToday.com*, 7 May 2002. southcoasttoday.com/article/20020507/news/305079993.
"Ferreira, Joao. "Reputed Gangsters Freed, Re-arrested." *SouthCoastToday.com*, 16 June 2007. southcoasttoday.com/article/20070616/news/706160342.
"Murder Trial Opens for Former Fugitive." *The Boston Globe* (Boston, Massachusetts), 10 November 2003.

MARLENE ROSE

Woman beaten and strangled to death on the railroad tracks near 1800 Purchase Street in New Bedford, Massachusetts, on July 7, 2002.

Victim: Marlene Rose, 43.

Accused: John Loflin, 34.

Details: John Loflin was indicted in November 2010 after the Bristol County's Cold Case Unit received an alert regarding a DNA match to a man who lived in Pulaski, Tennessee, and had served a jail sentence connected to a 2008 drug case there. Loflin's DNA matched the evidence gathered under Rose's fingernails and bite marks on her body.

At the time of his arrest, Loflin's family told reporters that he was barely able to walk due to brain damage he suffered before Rose's death.

Trial: John Loflin pleaded guilty to second degree murder in 2013 and was given a life sentence in state prison. He will be eligible for parole in 15 years.

Further Reading:

Dion, Marc Munroe. "Tennessee Man Sentenced to Life in Prison for 2002 Murder in New Bedford." *wickedlocal.com*, 9 November 2013. wickedlocal.com/article/20131109/news/311099677.

"Tenn. Man Pleads Not Guilty in '02 Slaying." *The Boston Globe* (Boston, Massachusetts), 3 March 2011.

ELIZABETH THOMAS & KENNETH AUBIN

Murder/Suicide at 39 Cole Street in the Ocean Grove neighborhood of Swansea, Massachusetts, on November 30, 2002.

Victim: Elizabeth Thomas, 46.

Accused: Kenneth Aubin, 48.

Details: Kenneth Aubin's wife, Joanne C. Aubin, had been left paralyzed by a stroke seven years previous to the incident. Elizabeth Thomas was her home health aide from People Inc., a nonprofit organization based in Fall River. She visited Aubin's home to help care for Joanne.

Ken Aubin had been having a relationship with Thomas.

Thomas was strangled to death. She had filed and then withdrew a complaint in court three days prior to the murder/suicide that Aubin had kidnapped and assaulted her with a gun.

Ken Aubin committed suicide by overdosing on Lorazapam and Hydrocodone as well as ethanol and acetaminophen.

Less than three weeks after the murder/suicide, Mrs. Aubin died in Charlton Memorial Hospital in Fall River.

Further Reading:

Gomstyn, Alice. "Deaths of 2 in Swansea Probed." *The Boston Globe* (Boston, Massachusetts), 1 December 2002.

Kenneth Aubin.
Photograph by Michael Brimbau.

ALBERT LOPES JR.

Shooting death of a man outside 94 Griffin Court in New Bedford, Massachusetts, on December 1, 2002.

Victim: Albert Lopes Jr., 34.

Accused: Louis Bizzarro, 16.

Details: Albert Lopes Jr. was gunned down in the early morning hours of December 1, 2002, in New Bedford.

The case remained unsolved until 2010 when Louis Bizzarro, who was already behind bars on a firearms conviction, was charged with the murder. Police had been called to 94 Griffin Court with reports of a fight and shots fired. Upon their arrival, state and local police that there had been a fight between Albert Lopes and a friend and another group of men. The fight ended when a male pulled out a handgun and fired multiple times at Lopes.

Bizzarro, a reputed Monte Park gang member, was serving a 12-14 year state prison sentence for a 2005 crime. He and two others were stopped in a car with body armor, a .357 Magnum revolver, and a .38-caliber revolver.

Trial: Louis Bizzarro was charged with murder in the death of Albert Lopes. No further information could be obtained regarding the outcome of the legal proceedings in this case.

Further Reading:

"New Bedford Inmate Charged in Cold Case." *Boston.com*, 2 April 2010. boston.com/news/local/massachusetts/articles/2010/04/02/new_bedford_inmate_charged_in_cold_case/

"Unsolved Cold Case Resolved in New Bedford." *Taunton Gazette* (Taunton, Massachusetts), 1 April 2010.

EDWARD J. TOLAN JR.

Man shot to death in his Fisher Road home in North Dartmouth, Massachusetts, on December 3, 2002.

Victim: Edward J. Tolan Jr., 34.

Accused: Peggy Ann Tolan, 32.

Details: Initially, Peggy Ann Tolan reported that when she came home to her North Dartmouth home she found her husband drunk and passed out in their bed. In his hand was a .38-caliber revolver.

The Tolan's had been experiencing extreme financial difficulties—their home had been foreclosed on by the bank and the couple was bankrupt. Mrs. Tolan believed that her husband was going to kill himself and she attempted to take the gun away from him. At that same time, Edward Tolan, she claimed, jerked his arm and the weapon fired, killing him. The shot was fired into Tolan's chin from 2 inches away.

Investigators did not believe her story and changed her with first-degree murder in the death of her husband. The state contended that Mrs. Tolan has placed the gun in her husband's hand and put his finger on the trigger, an apparent attempt to simulate suicide.

Mrs. Tolan contended that her husband was an abusive alcoholic who beat her and spent his days drinking up to 30 cans of beer and surfing the Internet.

The home on Fisher Road was declared unfit for habitation after the shooting. The couple lived with Mrs. Tolan's 80-year-old father and 16 dogs.

The couple had been married for five years and had no children. Edward Tolan's first wife had died of an aneurysm and he had two adult daughters from that marriage.

Trial: Peggy Ann Tolan was indicted for first degree murder in the death of her husband, Edward J. Tolan Jr. At her trial, police testified that Peggy Ann Tolan offered three different versions of where she was driving when she turned around to come home. In addition, during her 911 call, which was played for the jury, and which they replayed during deliberations dozens of times, she was asked by the dispatcher, "You shot the gun?" "Yes," Mrs. Tolan replied. When Mrs. Tolan claimed that her husband had bankrupted them with his massive spending on beer, evidence was presented that it was Peggy Ann who had spent more than $100,000 and caused the house to enter foreclosure.

A jury convicted Peggy Ann Tolan after three hours of deliberation. Judge Richard J. Chin sentenced her to life in prison without parole.

Trial: Peggy Tolan appealed her conviction in 2008 on the grounds that the judge erred in allowing her statements to the police during her lengthy interrogation to be admitted at trial and that her defense counsel did not render effective assistance. Her appeal was denied.

Further Reading:

"Commonwealth vs. Peggy Tolan." 453 Mass. 634, December 5, 2008-April 14, 2009. Bristol County. masscases.com/cases/sjc/453/453mass634.html.

Henry, Ray. "Tolan Guilty of Husband's Murder." *SouthCoastToday.com*, 10 November 2004. southcoasttoday.com/article/20041110/news/311109997.

"Wife Says Husband's Shooting Death an Accident." *The Boston Globe* (Boston, Massachusetts), 5 December 2002.

DAVID SILVA

Shooting death of a man outside a Cove Street apartment in New Bedford, Massachusetts, on January 2, 2003.

Victim: David Silva, 27.

Accused: Justin K. Gaouette, 19.

Details: According to Gaouett's appeal, the facts of the case are as follows: "In the fall of 2002, [Gaouette] and Matthew [Silva, David's brother] often spent time together because their respective girl friends, Letitia Boissoneault (Letitia) and Danielle Travers (Dee), were best friends. Sometime in November, 2002, the [Gaouette] gave Matthew twenty dollars to install a stereo in the [Gaouette]'s car. Soon afterward, [Gaouette] had a car accident, no longer wanted the stereo, and instead wanted his money back.

"Over the course of the next month, [Gaouette] saw less of Matthew, but relayed messages to him through their respective girl friends that he wanted his money returned. Dee told Matthew that [Gaouette] was getting angry about Matthew's failure to pay back the cash. During this same time period, between Thanksgiving and Christmas, 2002, [Gaouette] acquired a handgun. [Gaouette] stated that the purchase of the handgun had nothing to do with his dispute with Matthew.

"The hostilities between [Gaouette] and Matthew escalated on New Year's Eve. That afternoon, Matthew drove Dee to Letitia's house to pick her up so that the two young women could go shopping. As Matthew and Dee stopped at Letitia's house and waited for her to come outside, [Gaouette] drove up behind them with Letitia and two other individuals in his car.

"[Gaouette] asked Matthew if he had his money. Matthew said, 'No,' and told [Gaouette] that he could give it to him next week, when he got paid. [Gaouette] got angry and began yelling at Matthew, 'Are you trying to play me?' [Gaouette]t took off his coat and handed it to one of his friends who had been in the car with him. [Gaouette] wanted to fight: he yelled at Matthew, 'If you get out [of] this car right now, I'm going to bang you'; and 'I'll fucking crack you right here.' As [Gaouette] drove away from the scene, Matthew was smiling and laughing and told [Gaouette], 'I know where you live, and I got bigger boys than you.'

"[Gaouette] admitted to police that when he realized Matthew was not going to repay him, 'I knew that I wanted to hit him, at least.' [Gaouette] said he knew fighting was not going to get his money back, but explained that 'I felt disrespected, so I challenged [Matthew] to fight me.'

"On New Year's Day, at about 5:00 P.M., Letitia arrived at Dee's house to have birthday cake. Almost immediately, the two friends began to argue. Dee told Letitia that [Gaouette] 'shouldn't have did [sic] that,' referring to [Gaouette]'s challenge to fight. Letitia told Dee that Matthew should pay back the money. Letitia got angry and left. She called [Gaouette] to pick her up, and when he arrived, she told him what Dee had said. [Gaouette], who viewed the statement that he 'shouldn't have did [sic] that' as a threat, became very angry and called Dee. When Dee answered, [Gaouette] began to argue with her and said, '[Y]our faggot boyfriend's going to get it.'

"In short order, Matthew learned through a series of telephone calls from Dee that [Gaouette] was angry and still wanted to fight, so he called [Gaouette]. Upon receiving the call, [Gaouette] began to scream at Matthew, 'Where are you? I got something for you.' Matthew testified that his brother, Nicholas Silva (Nick), overheard the conversation and said into the telephone, 'He's at my house. You know where I live. Come get him. You know, if you want to fight him, come down here and fight him.' [Gaouette]'s account of the telephone call was similar. Dee testified that during the exchange of telephone calls, she received a call from Letitia in which she could hear [Gaouette] saying into the phone, to Dee, 'You're in it too'; 'I'm going to slap you'; and 'you're dead too.'

"[Gaouette] and Letitia headed towards Nick's house on Cove Street, but stopped first at [Gaouette]'s house. [Gaouette] retrieved the .38-caliber revolver that he had recently purchased and loaded it with six bullets. According to [Gaouette], he did not think the brothers 'would have weapons,' but he thought that 'it was a possibility,' and brought the gun for 'protection.' He stated that 'my intentions were not to use it.'

"Meanwhile, Matthew, Nick, and a third brother, David, gathered at a restaurant that was next door to Nick's house to 'have a beer' while they waited. There, they were joined by three friends.

"About thirty to forty-five minutes later, [Gaouette] and Letitia arrived on Cove Street. [Gaouette] put the car in park at a slant in front of Nick's house, thinking he was 'going to move my car out and park it.' There was a group of young men standing outside that included Nick, David, and the three friends; Matthew had gone into the house just before [Gaouette] arrived. Nick, who was near the stairs to his home, began to approach [Gaouette]'s car on the passenger side. Nick came within about three or four feet of the vehicle on the passenger side.

"According to [Gaouette]'s statement to the police, Nick said, '[W]hy don't you put down whatever you had in your hand.' [Gaouette] told the police that he was in the process of taking the gun out of his pocket and putting it under the seat, in preparation for a fist fight, when Nick walked toward the vehicle. [Gaouette] stated that he 'was nervous…So I kind of had my hand on [the gun].' At about the same moment, [Gaouette] realized that Matthew was coming quickly down the steps from the house carrying a baseball bat. Then [Gaouette] said, 'That's when I, like, grabbed it.

"[Gaouette] further said, '[A]fter that it was like a blur…[The n]ext thing I remember is Matt walking to the front of the car…and then he smashed my window [with a baseball bat]. And that's when I grabbed my gun…I think I shot, like three times.' In addition to seeing Matthew with the bat, [Gaouette] remembered a 'hand…coming [through the driver's side window] trying to… pull me.' He stated that he shot in the direction of both Matthew and the person trying to reach into the car. He described himself as 'just reacting.' He said that after he fired one shot they were 'still, like, coming after me. So I was still scared, so I fired two more shots.' He also remembered hearing banging on the car and commotion from those standing there.

"Matthew's testimony was similar. He stated that he ran or walked quickly to where [Gaouette] was parked and went around the front of the vehicle toward [Gaouette] as he held the bat up in the air. Matthew testified that as he 'ran around the front, [Gaouette] was in the driver's seat, and he pulled something up like this out of the side of the seat, and all I seen was the black and, like, the barrel.'

"Matthew testified that 'as soon as I seen that, I took the baseball bat…and smashed the window, the driver's side window.' Both [Gaouette] and Letitia were cut by the small shards of glass that flew toward them when the window was smashed. Matthew said that, 'As soon as I smashed the window, that's when I heard the first shot go off. That went out the windshield.' Matthew 'was struck in the elbow.'

"After the smashing of the window, Matthew's brother David had come around the rear of the motor vehicle on the driver's side and was reaching into the vehicle in an effort to grab the gun away from [Gaouette]. During the struggle, Matthew heard a second shot and then immediately heard David say, 'I'm hit,' and saw him jump back from the vehicle. David collapsed on the sidewalk and was pronounced dead at the hospital.

"After firing the gun, [Gaouette] drove away. He described himself as 'still…in shock' when the police pulled them over. He gave a statement to the police that evening.

"Letitia was the sole witness testifying for the defense at trial. Letitia testified that [Gaouette] had become increasingly angry over Matthew's failure to repay the money during the month preceding the shootings. Letitia added that when they stopped at [Gaouette]'s house, on their way to Nick's house, [Gaouette] changed his clothes. [Gaouette] had been wearing new clothes to meet Letitia's family, but changed into sweat clothes so that he would not get his new clothes dirty during a fight."

Trial: Justin Gaouette was convicted of murder in the second degree in the death of David Silva. He was also convicted on five other indictments: armed assault with intent to murder Matthew Silva; assault and battery by means of a dangerous weapon; unlawful possession of a firearm; unlawful possession of ammunition; and receiving stolen property (a firearm). He was sentenced to life in prison with the possibility of parole.

Afterword: Justin Gaouette appealed his conviction of murder in the second degree in 2005, claiming that he had ineffective assistance of council. The appeals court disagreed and his appeal was denied.

Further Reading:

"Commonwealth vs. Justin K. Gaouette." 66 Mass. App. Ct. 633, November 15, 2005-June 28, 2006. Bristol County. masscases.com/cases/app/66/66massappct633.html.
Gedan, Benjamin. "Friend Held in New Bedford Slaying." *The Boston Globe* (Boston, Massachusetts), 3 January 2003.
Ray, Henry. "Gaouette Convicted of Second-Degree Murder." *SouthCoastToday.com*, 7 February, 2004. southcoasttoday.com/article/20040207/News/302079993.

JOSHUA SANTOS

Beating death of a 2-year-old in his home in New Bedford, Massachusetts, on April 1, 2003.

Victim: Joshua Santos, 2.

Accused: Rui Novo, 30.

Details: The mother of Joshua Santos, Melissa Santos, was living with Rui Novo, a 30-year-old fisherman who had a history of domestic violence. The boy was beaten to death on April 1, 2003, and died from multiple internal injuries and bruises.

According to Novo's appeal record in 2007, the facts of the case are as follows: "Melissa Santos was the mother of two young boys when she began dating [Novo] in the summer of 2002. Christopher, her older son, was seven and one-half years of age, and Joshua, her younger son, was two. Christopher and Joshua were normal, active youngsters, who enjoyed wrestling together and pretending to be superheroes. According to her parents, Santos was very close with Christopher and Joshua. Santos's mother never saw her use physical force with her children. Santos's sister saw her hit Christopher when he misbehaved, but never saw her discipline Joshua, who 'got away with a lot.' In the fall of 2002, Santos, Christopher, and Joshua moved in with [Novo] at his New Bedford apartment, and around Thanksgiving, the couple became engaged. In late February or early March, Santos learned that she was pregnant with [Novo]'s child. According to Santos, family life with [Novo] was not perfect, but it was 'okay.'

"During the last week of March, Santos began experiencing abdominal cramping and vaginal bleeding and, on Friday, March 28, underwent emergency day surgery to terminate what was diagnosed as an ectopic pregnancy. Santos, [Novo], and the boys spent the weekend at home together. Santos was in pain from her surgery, and [Novo] was watching the children. Joshua appeared fine, and there was nothing unusual about his behavior. [Novo]'s behavior was unpredictable. He would be in a good mood one minute, and the next minute he would be angry with Santos, for no apparent reason.

"On Monday morning, Santos was feeling better and helped Christopher get ready for school. She, [Novo], and Joshua ran errands, and when Christopher came home from school, they all drove to Taunton so that [Novo] could obtain some legal papers for his mother. They stopped to eat at a McDonald's restaurant on the way home. The boys played in the restaurant's indoor playroom, and both boys appeared fine at that time. Arriving home around 5 P. M., Santos went to a nearby nail salon to get her nails 'filled,' and Joshua fell asleep in bed.

"Joshua woke up about twenty minutes after Santos returned home. [Novo] asked Joshua if he wanted to come out of his room, and Joshua said no. When [Novo] turned on the light, he saw that Joshua had vomited on his bed. [Novo] became angry and yelled at Joshua that, if he was going to throw up, he should go to the bathroom or tell his mother or [Novo]. Santos told [Novo] that Joshua was only a baby and that he did not know when he was going to throw up. [Novo] grabbed Joshua and brought him to the bathroom to give him a bath. Santos, meanwhile, put the soiled bed linens in a plastic trash bag (to take to her mother's house to wash) and put clean sheets on the bed.

"Tuesday morning (it was now April 1), Santos was awakened by Christopher, standing in her bedroom doorway, who told her that Joshua was on the living room floor and had thrown up everywhere. Santos went into the living room and saw Joshua lying on a pillow on the floor with his blanket. There was vomit on the coffee table and on the rug. Santos told Joshua to go into Christopher's room, and she began to clean up. [Novo] woke up and was angry with Joshua. He yelled, 'What did I tell you? I told you to tell me or mommy if you were going to throw up.' [Novo] followed Joshua into Christopher's bedroom. He picked Joshua up and threw him on the bed. Joshua landed with his face in the pillow. [Novo] yelled, 'Get your ass back in the room. Get your ass back in bed.' Santos tried to calm [Novo], and Christopher left for school.

"Santos tried to clean the vomit off the rug but was unsuccessful. [Novo] was angry and told Santos that she had to go rent a carpet cleaning machine. Santos later explained that 'whatever [Novo] had said, I obeyed and listened.' Santos, [Novo], and Joshua went together to a nearby store to rent a carpet shampooer...They returned home, and...Santos then left [Novo] and Joshua alone while she went to a nearby pharmacy to purchase pediatric electrolyte and nutritional supplement drinks.'

"When Santos returned to the apartment, Joshua was lying on Christopher's bed watching television. Santos asked him if he wanted to eat, and he responded no. He said yes, however, when she asked whether he wanted a drink. Santos poured some of the electrolyte drink she had purchased into a child's 'sippie' cup, and Joshua drank the liquid. Santos and [Novo] ate the breakfast sandwiches, and Santos began reading the operating directions for the carpet shampooer. When Santos turned the machine on, it made a loud shaking noise and went 'completely berserk.'

"Two hours after Santos returned from the pharmacy, at approximately

12:15 P.M., [Novo] noticed that Joshua had vomited again, this time on Christopher's floor. He became angry and 'grabbed [Joshua] off the bed and threw him in the tub.' Santos was in the living room attempting to work the carpet shampooer at this time, but could hear the sound of running water from the bathroom. [Novo] and Joshua were alone in the bathroom for about ten minutes. After she shut off the machine, Santos went into the bathroom. She saw [Novo] holding Joshua in the bathtub. Joshua's head was forward and he had red marks all over his stomach. Santos screamed, 'What the fuck?' [Novo] picked Joshua up, and Santos screamed again, 'What the fuck is happening?' [Novo] explained that Joshua had fallen in the bathtub. He carried Joshua into their bedroom and laid him on the bed. Joshua was unresponsive, and his eyes rolled back. [Novo] put Joshua in his pajamas, while Santos called his name. Joshua's eyes rolled back again, and his lips became blue. Santos yelled, 'This baby's sick. We have to take him to the hospital.' After a brief protest, [Novo] picked Joshua up and drove them to a hospital just a few minutes away. On the way to the hospital, Santos again asked, 'What the fuck happened?' [Novo] told her, 'If they say anything, you say Josh fell in the tub.'

"Santos ran into the hospital's emergency room at 1:10 P.M., carrying Joshua in her arms, very distressed and yelling, 'Something is wrong with my son.' A nurse at the triage desk took Joshua from his mother's arms and, realizing at once that he was not breathing, began performing mouth-to-mouth resuscitation and raced him to the emergency trauma room. The nurse later described the child as limp, unresponsive, pale, and turning cyanotic (blue-skinned, due to lack of oxygen in the blood). Vigorous efforts on the part of an entire team of medical professionals to revive Joshua were unsuccessful. Approximately thirty minutes after entering the emergency room with her son, Santos and [Novo] were informed by a physician that Joshua had died.

"The prosecution proceeded on the theory that [Novo] had beaten Joshua in anger because the child had vomited on the living room carpet (which, according to Santos, was new) and that Santos had given a different version of events to hospital personnel (and also, as we shall explain, to police officers) because [Novo] had asked her to lie. Uncontradicted testimony by the medical examiner who performed the autopsy established that the victim had twenty-five areas of bruising distributed over his entire body, from the head to the lower legs, on the front of the body and the back. Areas of bruising on the head and face included the left side of the head; in front of the ear; on the cheek; along the left side of the chin and on the right side of the chin; high on the right side of the head; and on the left side of the nose. Bruises also were found on the inside of the victim's lips. The left side of the victim's neck had three quarter-inch scrapes of the skin, and on the back of the neck, there was a small cluster of ruptured capillaries. Clusters of bruises were found on both sides of the victim's chest. The victim's body also had bruises on the back of one arm and on the left shoulder, behind one of the elbows and on the left knee area. There was a bruise on the victim's lower left leg, three bruises on the back of the thigh, and two bruises on the victim's back. There was bruising in the perianal region of the victim's body. One large band of bruising, extending across the victim's pelvic area, up the left side of his body, and over both sides of his back, covered between twelve and fifteen per cent of his body. The medical examiner testified that this large bruise appeared to be caused by the application of blunt force trauma by some mechanism such as fingers or hands, that the abrasions around the victim's neck could have been caused by fingernails, and that the small hemorrhages on his neck could have been caused by pinching. He also stated that the injuries were consistent with the victim's having been grabbed around the throat. The medical examiner described a purplish discoloration and swelling of the victim's genitalia due to injuries that had caused the scrotum sack to fill up with blood.

"The medical examiner testified to finding two tears in the victim's small intestine...air bubbles in and around that area of the body indicated that there had likely been an air embolism and hemorrhaging. These injuries were, in the opinion of the medical examiner, likely caused by a blunt traumatic injury consistent with a very hard punch to the stomach, which forced the victim's intestines up against his spine with force severe enough to sever the intestines. The medical examiner testified as well to finding some muscular tearing and hemorrhaging of the victim's back and scalp. The victim's brain was swollen.

"The medical examiner testified that all of the victim's injuries appeared to be new. He expressed the opinion that the victim's injuries were consistent with being punched or kicked and that death could have ensued from the bowel injuries, the loss of blood from internal bleeding, or a fatal heart arrhythmia caused by elevated potassium levels in the body. The victim's genital injuries would not have been fatal, but would have been very painful if they had been inflicted when the victim was conscious. The bowel injuries, which were fatal, also would have been very painful if inflicted when he was conscious. The medical examiner testified that the injuries would have left the victim immobile, and if he had remained conscious after they were inflicted, he would have been unable to speak normally. Considering the magnitude of the victim's injuries, the medical examiner estimated that, once they were inflicted, the victim's survival time would have been between a few minutes and one, or at most two, hours."

Trial: "[Novo] did not testify at trial. His theory of defense was that Santos had inflicted the fatal injuries. In support of this theory, his trial counsel called three defense witnesses, who provided testimony supporting [Novo]'s contentions that (1) the living room carpet in [Novo]'s apartment was not new; (2) Santos turned to [Novo] for comfort at the hospital on being told that her son had died; (3) Santos could not have been changing the bedding on Christopher's bed while [Novo] gave the victim a bath (as Santos, three times, had recounted to prosecutors and police). There was no contention that the victim had not died as a result of a brutal beating inflicted some time after 11 A.M. on the morning of April 1. The only point of contention at trial was whether Santos or [Novo] had inflicted the fatal injuries."

Rui Novo was convicted of murder in the beating death of his former girlfriend's 2-year-old son and sentenced to a mandatory life sentence without the possibility of parole.

Afterword: Rui Novo appealed his conviction in 2004 and 2007. In 2004, he claimed that the police had used coercive interrogation techniques and that because of this his confession was irretrievably tainted. His appeal was denied.

In 2007, Novo claimed that judge abused his discretion in admitting in evidence a witness's prior consistent statement and for inadequate assistance of counsel. Again, the appeal was denied.

Further Reading:

"Commonwealth vs. Rui Novo." 444 Mass. 262, May 4, 2004-August 6, 2004. Bristol County. masscases.com/cases/sjc/442/442mass262.html.
"Commonwealth vs. Rui Novo." 449 Mass. 84, March 9, 2007-May 8, 2007. Bristol County. masscases.com/cases/sjc/449/449mass84.html.
"Man Gets Life Term for Killing Toddler." *The Boston Globe* (Boston, Massachusetts), 20 November 2004.
"Mother Faces Charges in Child's Death." *The Boston Globe* (Boston, Massachusetts), 10 April 2003.

ROBERT BERNARD

A Rhode Island gang-related drug murder in a Third Street apartment known for drug sales in Fall River, Massachusetts, on May 5, 2003.

Victim: Robert Bernard, 34.

Accused: Wayne Rogers, 38.

Details: Both the victim and the accused were known to each other from the Rhode Island drug culture. Bernard was shot three times allegedly by Rogers and died in the Corky Row section of Fall River where drug transactions and problems between neighbors frequently took place.

Trial: Wayne Rogers was acquitted of the charges at trial.

LEONARD SILVIERA

Man beaten and burned in an arson fire on the second floor of his West End, New Bedford, Massachusetts, home at 18 Homer Street on July 11, 2003.

Victim: Leonard Silviera, 86.

Accused: Christopher Viger, 24.

Details: Leonard Silviera was found dead on July 11, 2003, on the second floor of his 18 Homer Street home that was on fire. An autopsy showed that Silviera had been struck by a blunt object that killed him before the fire had been set.

Christopher Viger had worked for Silviera and was the last person to see him alive. In addition, he often stayed in the residence.

"According to testimony, on July 10, 2003, at 10:45 p.m., Mr. Viger left a house party at his mother's house with Mr. Silviera. They both left in a taxi. Mr. Viger told police he escorted Mr. Silviera to his home at 18 Homer St. and then walked to a bar in downtown New Bedford, approximately 1½ miles from the North End neighborhood...At 5:45 a.m. the next morning, Mr. Silviera was found dead inside his house. The doors inside the apartment were locked, and there were no signs of a break-in.

"Mr. Viger told investigators he walked back to his mother's house on Bullard Street after leaving the bar. However, that conflicted with a statement provided by his brother's girlfriend, who stayed at the house that night. She did not see the defendant in the house when she woke early the next morning.

"The defendant's mother testified she saw Mr. Viger at 5:45 a.m. the next morning inside her apartment, smoking a cigarette on the couch.

"Two witnesses, Lamar Antone and Eric Oliveira, testified they saw Mr. Viger on Homer Street during the early morning hours of July 11. They said Mr. Viger threw an object on a front lawn around the corner from Mr. Silviera's house. Police later recovered a wristwatch at the location.

"Roger Dubois, a former cellmate of Mr. Viger's, testified the defendant admitted to him twice in 2006 that he killed Mr. Silviera.

"'I did it. But it's not the way you guys think,' Mr. Dubois said Mr. Viger told him in their jail cell one night.

"Mr. Dubois said the defendant told him he killed the victim by hitting his head with a hammer nine times, and then said he made a mistake by not breaking a window in Mr. Silviera's house to make police think he was killed during a home invasion.

"The prosecution's case was also not helped by the forensic evidence, which was inconclusive. An ax and two hammers found inside Mr. Silviera's home did not have enough DNA for testing, officials said.

"Also, DNA samples taken from two small hairs found on the watch police found were determined to have come from an adult male. A forensic scientist testified there was a 1-in-21,000 chance the hairs could have come from Mr. Silviera.

"Mr. Silviera was a decorated World War II veteran who was described as a modest and generous landlord. He bought 14 properties in the city assessed at more than a million dollars, according to city records. ("Jury Acquits").

Police indicted Viger in December 2005.

Trial: Christopher Viger was tried on charges of murder, assault and battery with a dangerous weapon, and arson. In the week-long trial, the DA argued that Viger had an uncorroborated alibi. The state believed that this murder was not a random act, and Viger's "complex relationship" with the deceased indicated that he was the killer. The jury deliberated for 16 hours and acquitted Viger of the crimes.

Further Reading:

Fraga, Brian. "Jury Acquits Christopher Viger of 2003 Slaying of Leonard Silviera." *SouthCoastToday.com*, 27 July 2007. southcoasttoday.com/article/20070727/NEWS/707270375.

"New Bedford Man Charged with Fire Death." *The Boston Globe* (Boston, Massachusetts), 30 December 2005.

KEONE MENDES

Stabbing death of a man outside the Main Event Club at 250 Union Street in New Bedford, Massachusetts, on July 25, 2003.

Victim: Keone Mendes, 25.

Accused: Miguel Lozada, 22.

Details: After getting into a fight with four men, all of whom were arrested at the scene, Keone Mendes was stabbed in the chest and died at the scene on Union Street in New Bedford, around 1:40 a.m.

The fight that led to the death began inside the Main Event Club at 250 Union Street. An argument over a barstool escalated around 1:30 a.m. when Jonathan Barros, one of Miguel Lozada's friends, confronted Mendes inside the club. The men left the bar when a bouncer told them to leave. Police found Keone Mendes between two parked cars bleeding from the stomach. He died soon after.

Lozada admitted to police that he had stabbed Mendes but the jury never saw the videotaped confession. It was suppressed because the judge found that the police had improperly questioned Miguel Lozada.

Miguel Lozada was charged with murder and Raymond Velez, 30, was charged as being an accessory after the fact. Johnathan Barros, 26, and Alexis Nunez, 25, were charged with assault and battery with a dangerous weapon.

Trial: Miguel Lozada was indicted for murder of Keone Mendes, but was found guilty of voluntary manslaughter and sentenced to 8 to 12 years in prison.

Further Reading:

"Four Men Face Charges in Fatal Stabbing." *The Boston Globe* (Boston, Massachusetts), 26 April 2003.
Henry, Ray. "Man Found Guilty of Fatal 2003 Stabbing." *SouthCoastToday.com*, 5 May 2005. southcoasttoday.com/article/20050505/news/305059988.

PATRICK MURPHY

Stabbing death of a youth at 89 Purchase Street in New Bedford, Massachusetts, on August 10, 2003.

Victim: Patrick Murphy, 14.

Accused: Lydell Pina, 27.

Details: Lydell Pina had paid a visit to 89 Purchase Street in the early morning of August 10, 2003, to purchase drugs from Patrick Murphy. A few hours later, Pina returned for more drugs and entered the first floor apartment where the teen and other had been staying. An argument ensued that carried out into the hallway. Witnesses told police that they heard Pina demand that Murphy give him all of his drugs. Murphy yelled for help from another person in the apartment. It was at this point that Pina stabbed Murphy, who stumbled into the doorway of the apartment as Pina fled the building. Murphy had been stabbed in the shoulder and the chest and had two defensive-type wounds on his left arm.

Three juveniles, two of them female, reported to police that they witnessed Pina at the apartment. There were no witnesses to the actual stabbing.

Pina had a criminal record—convictions for stalking and arrests for other crimes including assault and battery. Pina's brother Myron was recently indicted in federal court for running an Oxycontin ring. Both Pina and Myron are nephews of Ward 4 City Councilor Joseph P. Fortes.

Just hours after the murder of Murphy, the seventh of the year, then Mayor Frederick M. Kalisz Jr. forced the resignation of Police Chief Arthur J. Kelly III.

Trial: Lydell Pina was charged with murder in the stabbing death of Patrick Murphy. In 2006, a jury deliberated for 2 hours and acquitted Pina of all charges.

Further Reading:

Ferreira, Joao. "City Man Acquitted in Slaying of Teen." *SouthCoastToday.com*, 19 August 2003. southcoasttoday.com/article/20060224/opinion/302249997.

BRENDON CAMARA

Toddler beaten to death in Somerset, Massachusetts, on October 20, 2003.

Victim: Brendon Camara, 4.

Accused: Eric Durand, 31.

Details: According to Eric Durand's first appeal, the facts of the case are as follows:

"At the time of the victim's death in October, 2003, [Brendon Camara] was living with his mother, Laura Bowden, and his twin brother Michael in the basement of a house belonging to Paul Paquette in Somerset. Also living in the house at the time were Paquette, his two daughters, Priscilla and Patricia Paquette, and their children. Bowden was a close friend of Patricia Paquette (Patricia), in particular. [Durand] was Bowden's boy friend, and had been, off and on, for approximately one year. He was not the father of her twins, who were born in November of 1998, but he had two young children of his own. He frequently stayed with Bowden at the Paquette house.

"Although [Durand] appeared to develop a good relationship with the victim's brother, treating Michael like his own child, it did not seem that he cared for the victim. [Durand] called the victim -- who was a little smaller than his brother, was very attached to his mother, had speech difficulties, and would wet his bed and his pants -- 'cry baby' and 'pissy pants,' and at times seemed as though he liked to upset the victim. He wanted the victim to be tougher, to cry less often, and to be more like Michael. The victim, in turn, was intimidated by [Durand], and would sometimes become visibly upset by [Durand]'s presence. Bowden gave [Durand] permission to discipline Michael and the victim, but never saw him hit either one of them. However, Bowden would herself sometimes discipline her sons by hitting their hands or bottoms, and on one occasion, she slapped them in the face.

"On the day before the victim's death, [Durand] and his two children spent time with Bowden, Michael, and the victim, as well as Patricia and her son, in the basement of the Paquette house. [Durand] spent the night at the house. The following morning, October 20, Bowden woke at approximately 6 A. M.; she was scheduled to be at work at 7 A.M. She woke [Durand], but [Durand] said it was already too late for him to go to work and he went back to sleep. When Bowden left the house at 6:30 A.M., the victim and Michael also were asleep.

"At around 9 A.M., Patricia woke up and went into the twins' bedroom. She found them partially awake and still in bed. At around 10 or 10:30 A.M., she returned to the boys' bedroom, and found them out of bed and playing. At that time, [Durand] was on the bed in Bowden's room, and Patricia went to talk to him. At some time around 10 A.M., Bowden telephoned while she was on her half-hour break. She spoke briefly to Patricia, who answered the telephone, and then to [Durand] for the rest of her break. During the conversation, Michael and the victim went into Bowden's room and [Durand] asked the victim if he 'peed his pants.' When the victim did not say anything, Patricia felt his pants and told [Durand] they were wet. The victim then asked if he could use the bathroom and [Durand] asked, 'Why do you need to go to the bathroom if you peed your pants?' [Durand] also told Bowden that the victim was asking to go the bathroom but that he did not think he had to go because he already urinated on himself. Bowden told [Durand] to let him go. The telephone conversation ended shortly thereafter.

"[Durand] put the victim 'in the corner' as punishment. While Patricia and [Durand] talked, the victim stayed in the corner with his face to the wall, but kept moving around. At some point, [Durand] called him 'piss pants,' and when the victim turned around in response, [Durand] threw a toy shark at his face. The victim cried when the shark hit him in the mouth, but [Durand] told him that he did not throw it that hard. Still crying, the victim turned back to face the corner.

"When the victim 'got out of the corner,' Patricia brought [Durand] a face cloth, and seeing [Durand] begin to take care of the victim's wet clothes, she started upstairs to the kitchen. Before she got there, however, [Durand] walked up to her with the victim and told her that the victim had urinated on [Durand]'s leg, and showed her the wet spot on his pants. Although Patricia thought [Durand] seemed upset, [Durand] said he could just go home and get another pair of pants. [Durand] took the victim into the upstairs bathroom to wash him while Patricia went to the kitchen and began washing dishes. At some point, Patricia saw [Durand] walk by the sink with the victim and believed they were going downstairs to the basement.

"After finishing the dishes, Patricia went into the living room to check on her son. She saw Michael in the living room and told him that she was going to bring him downstairs to [Durand]. When she did so, Patricia saw [Durand] next to the door of Bowden's room and the victim lying on the bed in his own room. Patricia observed that the victim was not moving, but also that he did not look as though he were in any distress.

"Patricia returned upstairs and used the computer in the living room. At some point, [Durand] approached her and told her that Michael had come upstairs and told him that the victim had fallen down the stairs. Although Patricia remained at the computer after hearing this, [Durand] retreated to the basement. A few minutes later, however, [Durand] reappeared and told her that the victim was 'acting weird.' Again, Patricia remained at the computer, and [Durand] went downstairs to the basement. A couple of minutes later, [Durand] returned a third time and told Patricia that there was something seriously wrong with the victim. Patricia ran down the stairs and into the twins' bedroom; the victim was lying on the bed, not moving, and his eyes were rolled back. Patricia tried talking to him, checked for his pulse and heartbeat, and held the victim in her arms. [Durand], who had followed Patricia down the stairs, looked scared and was asking why this happened; he asked the victim if the victim was not responding because he was mad at [Durand].

"[Durand] told Patricia to telephone Bowden at work. After Patricia made the telephone call, [Durand] took the telephone from her and told Bowden that the victim had fallen down the stairs, walked to the bed, and was now not responding. Bowden instructed [Durand] to telephone 911, and he did so. Bowden immediately left work to go home.

"The Somerset police 911 dispatchers received two calls from the Paquette house, one at approximately 12:15 P.M., and one four to five minutes later. The responding police officers were told by [Durand] that the victim had fallen down the stairs and was not breathing; [Durand] then directed the officers to the basement where the victim was on the bed. The officers administered cardiopulmonary resuscitation to the victim, who did not respond. Paramedics arrived within minutes. [Durand] similarly told the paramedics that the victim had fallen down four to five stairs and was not unconscious at the time of the fall, but rather had gotten up, walked to the bed, lay down, and did not cry or complain that anything hurt.

"Bowden arrived after the police and ambulance were at the scene. She went to the basement and observed Patricia and [Durand], who was crying and saying he was sorry. The paramedics transported the victim to the emergency room of Charlton Memorial Hospital in Fall River. After continued attempts to revive the victim at the hospital, he was pronounced dead by an emergency room doctor."

Trial: In 2006, Eric Durand was found guilty of murder in the first degree on the theory of extreme atrocity or cruelty. He was also found guilty of assault and battery with a dangerous weapon, a plastic toy shark.

Afterword: Eric Durand appealed his conviction in 2010 and again in 2016. In 2010, he objected to a substitute medical examiner presenting testimony at trial instead of the medical examiner who had conducted the autopsy, the admission of a statement made by Durand about throwing an object, despite the fact that the statement was ordered suppressed, and the admission of incriminating statements made by Durand that were obtained through improper interrogation techniques.

The appeals court reversed Durand's convictions and the verdicts were set aside, and a new trial was ordered.

On August 29, 2011, Durand was again convicted of murder in the first degree by extreme atrocity or cruelty, and assault and battery by means of a dangerous weapon. He was sentenced to life in prison without the possibility of parole with a concurrent sentence of 2 to 4 years for the assault and battery conviction.

In 2016, Durand appealed his second conviction asserting that there were errors in his right to cross-examine the medical examiner, a denial of his motion to suppress statements, a denial of a motion for a mistrial after the jury was exposed to inadmissible evidence, the admission of hearsay testimony of a Commonwealth expert witness, the denial of the motion for a mistrial related to improper statements made during closing arguments, the denial of the motion to dismiss on double jeopardy, and, finally, the denial of a requested jury instruction.

The appeals court denied his claims and did not grant the request by Durand. The conviction holds.

Further Reading:

"Commonwealth vs. Eric J. Durand." 457 Mass. 574, March 5, 2010-August 19, 2010. Bristol County. masscases.com/cases/sjc/457/457mass574.html.

"Commonwealth vs. Eric J. Durand." 475 Mass. 657, May 6, 2016-October 7, 2016. Bristol County. masscases.com/cases/sjc/475/475mass657.html.

JOSE TORRES

Shooting of a man at 29C Pleasant View in Fall River, Massachusetts, on October 25, 2003, who later died of his injuries on October 27, 2003.

Victim: Jose Torres, 33.

Accused: Alberto Diaz Jr, 25, Luiz Diaz, 20, and Luis Tejaeda, 28.

Details: Jose Torres was shot three times in the abdomen in the doorway of his apartment at the Pleasant View housing project. Around 10:30 in the evening of October 31, 2003, Torres answered his door and was confronted by two men who asked if there was another man inside. When Torres answered no, one of the men, believed to be Alberto Diaz, shot him.

Police pursued a car they believed was linked to the crime. They saw a gun being thrown out of the car and also began searching for it. The gun was eventually discovered near Route 128 by state police.

A mortally wounded Torres was able to identify Alberto Diaz before he died as the shooter.

Trial: Alberto Diaz Jr, Luiz Diaz, and Luis Tejaeda were all charged with second-degree murder. Alberto pleaded guilty and received a life sentence in prison, eligible for parole in 13 years, Tejaeda was convicted of involuntary manslaughter and sentenced to 15-16 years in prison, and Luiz received a 6 to 13 year sentence.

Further Reading:

Ranalli, Ralph. "3 Charged in Slaying in Fall River." *The Boston Globe* (Boston, Massachusetts), 28 October 2003.

MICHAEL WHITE

Stabbing death of a man outside the Dream Cafe on Acushnet Avenue in New Bedford, Massachusetts, on November 1, 2003.

Victim: Michael White, 34.

Accused: Patricio Oscar Santiago, 24.

Details: According to Santiago's appeal, the facts of the case as presented at trial were the following:

"On the evening of October 31, 2003, which was Halloween, Allan Anthony Monteiro, Peter Ruby, Anthony Francisco Faria, Jr., and Michael White (victim), a close friend of Monteiro, went out together to celebrate Monteiro's birthday. They met at Monteiro's sister's house. The men went to the Dream Café, a bar on Acushnet Avenue in New Bedford, arriving at approximately 11 P.M.

"Joseph Santos was checking the identification cards of patrons as they entered the front door (the only door for patrons) to the bar. Inside there was a bar and an area in which there were two pool tables, as well as some tables and chairs. That evening the bar was more crowded than usual because it was Halloween and there was a professional baseball game being televised. By 10 P. M., the bar and pool table area were very crowded.

"Once inside the Dream Café, Faria went to the bar to get some drinks. He then joined Monteiro and the victim to play some pool. Ruby watched television.

"In the pool room, Monteiro saw [Santiago], whom he knew from having grown up 'in the same area.' [Santiago] had arrived at the bar that night at about 10 P.M. with about five or six friends. Monteiro went to one table and played pool with a man who had just won a game. During the game, that man, along with some other men who were watching, and whom [Santiago] appeared to be with, made some unspecified 'wise remarks.' Monteiro lost the game and told the victim, who was next up to play, that he no longer wished to play at that table. Monteiro proceeded to play pool at the other table with Faria and two women. The victim stayed to play against the same man who had played Monteiro.

"Monteiro left to make a telephone call. When he returned, the victim met him at the pool table that Monteiro and Faria had been using. One of the men in the group with [Santiago] went over to the victim and said something to him, starting a verbal altercation. The victim moved away, but the man returned, with a friend, and punched the victim.

"Santos quickly moved in, grabbed the victim from behind, and ejected him from the bar. While doing so, a different man was trying to punch the victim. About ten to fifteen people followed the victim outside the bar after he was thrown out. On the sidewalk, just outside the door to the bar, several of the men surrounded the victim and began beating him. Santos shut the door and attempted to block others from leaving. Monteiro, however, was able to get by Santos.

"Monteiro was attempting to stop the beating of the victim. He yelled for the men to stop and physically tried to push some of the men off of and away from the victim. While doing so, Monteiro saw [Santiago] approach the fight. Monteiro observed that [Santiago] was holding a knife and watched as [Santiago] 'thrust [the knife] into the pile.' [Santiago] did this 'a couple' of times. Then, the men surrounding the victim 'gathered up' and dispersed, running across the street toward a parking lot at a Brooks Pharmacy.

"Faria, who was not able to leave the Dream Café until after Monteiro, testified about his observations once he was outside. Faria saw [Santiago] and that [Santiago] was holding a knife 'tucked under his arm.' Faria watched [Santiago] go into the pile with the victim. Then he watched everyone take off running.

"There was blood on the ground near the victim. Monteiro went over to him, grabbed his hand, and yelled for someone to call an ambulance. Ruby was finally able to leave the bar. When he got outside, he saw Monteiro with the victim in between a van and a white automobile. Monteiro walked the victim over to the automobile. The victim's eyes rolled back, and he slumped down alongside the automobile, leaving blood smears along its side. The victim then fell face forward to the ground. Monteiro moved the victim onto his back. The victim was 'gurgling,' and blood was 'pouring out' of him. Monteiro instructed Faria to get the automobile, which was in the Brooks Pharmacy parking lot across the street. When Faria returned with the automobile, Monteiro and Ruby got inside and left. Monteiro wanted to go to 'Presidential,' but Faria drove back to Monteiro's sister's home.

"Police arrived shortly after Monteiro, Faria, and Ruby had left. They found the victim lying on his back on the sidewalk outside the Dream Café. He was taking shallow breaths and was bleeding. A detective used 'trauma pads' in an attempt to stop the bleeding. At one point, the victim made a loud gasp and stopped breathing. Emergency medical technicians arrived and took over the medical care. The victim died at the scene as a result of multiple stab wounds, including wounds to his back and chest. He also had numerous abrasions on his face and extremities.

"After the victim's stabbing, police questioned various individuals. Monteiro first lied to them and told them he 'didn't see nobody' because he needed to 'protect' his children, 'was scared,' and '[j]ust didn't want the problems.' Eventually he told them that [Santiago] was the person with the knife and identified [Santiago] in a photographic array as the man who had thrust the knife into the pile with the victim.

"Faria also spoke with police. From a photographic array, he identified [Santiago] as the man with the knife. A patron of the bar and a friend of Santos, Timothy Pereira, told police that the group of men who were beating up the victim outside the bar were from the 'Presidential Heights' housing project. Pereira identified [Santiago] from a photographic array as one of the men who had been involved in the fight with the victim outside the bar.

"On November 3, 2003, [Santiago], after being taken into custody and after waiving his Miranda rights, agreed to speak with police. [Santiago] stated the following. He had been at the Dream Café on October 31, 2003. He had arrived at approximately 11:30 P.M. and stayed for only about ten minutes. [Santiago] had one drink, spoke with one friend, and said hello to 'some girls.' [Santiago] recounted that he went to purchase some gasoline and then went to another bar, the Highlander, which was one block away. There [Santiago] had one drink with his cousin, left after closing at around 2 A.M., and thereafter went to his mother's house to sleep. While he was at the Dream Café, nothing remarkable had occurred, and he had not been inside the pool table area. [Santiago] recalled that he had been wearing gold hoop earrings, a white shirt, and dark blue jeans.

"Police subsequently interviewed two employees of the Highlander and showed them photographic arrays containing [Santiago]'s photograph. Neither employee recognized the defendant as having been a patron at the Highlander on the night of October 31, or the early morning of November 1.

"It was stipulated that the victim's blood was recovered from the exterior of a truck in the parking lot at Brooks Pharmacy, which was across the street from the Dream Café. Pursuant to a warrant, police searched [Santiago]'s automobile and recovered, from the front passenger side carpet, blood from which the deoxyribonucleic acid profile obtained 'matched' the victim's. [Santiago] did not testify. His trial counsel called one witness, Santos, who testified that [Santiago] had not been involved in the fight with the victim. [Santiago]'s trial counsel argued that [Santiago] had not been involved in the fight and that there was a lack of physical evidence against him because no blood was recovered from his clothing or from the driver's side of his automobile. Defense counsel argued that the police investigation was flawed, and that witnesses were not credible because they had lied to police and were inconsistent with their descriptions of the man who held the knife. Defense counsel also pointed out a lack of motive."

Michael White's murder was the 10th of 11 homicides in 2003. He was a chef at a pizza parlor in New Bedford and the father of two children. Michael White was the cousin of former Boston Celtics point guard Dana Barros.

Trial: Patricio Santiago was tried in October of 2004, but a mistrial was called when the jury could not reach a unanimous decision.

In January of 2006, after the jury deliberated for 10 hours over 2 days, Patricio Oscar Santiago was found guilty of murder in the first degree on each of the two theories on which he was prosecuted: murder with premeditation and murder with extreme atrocity and cruelty.

Afterword: In February, 2009, Santiago appealed his conviction based on claims of the conduct of the prosecutor and due process and asked for a new trial. His appeal was denied.

Further Reading:

"Commonwealth vs. Patricio Santiago." 458 Mass. 405, September 14, 2010-December 7, 2010. Bristol County. masscases.com/cases/sjc/458/458mass405.html.

Ferreira, Joao. "Police Make Arrest in City Slaying." *SouthCoastToday.com*, 4 November 2003. southcoasttoday.com/article/20031104/News/311049995.

Nicodemus, Aaron. "Witnesses ID Suspect in Fatal Halloween Shooting." *SouthCoastToday.com*, 25 October 2005. southcoasttoday.com/article/20051025/news/310259988).

WILLIAM CASSAVANT

Man smothered to death in his home in New Bedford, Massachusetts, on November 2, 2003.

Victim: William Cassavant, 50.

Accused: Kathleen Ferreira, 30.

Details: William Cassavant was smothered to death by his girlfriend, Kathleen Ferreira, in their home on November 2, 2003.

Court documents show that William had a record of assault against Ferreira. On February 1, 2003, Cassavant was arrested for assault and witness intimidation, with prior charges pending at the time of his death.

The violence dated back to at least August 2001, when an emergency restraining order was issued to Ferreira after police were called to her home. Cassavant had been punching her and there were bruises evident on her. Some of the earlier charges were dismissed, Cassavant received probation for two instances of assault and battery and for resisting arrest in 2002.

"William also had two separate prior incidents with local police. A 1998 article from the *Providence Journal* detailed a stand-off in which police were called to William's home upon report of him having a gun and acting suicidal. He surrendered to police. In 1997, police were called to his home for a domestic disturbance where they seized several weapons and charged William with weapons violations."

Trial: Kathleen Ferreira was arraigned in New Bedford Superior Court on July 6, 2004 and charged with second-degree murder. The charges against her were dismissed as she successfully used the battered woman defense.

Further Reading:

2003 Massachusetts Domestic Violence Homicide Report. 2006. Jane Doe Inc. janedoe.org/site/assets/docs/Learn_More/DV_Homicide/2003_MA_DV_Homicide_Report_JDI.pdf

ALBERTO GONZALEZ

Fatal shooting of a man at 115 Hillman Street in New Bedford, on November 20, 2003.

Victim: Alberto Gonzalez, 20.

Accused: Shawn Hunt, and Michael Pittman, ages unknown.

Details: According to the successful appeal of Shawn Hunt, the facts of the case are as follows:

"On November 20, 2003, at approximately 6:00 P.M., the victim, Alberto 'Tito' Gonzalez (Tito), was shot from a passing motor vehicle at the corner of Hillman and Spruce Streets in New Bedford. Fernanda Gonzalez, Tito's mother, was unloading groceries in front of her home on Spruce Street when the shooting occurred. Tito had just left their home to visit a neighbor who also lived on Spruce Street. As Tito walked in a northerly direction across Hillman Street, Fernanda observed a dark-colored vehicle turn right from Spruce Street onto Hillman Street. As the vehicle made the turn, she heard shots and observed that someone in the vehicle was firing at Tito. Tito bent over at the waist, stumbled a bit, and ran up Hillman Street. As he did so, he yelled at her to go into the house. She watched until Tito disappeared from sight as the vehicle pursued him up Hillman Street.

"The police arrived on the scene within minutes after the shooting. They searched the area for Tito but were unable to locate him or find any evidence that a shooting had occurred. After the police left, Tito's family and friends organized a search of the neighborhood. At or around 8:00 P.M., almost two hours after the shooting, one of Tito's friends found Tito's body in the backyard of a residence on Hillman Street. He had suffered a fatal gunshot wound.

"Later that night, a team of police officers from the New Bedford police department and the State police returned to the area to begin their investigation into the shooting. Their first lead came from an area resident who told them he had heard shots and had looked toward Hillman Street, where he saw a dark blue or green Ford Focus automobile racing up the street. This person also told the police that the driver was a black male wearing a black 'doo rag.' He was unable to see the driver's face or whether other individuals were in the vehicle.

"In their interviews with Tito's family and friends that night, the police elicited information suggesting a motive for the shooting and the possible identity of the perpetrators. The police were told that on October 19, 2003, a month prior to the shooting, Tito and some of his friends had been involved in a brawl at a local restaurant. The combatants were two groups of individuals, one group associated with Tito and the other with [Hunt and Pittman]. During the fracas, Hunt suffered a serious head injury and was said to be angry and bent on taking revenge. Pittman, also present that night, was angry because of the injury to Hunt, his associate.

"Prior to the fight, Pittman and Tito had been friendly; after the fight, their relationship became hostile. Pittman was also upset with Tito because he heard that Tito was bragging that his group had gotten the better of Pittman's group. Tito stopped associating with Pittman, and he told his friends he was afraid of Pittman and his group.

"The hostilities continued into the weeks leading up to the shooting. Two days after the fight, Pittman, Hunt, and some of their friends went to a house frequented by Tito and his friends. The owner of the house, the sister of one of the combatants on Tito's side, refused to open the door and threatened to call the police. Pittman and his group left. Tito became aware of Pittman's presence and ran out of the back door to avoid a confrontation.

"After the fight, but before the shooting, Hunt went by Tito's house. He accosted Tito's downstairs neighbor, mistaking him for Tito. Hunt told the neighbor that he should tell Tito that he (Hunt) was coming back to get him. Because of this and other threats, one of Tito's friends gave Tito a gun for protection.

"Members of the Gonzalez family and other individuals implicated [Hunt and Pittman] more directly in testimony about events occurring on November 20, 2003, the day of the shooting. In the early afternoon of that day, Tito and some of his friends were visiting with another friend, who lived just up the street from Tito's residence. At or around 5:00 P.M., Tito received a call on his mobile telephone (mobile phone) from Pittman and several of his associates. Tito activated the speaker so that his friends could hear the conversation. They heard a voice, identified by Tito as that of Pittman, tell Tito that today was the day he was going to die. Pittman also warned Tito to 'bring your heater [gun] home with you tonight because we are going to kill you.' Tito was told to come to the Bullard Street area where Pittman and his associates congregated and that if he did not do so, the group would go to his mother's house to get him. The shooting occurred just an hour or so later near Tito's residence.

"After the shooting, Pittman called Tito's mobile phone while the family was still at the hospital. There was evidence before the grand jury that Pittman taunted Tito's sister about what had just happened to Tito, asking, 'How do you feel now that he's dead? How does it feel that he is dead, that we killed him?'

"In the hour after the shooting, Pittman, Hunt, and a third man, known to the police as Rakeem 'Ty' Wallace, appeared at the third-floor apartment of Corey Hubbard, one of their associates. They arrived in a dark-colored Ford Focus. The driver parked the vehicle in a concealed location near the apartment. Hubbard's second-floor neighbor heard loud footsteps headed to Hubbard's apartment and decided to go upstairs to see what was happening. Hunt had a gun in his hand. All of the men appeared to be nervous and scared.

"During the conversation after the neighbor's arrival, Hunt implicated himself in the shooting, volunteering that he had to 'get out of here' because 'we' 'just took out the kid.' There was evidence before the grand jury that Hunt said that they shot Tito '[f]rom the car' and that he (Hunt) had been driving. There was also evidence that Hunt handed the gun and the car keys to Hubbard, ordering him to get rid of the gun and clean out the vehicle. Hubbard then handed the car keys to the second-floor neighbor, who took the vehicle to a car wash and vacuumed up a shell casing he found in the back seat area. There was evidence, based on a police officer's notes from an interview, that later Hubbard wrapped the gun in a sock, tied it to a brick, and threw it into the ocean.

"Within a few days of the shooting, the police linked Hunt to the Ford Focus seen leaving the scene of the shooting. They learned that Hunt had rented a blue Ford Focus from a local car dealer, and that the vehicle had not been returned after the shooting. After the police issued a BOLO ('Be On the Lookout') bulletin for the vehicle, a police officer spotted it at a gasoline station in Taunton. Hubbard, in whose apartment [Hunt and Pittman] gathered in the immediate aftermath of the shooting, was operating the vehicle. A search of the vehicle revealed a black 'doo rag' in the center console and a spent shell casing inside the pocket of the front passenger side door. Investigators also discovered Pittman's fingerprints in the vehicle, as well as an electricity bill in Hunt's name, a receipt from the rental car company in his name, and a piece of mail addressed to him.

"The prosecutor presented Fernanda as the only eyewitness to the shooting. She testified that she recognized Pittman as the person in the front passenger seat of the vehicle from which the shots had been fired. She said that she saw Pittman put his head outside the vehicle and fire a gun at her son. She also testified that she recognized Hunt as the passenger in the back seat of the vehicle.

"The police first became aware of Fernanda's new claim that she could identify the perpetrators on February 14, 2004, some three months after the shooting. She appeared at the New Bedford police department, where she spoke to Beaudoin, the lead investigator in the case. Fernanda told him that she now remembered that Pittman was the person who shot her son. She claimed that she saw Pittman lean his body out of the car and fire shots at Tito. She explained her ability to provide this new information by claiming that she realized that Pittman was the person who had shot her son when, in January, 2004, she saw his image on television in connection with his court appearance in another matter. She described to Beaudoin how she had visited the court on January 23, 2004, the day when Pittman was scheduled to appear, and that she had said to him, 'You killed my boy.' When confronted, Pittman denied any involvement in her son's death.

"Prior to the presentment of the Gonzalez case to the grand jury in June, 2008, the district attorney's newly formed 'cold case' prosecution team received the entire investigative file on the Gonzalez shooting and had access to the original investigators and their reports. The prosecutor was aware, therefore, of Fernanda's original statement, her motivation to secure [Hunt and Pittman]' arrest, the investigators' concerns about the credibility of this new identification, and the prior district attorney's decision not to present the case to the grand jury. Nonetheless, the prosecutor took no steps to vet the plausibility or credibility of Fernanda's proposed grand jury testimony before presenting it to the jury. The witness preparation session on the eve of the hearing on Pittman's motion to suppress Fernanda's identification was the first time she was asked to explain how she saw what she now claimed to have seen on the night of the shooting.

"On the eve of trial, the Commonwealth learned that Fernanda Gonzalez, the victim's mother, had fabricated her grand jury testimony identifying Pittman as the person who shot her son and Hunt as an accomplice. In accordance with established law, the Commonwealth promptly disclosed the witness's false statements to the court and [Hunt and Pittman]. In response, [Hunt and Pittman] filed motions to dismiss the indictments with prejudice, claiming that prosecutorial misconduct in the presentation of the false identification testimony impaired the integrity of the grand jury proceedings.

"After a lengthy evidentiary hearing on the motions to dismiss, the judge allowed the motions without prejudice on the grounds that the Commonwealth 'proceeded with reckless disregard for the truth of the identification evidence' and that the false identification testimony 'probably influenced the decision to indict.'

Alberto Gonzalez was the eleventh slaying in New Bedford in 2003, a year which marked the highest murder rate in the city's history.

Trial: In 2009, Shawn Hunt and Michael Pittman were indicted by a Grand Jury of murder in the first degree and carrying a firearm with out a license. A Grand Jury witness, the mother of Alberto Gonzalez, admitted to fabricating her identification of the Hunt and Pittman as the perpetrators of the crime. The indictments were dismissed.

There is no other information regarding a retrial in the case of Alberto Gonzalez.

Further Reading:

"Commonwealth vs. Shawn Hunt." 84 Mass. App. Ct. 643, April 10, 2013-December 20, 2013. Bristol County. masscases.com/cases/app/84/84massappct643.html.

Rosenwald, Michael S."New Bedford Probes 11th Slaying." *The Boston Globe* (Boston, Massachusetts), 22 November 2003.

LAURIE TAVARES

Woman killed in a vehicular homicide in New Bedford, Massachusetts, on November 27, 2003..

Victim: Laurie Tavares, 28.

Accused: Tracey Andre Douglas, 37.

Details: According to Douglas' appeal on his conviction, the facts of the case are as follows:

"On November 27, 2003, at approximately 8:30 P.M., [Douglas]'s jeep and the victim's vehicle collided at an intersection in New Bedford. Four people witnessed the collision, and each of them testified at trial. According to the witnesses, [Douglas]'s jeep went through a stop sign at a high rate of speed and struck the victim's vehicle. A New Bedford police officer arriving at the scene after the accident saw [Douglas] pacing back and forth in an agitated manner. The officer spoke to [Douglas] and did not detect the odor of alcoholic beverages. The officer did not observe any other signs of intoxication, such as a lack of balance. The victim died at the scene from multiple traumatic injuries. Paramedics took [Douglas] to the nearest hospital for treatment.

"Shortly after the collision, a New Bedford Police Department accident reconstruction expert investigated the cause of the crash. She analyzed the damage to the vehicles and made numerous measurements of the crash scene. Based on her investigation, the expert concluded that [Douglas]'s jeep had been traveling at sixty-four miles per hour when it entered the intersection.

"Soon after [Douglas] arrived at the hospital, two New Bedford police officers interviewed him. According to the officers, [Douglas] was 'angry [and] agitated' and his breath smelled of alcoholic beverages. He told the officers that he had consumed 'a forty of OE,' a forty-ounce bottle of Olde English brand beer. Both officers testified that [Douglas]'s demeanor changed when one of the officers notified him of the victim's death.

"While at the hospital, [Douglas] complained of pain in his chest. In response to his complaint, hospital staff drew a blood sample from him and analyzed it. The doctor who had treated [Douglas] testified that his blood serum sample had an alcohol reading of 185 milligrams per deciliter. A laboratory supervisor from the Massachusetts State police crime laboratory testified that the reading translated to a whole blood alcohol level of .15 to .16."

Trial: Tracey Andre Douglas was convicted on May 19, 2006 of motor vehicle homicide under the influence and was sentenced to consecutive jail terms of 2½ and 2 years.

Afterword: In his appeal in 2009, Douglas asserted that the judge erred in admitting evidence of the defendant's blood alcohol content without expert testimony to explain its relationship to intoxication, and in instructing the jury, given that the judge did not give an instruction on the *per se* theory of operation under the influence and incorrectly instructed the jury on the permissible inference of operating under the influence, the errors may have materially influenced the verdict and therefore created a substantial risk of a miscarriage of justice.

The appeals court agreed and the verdicts were set aside. A new trial was ordered.

No records could be located of a retrial.

Further Reading:

"City Man Sentenced in Fatal Collision." *SouthCoastToday.com*, 20 May 2006. southcoasttoday.com/article/20060520/News/305209984.

"Commonwealth vs. Tracey Douglas." 75 Mass. App. Ct. 643, March 6, 2009-November 2, 2009. Bristol County. masscases.com/cases/app/75/75massappct643.html.

FRANK PEREIRA JR.

Shooting death of a suspected burglar at 134 Ashley Boulevard in New Bedford, Massachusetts, on June 17, 2004.

Victim: Frank Pereira Jr., 24.

Accused: Charles Chieppa, 56.

Details: Frank Pereira was shot and killed on June 17, 2004, after, it was initially believed, he had broken into the home of Charles Chieppa—his home for 50 years. Investigators later doubted that Pereira had ever entered the home, and, instead, had tried to break into several vehicles in Chieppa's driveway.

According to testimony, Pereira had just broken into Chieppa's basement. Chieppa awoke about 4 a.m. to the sounds of an intruder. He woke a tenant in the second-floor apartment, asking him to call the police.

Charles Chieppa, an expert rifleman and Vietnam veteran, was charged with second-degree murder in the killing, after firing four shots from a semi-automatic Walther P38 handgun at Pereira.

Witnesses reported that they heard Chieppa yelling and swearing at Pereira, demanding to know why he was breaking into his home. They also saw the shots fired and Pereira running from the scene and collapsing in the street. It was later determined that Pereira was carrying a knife. According to the Medical Examiner, Pereira had been shot in the back.

Trial: In 2007, a jury deliberated for 3 hours and acquitted Charles Chieppa of second-degree murder in the death of Frank Pereira Jr.

Further Reading:

"New Bedford Man Cleared of Murder." *The Boston Globe* (Boston, Massachusetts), 27 March 2007.
"Rifleman Won't Face Bail in Shooting Case." *News-Press* (Fort Myers, Florida), 6 February 2005.

REY DAVILA

Paraplegic man stabbed and thrown down the stairs to his death at Ships' Cove Apartments at 130 Canal Street in Fall River, Massachusetts, on June 29, 2004.

Victim: Rey Davila, 29.

Accused: Fred Dixon, 35, and Felix Marrero, 23.

Details: According to Fred Dixon's appeal, the facts of the case are as follows:

Rey Davila "was found at approximately 9:30 P.M. on a landing between the third and fourth floors of a stairwell located next door to [Dixon]'s apartment. The victim's jeans had been pulled down and his right pocket had been turned inside out. According to the medical examiner, the victim suffered two fractures of the jaw, a dislocated neck and numerous lacerations and abrasions. He opined that the victim had sustained blunt trauma to his head and neck and had died as a result of those injuries.

"The victim and [Dixon] both lived on the fourth floor of Ship's Cove; the victim lived in apartment 412 at the south end of the complex while [Dixon], along with his girlfriend and their son, lived in apartment 401 at the north end. Ship's Cove was equipped with security cameras which recorded the following sequence of events before the victim's body was found.

"At approximately 9:16 P.M., the victim entered the building through the first-floor lobby and took the elevator to the fourth floor. [Dixon], Marrero, and several other persons entered the lobby seconds later. The group, which included another resident of Ship's Cove, Karrah Kenner, entered the lobby elevator. Kenner, who lived across the hall from [Dixon], went to the fourth floor while [Dixon] and Marrero remained in the elevator, exiting on a higher floor. Within minutes, however, [Dixon] and Marrero took the elevator back to the fourth floor.

"Shortly thereafter, [Dixon]'s next door neighbor, Maria Carreiro, heard a man scream more than once, 'No, no, please, no, no.' The voice was coming through the wall adjacent to [Dixon]'s apartment. Carreiro called the police. She then observed the wall near her front door shaking, and heard the door to [Dixon]'s apartment open. Next, she heard the door to the fire stairs (stairwell) open, followed by the sound of '[s]omething rolling down the stairs.'

"Around the same time, Kenner and her boyfriend, Jason Alves, heard loud noises coming from [Dixon]'s apartment. Alves knocked on [Dixon]'s apartment door and asked if everything was all right. No one opened the door but a voice which both Kenner and Alves recognized as [Dixon]'s answered, 'Everything is all right, Fam.'

"At approximately 9:38 P.M., two Fall River police officers arrived in response to Carreiro's call, just as [Dixon] and Marrero were leaving the building through the door at the south stairwell. After the police discovered the victim's body, they secured the scene and obtained a search warrant for [Dixon]'s apartment. During the execution of the warrant, police observed blood stains on the wall which separated [Dixon]'s apartment from Carreiro's apartment. They also recovered a baseball cap similar to the one Marrero was observed wearing when he entered the lobby earlier that evening, and a paper bag similar to the bag that [Dixon] had been carrying when he first entered the elevator. The police also observed blood in the stairwell where the body was found. Deoxyribonucleic acid (DNA) testing revealed that the blood in [Dixon]'s apartment and the stairwell matched the victim's DNA profile. DNA testing on the baseball cap revealed the presence of three DNA profiles, one of which matched Marrero's DNA profile. Also, Marrero's fingerprints matched a latent fingerprint found on the paper bag.

"Later in the evening of June 29, [Dixon] and Marrero were seen together at Marrero's apartment building. Marrero had changed his shirt and was no longer wearing a cap. In the late afternoon on the following day, June 30, 2004, [Dixon] and Marrero stopped briefly at the home of [Dixon]'s cousin, Helen Deans. During the visit, [Dixon] told Deans that 'something happened.' [Dixon] and Marrero were also observed together on July 1, and were arrested together in Boston on July 2, 2004."

Trial: "[Dixon] made a number of incriminating statements during the booking process at the Fall River police station. The jury heard testimony that in response to a question posed by the booking officer about whether a weapon had been used during the incident, [Dixon] stated, 'The dude hit us.' The Commonwealth also introduced evidence that while [Dixon] was using the telephone in the booking room, he was overheard saying, 'You're pregnant?' and 'I fucked up. I fucked up.'

In 2006, Fred Dixon was convicted of second-degree murder and sentenced to life in prison. He will be eligible for parole in 2021.

Felix Marrero was acquitted in his trial in June of 2006.

Afterword: Fred Dixon appealed his conviction in 2010 on the grounds that the judge at a pretrial motion erred in denying the suppression of three statements that Dixon had made to the police. The appeals court disagreed and affirmed the conviction.

Further Reading:

"Commonwealth vs. Fred Dixon." 79 Mass. App. Ct. 701, November 18, 2010-June 23, 2011. Bristol County. masscases.com/cases/app/79/79massappct701.html.

"Two Held in Disabled Man's Killing." *The Boston Globe* (Boston, Massachusetts), 7 July 2004.

JESSICA CORVELO

Woman stabbed to death in Fall River, Massachusetts, on August 9, 2004.

Victim: Jessica Corvelo, 22.

Accused: Andres Rivera, 22.

Details: Andres Rivera told police that his girlfriend and mother of their three-year-old twin daughters, Jessica Corvelo, was attempting suicide on August 9, 2004. In an effort to stop her, he tackled her to get the knife away from her. The initial cause of death was a single cut to the throat.

The autopsy report listed multiple stab wounds on Jessica's body, not just the one wound to her throat. The fatal injury was the neck wound, but it was six-inches long and severed her trachea, making any efforts to resuscitate her futile. None of the wounds were consistent with being self-inflicted.

The father of the victim later said that he found more than 50 different knives and swords in his daughter's apartment. The murder weapon had been a 5-inch long steak knife that he had given the couple as a part of a set.

Trial: Andres Rivera pleaded guilty to involuntary manslaughter in the stabbing death of his girlfriend, the mother of their twins. He was sentenced to 8 years in prison.

Afterword: Andres Rivera was scheduled to appear before the parole board in 2010 but no information could be located as to the board's decision. In searching inmate records through Vinelink.com (a victim and concerned citizen network of prison inmates), there is no Andres Rivera currently serving a prison term in Massachusetts.

Further Reading:

Pateakos, Jay. "Slain Woman's Family Grapples with Alleged Killer's Parole." *Herald News* (Fall River, Massachusetts), 16 February 2010.

COURTNEY SAU

Woman stabbed to death in front of 136 John Street in the Corky Row neighborhood in Fall River, Massachusetts, on February 5, 2005.

Victim: Courtney Sau, 19.

Accused: Carla Carvalho, 20, and Karen Cordeiro, 20.

Details: Carla Carvalho and Karen Cordeiro were roommates. Carvalho, Cordeiro, and Courtney Sau apparently had an argument at a Providence night club hours before Sau's death, the subject of which was Carvalho's relationship with Sau's ex-boyfriend.

"The lives of the three young women became intertwined forever during the early morning hours of Feb. 5, 2005. As they exited a Providence nightclub, Carvalho and Cordeiro became engaged in a fight with Sau over an ex-boyfriend of Sau's who had gone home with Cordeiro a couple of weeks before.

"While the sides eventually separated, Sau, with directions provided by a friend who also knew Carvalho and Cordeiro, decided to drive to Fall River with a car full of friends instead of returning to her home in Taunton. Knowing Sau was en route — she called Carvalho twice on the way —Carvalho and Cordeiro readied themselves for a fight.

"According to Carvalho's police interview during the hours after the incident, Carvalho armed herself with a beer bottle. Cordeiro, to Carvalho's surprise, had also grabbed a kitchen knife. As Sau exited her car, Carvalho attacked, smashing the bottle over Sau's head. She told police that she then backed off as Cordeiro jumped into the melee.

"After those two struggled with each other on the ground, Cordeiro, now covered in blood, jumped up and she and Carvalho retreated back into their apartment. Cordeiro had stabbed Sau in the neck and back with the knife, leading to Sau's death.

"Carvalho said she wasn't aware Cordeiro had armed herself with the knife and would have stopped her if she had. It's an event that Carvalho doesn't like to talk about, but also one that regularly plays back over and over again in her mind" ("Out of Prison").

Sau was born in Auckland, New Zealand, and had moved with her family to Taunton, Massachusetts, four years before her death. She was studying to be a police officer at Bridgewater State College.

Trial: Karen Cordeiro was charged with first-degree murder. A jury in 2007 determined her guilty of second-degree murder and she was sentenced to life in prison with the chance of parole after 15 years.

Carla Carvalho was acquitted of the crime of murder, but sentenced to 5 to 7 years in prison on a charge of assault and battery with a dangerous weapon for her role in the fight.

Further Reading:
"Auckland Teen Stabbed to Death in US." *New Zealand Herald*, 12 February 2005. nzherald.co.nz/nz/news/article.cfm?c_id=1&objectid=10010792.
"Fall River Woman Convicted of Murder." *Boston.com*, 24 January 2007. archive.boston.com/news/local/rhode_island/articles/2007/01/24/fall_river_woman_convicted_of_murder/.
Richmond, Will. "Out of Prison, Carla Carvalho Tries to Move on with Life after Courtney Sau Case." *Herald News* (Fall River, Massachusetts), 7 November 2011.

TOM MURRAY

Disabled veteran shot to death in his home on Welcome Street in New Bedford, Massachusetts, on February 28, 2005.

Victim: Tom Murray, 61.

Accused: Robert Geliga, 18, Ramon Geliga, 17, and Bobby Joe Lecroy, 18.

Details: Ramon and Robert Geliga were well known to the Murray family, whom they met through one of their daughter's friends. The brothers hung out at the Murray house, they come over for dinner, and had even stayed overnight at times when they said they had no place else to go.

A month before the incident, Cheryl Murray noticed that $500 in rent money was missing from her purse after the brothers had visited. Then Tom Murray asked a neighbor to stop lending his car to the Geligas. There were other minor confrontations.

On the day of the killing, the Geliga brothers knocked on the side door and entered in a rage while Bobby Joe Lecroy stood guard in the hallway. Cheryl said that Ramon pulled a gun out of his pants and pointed it at her husband Tom's head and said, according to a friend who witnessed the altercation, "You're not going to tell us what to do." Tom Murray allegedly retorted, "What are you going to do? Shoot me?" And they did.

Tom Murray was hit in the abdomen and died at St. Luke's Hospital.

Ramon Geliga confessed his role in the killing. Lecroy denied that Ramon Geliga had fired in self-defense. He led the police to a Holly Street home where they found the .22-caliber Smith & Wesson semi-automatic used in the shooting. Lecroy said that at no time did Murray arm himself.

The Geliga brothers came from a deeply unstable household and bounced back and forth between state custody and public housing. Their father, now dead, was a drug addict who had once attacked their mother with a knife. Their mother, Darlene Sanchez has a long criminal history that includes time served for assault and battery with a razor. The children were present and witnesses to most of this violence. In one video of an altercation, the brothers could be seen in the background, frightened.

In a detailed reporting of the violence that shaped the lives of these teens, the background of the victim, Tom Murray, was also examined.

"Born in Cambridge to a family of 14 children Mr. Murray angered his parents by quitting high school and working as a short-order chef in Malden as a young man.

"'He was bored with school' said his sister Barbara Scarlata 64 of Carver. 'He was too smart for his own good.'

"Even before he had a family of his own Mr. Murray had fatherly impulses. When times were tough he once purchased Christmas presents for Ms. Scarlata's children. 'My own kids wouldn't have had Christmas one year if it wasn't for him' she said.

"But there was another side to Mr. Murray one his sister wouldn't talk about. Convicted of rape in 1966 Mr. Murray was sentenced to 4 to 10 years in state prison said Dianne Wiffin a spokeswoman for the state Department of Correction.

"At the same time Mr. Murray received concurrent prison sentences for robbery by force forgery assault with a dangerous weapon and receiving stolen goods the spokeswoman said.

"As recently as five years ago he was charged in Somerville District Court with forging documents and uttering a false prescription according to court records. The connection between the teenagers and retiree remains a matter of dispute.

"Ms. Sanchez claims Ramon and Robert supplied Mr. Murray and his wife with crack cocaine in return for letting them stay in their apartment at 34 Welcome St. Toward the end the brothers had allowed the couple to purchase the drug on credit, his mother said. Robert told Ms. Sanchez that Mr. Murray owed about $300.

"Mr. Murray's wife Cheryl denied that she or her husband had ever purchased drugs from the Geliga brothers" ("Violence Shaped Brothers' Lives").

Trial: Robert Geliga pleaded guilty to manslaughter and was sentenced to 8 to 10 years in prison. He was released on May 28, 2014. Ramon Geliga was convicted of murder in 2006 and sentenced to life in prison.

Afterword: In 2016, Robert Geliga was arrested for stabbing Eliseo Ramirez, 20, four times on February 17 during a fight at Dublin's Sports Bar at 1686 Acushnet Avenue in New Bedford. Ramirez suffered wounds to his neck, back, and torso.

In 2017, Robert Geliga, while out on bail for the stabbing in 2016, was arrested for trafficking in Fentanyl. When police conducted a search warrant of his apartment, they found 20 bags of Fentanyl, weighing 16.5 grams, $90 in cash, a digital scale, and cutting agents and packaging materials.

Further Reading:

Brown, Curt. "Update: New Bedford Man, Who Served 9 Years for Manslaughter, Arrested for Stabbing at Sports Bar." *SouthCoastToday.com*, 24 February 2016. southcoasttoday.com/article/20160224/NEWS/160229690.

Daniel, Marc. "3 Teenagers Face Murder Charges." *The Boston Globe* (Boston, Massachusetts), 9 March 2005.

Henry, Ray. "3 Teens Charged in Slaying." *SouthCoastToday.com*, 9 March 2005. southcoasttoday.com/article/20050309/news/303099997.

Henry, Ray. "Violence Shaped Brothers' Lives." *SouthCoastToday.com*, 13 March 2005. southcoasttoday.com/article/20050313/news/303139997.

"New Bedford Felon Arrested for Trafficking in Fentanyl While Out on Bail for Stabbing." NewBedfordGuide.com, 27 January 2017. newbedfordguide.com/new-bedford-felon-arrested-for-trafficking-in-fentanyl-while-out-on-bail-for-stabbing/2017/01/27.

JAMES GAUOETTE

Man shot and killed in New Bedford, Massachusetts, on March 30, 2005.

Victim: James Gauoette, age unknown.

Accused: Alexander Molina, age unknown.

Details: According to Molina's appeal of his conviction, the details of the case are as follows:

"James Gauoette (victim) was shot and killed in New Bedford on March 30, 2005, during daylight. Three people saw the events surrounding the shooting. We refer to them by pseudonyms as Alice, Barbara, and Claire. Their testimony, although differing in some details, was consistent in part. Alice testified that she heard gunfire, saw the victim lying on the sidewalk, and observed a man with a short-sleeve, mustard colored T-shirt and light colored jeans standing over the victim, hitting him with an object. That man was of medium build with a tanned complexion, but she could not see his face. He ran down Salisbury Street.

"Barbara, who was acquainted with [Molina], testified that she was talking with him around 5:00 P.M. on a porch in the vicinity of the shooting. He was wearing jeans and a yellow shirt. She observed 'Jimmy' (the victim) approach [Molina], saying, 'I'm just here to talk.' She saw [Molina] go to the trunk of his car, which was parked nearby, retrieve a gun and shoot Jimmy. Barbara saw [Molina] ten to fifteen minutes later, after police and medical personnel had arrived, but he had changed into a brown jogging outfit.

"Claire testified that she heard a gunshot and, looking out of her window, saw a man walk across Salisbury Street to the corner of Ruth and Salisbury Streets and shoot the 'kid' lying on the sidewalk four times before running back across the street and giving the gun to another man, who threw it inside a green car parked on Salisbury Street.

"Claire knew the green car to have been previously driven by [Molina], whom she knew from the neighborhood. She saw the shooter and his friends running away and, some twenty or thirty minutes later, saw the shooter come up Salisbury Street and go into a beige house, emerging in different clothing, having changed to a brown sweatshirt. Claire identified [Molina] in court as the shooter. At the police station, [Molina] was described as wearing a brown corduroy or velour suit."

Trial: Alexander Molina was convicted of murder in the second degree and sentenced to life in prison with the possibility of parole in 15 years.

Afterword: Alexander Molina appealed his conviction in 2011 on the grounds that a witness received a cash reward from a local chamber of commerce for testifying, errors in the judge's instructions to the jury, and denying a pretrial motion to suppress statements that Molina made to the police, claiming that he had invoked his right to counsel. The court affirmed the conviction and denied Molina's appeal.

In 2007, Molina petitioned a US District Court for habeas corpus relief. The court denied his petition.

NOTE: There are variant spellings of the victim's name: James Gaouette and James Gauoette. We have been unable to confirm the correct spelling.

Further Reading:

"Alexander Molina v. Kelly Ryan." United States District Court, District of Massachusetts, Civil Action No. 14-cv-11104. gpo.gov/fdsys/pkg/USCOURTS-mad-1_14-cv-11104/pdf/USCOURTS-mad-1_14-cv-11104-0.pdf

"Commonwealth vs. Alexander Molina." 81 Mass. App. Ct. 855, October 14, 2011-June 13, 2012. Bristol County. masscases.com/cases/app/81/81massappct855.html.

Fraga, Brian. "Molina Convicted of Second-Degree Murder, Sentenced to Life in Prison." *SouthCoastToday.com*, 29 February 2008. southcoasttoday.com/article/20080229/NEWS/802290332

SUSY GOULART

Stabbing and hacking death of a woman at Pleasant View Apartments in Fall River, Massachusetts, on April 16, 2005.

Victim: Susy Goulart, 23.

Accused: Jermaine Holley, 27.

Details: According to Jermaine Holley's appeal in 2016, the facts of the case are as follows:

"[Susy Goulart] lived in a multibuilding public housing development in Fall River. On the day of her death, the victim's former friend and neighbor, Patricia Moran, moved out of her apartment because she had been evicted as the result of both nonpayment of rent and a then-pending criminal charge of assaulting the victim during a dispute over a debt. Moran's boy friend and his brother, [Holley], had often visited Moran at the development. [Holley] was among those who helped move Moran's belongings into a truck after which the group drank alcohol outside her building. [Holley] told one of these people that the victim owed Moran money.

"[Holley] was still at Moran's building at approximately 8 p.m. At approximately 9 p.m., a neighbor saw the victim walking home from the direction of Moran's building. The victim then stopped to smoke a cigarette while with her downstairs neighbors near the back door of her own building. As the victim was walking upstairs afterward, the neighbors saw an African-American man also walk upstairs. He did not respond when the victim asked him, 'Are you here for me?' The hood the man was wearing blocked most of his face. Earlier in the day, a resident had seen [Holley] wearing a 'hoodie.'

"Soon after the victim and the man walked up the stairs, the neighbors she had been smoking with heard the victim's apartment door lock and then the sound of loud music. A neighbor who lived next door to the victim, also heard people enter the apartment. Later, this neighbor heard a scream but could not tell the source. Shortly after that, she saw smoke coming from the victim's apartment and telephoned the fire department. No one saw or heard anyone else enter or leave the apartment, and the victim did not answer her friend's telephone calls at 10:13 p.m. and 11:32 p.m.

"Police, fire fighters, and paramedics responded to the scene. A pot on the stove was on fire, blood was seen throughout the living room and kitchen, and the victim was dead on the floor, wearing only a shirt and holding a severed telephone line. An autopsy showed that she had died as a result of forty stab wounds and thirteen cutting wounds. The knife used in the killing was never found.

"Investigators took samples of blood, clothing (including a bloody sock), and powder and gelatin lifts of fingerprint and footwear impressions from the victim's apartment, as well as fingernail scrapings, a blood sample, and oral, vaginal, and anorectal swabs from the victim's body. The State police crime laboratory compared deoxyribonucleic acid (DNA) samples from the evidence collected to DNA samples from the victim, [Holley], [Holley]'s brother, and the first police officer to respond to the fire. Over the course of the investigation, the police also found and seized a pair of [Holley]'s shoes, the soles of which were consistent with footprint impressions found in blood in the victim's apartment.

"Residents of the housing complex told police that they had seen [Holley] with a knife on the day the victim was killed. At around noon, [Holley] showed his knife to one resident who had stopped by Moran's apartment. It was approximately eleven inches long with a black handle and black sheath. That afternoon, [Holley] visited another resident's apartment to demand money that the resident's former boy friend owed to [Holley]. When the resident told [Holley] that she was not responsible for the debt, [Holley] lifted his hoodie and shirt to show her a knife with a black and silver handle in a 'holster,' and said he would be back. A third resident, José Torres, said that [Holley] had waved a large knife at Torres and his friends on the day of the murder.

"Five days after Goulart's death, the police went to speak with [Holley]. He was brought to the police station, where an officer noticed a cut on [Holley]'s hand. A test for blood on both of his hands was negative.

"After giving [Holley] the Miranda warnings, the police interviewed him about the victim's death. During the interview, [Holley] denied being at the housing complex on the day of the murder and denied knowing personally or having sex with the victim (he even initially denied knowing Moran). He also falsely stated that he and his girl friend had gone to Newport, Rhode Island, on the day of the victim's death. When the police asked [Holley] if he could think of anything worse than murder, he said, 'You can snitch on somebody. That's like taking somebody's life.' At some point, [Holley] apparently had told his girl friend that the victim was a snitch."

Trial: "At trial, [Holley] pointed to the victim's former boy friend as the murderer, suggesting that the police had narrowed their search too quickly to African-American men, and highlighting a number of reasons that the boy friend had to kill the victim, including their turbulent relationship and the fact that she had had sex with [Holley]. [Holley] also presented evidence that the boy friend had been in the housing complex on the day of the murder. The defense stressed the lack of fingerprint evidence linking [Holley] to the murder and argued that the number and type of stab wounds were indicative of the victim's boy friend's obsession with and anger at her. The victim's boy friend had been seen elsewhere on the evening of the murder."

In December, 2011, Jermaine Holley was convicted by a jury of murder in the first degree on a theory of extreme atrocity or cruelty. He was sentenced to life in prison without the possibility of parole.

Afterword: In 2016, Jermaine Holley's lawyers petitioned for a new trial, asserting multiple errors in the trial by the police and the judge. The appeals court denied Holley's arguments and affirmed his conviction and denied his motion for a new trial.

Further Reading:

"Commonwealth vs. Jermaine Holley." 476 Mass. 114, September 9, 2016-December 19, 2016. Bristol County. masscases.com/cases/sjc/476/476mass114.html.

DANA HAYWOOD

Man shot and killed in the Monte Park neighborhood of New Bedford, Massachusetts, on July 4, 2005.

Victim: Dana Haywood, age unknown.

Accused: John Burgos, age unknown.

Details: According to John Burgos' appeal in 2014, the *complicated* facts of the case and the evidence presented at trial is as follows:

"Dana Haywood was shot and killed on July 4, 2005, in the Monte Park neighborhood of New Bedford. Over three years later, in February of 2009, an assistant district attorney in the Bristol district received a letter from Rico Almeida, who was then sharing a cell with [John Burgos] in the Bristol County house of correction. Almeida wrote that [Burgos] had been one of the participants in the shooting death of Haywood on July 4, 2005, that [Burgos] had told Almeida 'how they did it, where, and when,' and that Almeida would be able to arrange for [Burgos] to repeat this admission to the shooting of the victim. Almeida offered to wear a concealed recording device and record the proposed conversation. In response to the letter, the Commonwealth submitted an affidavit of Trooper Anthony Spencer of the State police to a judge in the Superior Court, and obtained a search warrant authorizing the electronic recording of conversations between the cooperating witness (i.e., Almeida) and [Burgos]."

John Burgos was a member of the United Front Gang (a group of individuals that operate in and around the United Front Homes located adjacent to Chancery and Kempton Streets) for a dozen years. "The members are known to be heavily involved in the distribution of illegal narcotics. The members are also known to commit violent crimes including possession of firearms and multiple shootings. Mr. Burgos himself was also a target of a shooting on May 21, 2006 along with Justin Barry who was murdered in the shooting. This shooting was perpetrated by rival Monte Park members including David DePina. Mr. DePina is presently awaiting trial in the fatal shooting of Barry and the shooting of Mr. Burgos."

Dana Haywood was a known member of the rival Monte Park Gang (a group of individuals that are known to distribute illegal narcotics by Monte Park on Acushnet Avenue in the city of New Bedford) at the time of his death. "The gang members are also known to commit violent crimes including illegal possession of firearms and multiple shootings…Dana Haywood's murder is suspected to be in retaliation for the fatal shooting of Cecil Lopes which occurred on October 31, 2004. The Cecil Lopes murder took place at the United Front Homes on Chancery Street in the city of New Bedford. The Cecil Lopes murder involved a shooting directly outside a residence in the United Front Housing complex…Mr. Haywood was shot one block from the Monte Park Housing complex on Russell Street in the city of New Bedford…eyewitnesses to Mr. Haywood's shooting saw 3 young black males, at least 2 of who [sic] were shooting. The 3 males fled from Mr. Haywood's body to an awaiting vehicle."

"Police officers then provided Almeida with an electronic recording device that Almeida hid on his person and used to secretly record a conversation with [Burgos] in their jail cell on March 3, 2009. During the conversation, which lasted over sixty minutes, [Burgos] admitted to being one of the shooters involved in killing the victim on July 4, 2005, and described the actual shooting incident in some detail, as well as his attitude toward it.

"On October 31, 2004, some nine months before the victim was killed on July 4, 2005, Cecil Lopes, a resident of the United Front housing development in New Bedford, had been killed. In November, 2004, [Burgos], who also lived in the United Front development, had made a telephone call to his brother. In this conversation, he and his brother had talked about how Lopes's photograph was in the newspaper and [Burgos] had stated that he had put the image from the newspaper on his wall. They also had discussed that someone named 'Aceon' was responsible for the killing. Aceon was known to be associated with the Monte Park area of New Bedford. The Commonwealth's theory at trial was that [Burgos] and his friend William Payne killed the victim in retaliation for Lopes's murder.

"At the scene of the shooting resulting in the victim's death, police recovered a blue baseball cap and some bullet shell casings. A bystander had seen three individuals at the scene, all of whom were wearing white T-shirts. Later that night, [Burgos] and Payne were at the home of Payne's grandfather who observed [Burgos] to be laughing and behaving differently than he usually did.

"Almeida, who had entered into a cooperation agreement with the Commonwealth, was a witness at trial…A recording of the recorded conversation was then played for the jury and entered into evidence as an exhibit. In that conversation, [Burgos] agreed with Almeida's assertion that he and Payne shot the victim, described the shooting as 'executionist style,' and made statements suggesting a lack of any feelings of guilt or remorse. He also indicated that he had been wearing a white T-shirt at the time of the shooting, and that the victim had been killed in retaliation for the death of Cecil Lopes.

DNA testing was performed on the baseball cap found at the scene revealed that Burgos wore the cap. Haywood's DNA was not on the cap. In addition, "shell casings found at the scene were compared to a shell casing found three months later in a car driven by Payne. The State trooper who did the comparison opined that the casings were fired from the same unknown weapon."

Trial: John Burgos was indicted in 2009 was convicted in November, 2010, by a jury of murder in the first degree.

Afterword: In 2014, John Burgos appealed his conviction on the basis that his motion to suppress a secretly recorded conversation between him and an informant working with the police was erroneously denied and that the evidence of that conversation should have been excluded at trial. He asked that his conviction be reversed as a result. The appeals court agreed and reversed Burgos' conviction.

In 2016, John Burgos pleaded guilty to second degree murder and was sentenced to serve 15 to 17 years in state prison.

Further Reading:

"Commonwealth vs. John Burgos." 470 Mass. 133, September 5, 2014-November 21, 2014. Bristol County. masscases.com/cases/sjc/470/470mass133.html.

Finucane, Martin. "Conviction Thrown Out in 2005 Slaying in New Bedford." *The Boston Globe* (Boston, Massachusetts), 22 November 2014.

"31-Year-Old New Bedford Man Sentenced to 15-17 Years in Prison for 2005 Murder." NewBedfordGuide.com, 1 April 2016. newbedfordguide.com/31-year-old-new-bedford-man-sentence/2016/04/01.

SUZANNA M. SOARES

Woman shot to death in her 71 S. Sixth Street home in New Bedford, Massachusetts, on September 5, 2005.

Victim: Suzanna M. Soares, 30.

Accused: John D. Sylvia Jr, 30.

Details: Police responded to a 911 call reporting that shots had been fired in the neighborhood of S. Sixth Street in New Bedford at 3:47 a.m. on September 5, 2005. They found Suzanna Soares, 30, mother of three (ages 1, 8, and 10) lying on the bed, shot five times, including once in the head. John Sylvia, her boyfriend, was in the apartment at the time of her death.

Sylvia claimed that two masked men stormed into the house demanding money and aimed the gun at Sylvia and fired, but he was not injured. Then, Sylvia said, the men turned to Soares and fired five times, killing her. Then the men ran out of the home.

John Sylvia was later arrested and charged with the execution style killing. He was indicted in June of 2006.

Authorities allege that Sylvia shot Soares, manipulated the crime scene, and gave false and misleading statements to the police. Oddly there was a large amount of cash on the nightstand which did not jibe with the demands for money when the men broke into the house.

The motive, investigators believed, was not only that they had a troubled relationship (Soares was supposedly seeing someone else) and she was going to break up with Sylvia, but also that Soares, who worked for an insurance company, had nine months before her death insured her life for $535,000, listing John Sylvia as the sole beneficiary.

It was reported that Mr. Sylvia was seeing a few other women at the time he was supposedly trying to fix his broken relationship with Soares, and within days of her death, had moved in with one female friend.

Trial: John D. Sylvia Jr. was tried in June of 2008 for the murder of Suzanna Soares. He was found not guilty.

Further Reading:

Cramer, Maria "Shooting Victim had Wanted Out of New Bedford." *The Boston Globe* (Boston, Massachusetts), 8 September 2005.

Fraga, Brian. "Murder Trial Notebook." *SouthCoastToday.com/Blogs*, 26 June 2008. southcoasttoday.com/new-bedford-crime/2008/06/26/murder-trial-notebook/.

Fraga, Brian. "Murder Trial Wrap-Up." *SouthCoastToday.com/Blogs*, 28 June 2008. southcoasttoday.com/new-bedford-crime/2008/06/28/murder-trial-wrap-up/.

Fraga, Brian. "Opening Statements Given in Murder Trial of New Bedford Man" *SouthCoastToday.com*, 18 June 2008. southcoasttoday.com/article/20080618/News/80618011.

Fraga, Brian. "Prosecution Rests in New Bedford Murder Case" *SouthCoastToday.com*, 27 June 2008. southcoasttoday.com/article/20080627/News/806270353.

ANDERSON ROSA

Man shot to death at the corner of Cove and Stapleton Streets in New Bedford, Massachusetts, on October 6, 2005.

Victim: Anderson Rosa, 21.

Accused: Kyle Sylvia, age unknown.

Details: According to Kyle Sylvia's appeal in 2010, the facts of the case as presented at trial are as follows:

"At approximately 12:50 P.M., on October 6, 2005, Victoria Dudley and her son Christopher, who was twelve years of age, were walking east on Cove Street in the south end of New Bedford. They passed the victim, Anderson Rosa, who was unknown to them, and who was pacing back and forth on the sidewalk outside a house on the corner of Cove Street and Stapleton Street. Across that corner, on Cove Street, was the 'station 2' police station, which the New Bedford police department had closed to the public, but utilized as an office for its division of professional standards.

"After passing the victim, the Dudleys noticed a man, [Sylvia], walking quickly westbound toward them, dressed in a bulky, black hooded sweatshirt or jacket, and black pants. Victoria's attention was drawn to [Sylvia] because his clothing seemed inappropriate for that day's warm weather. [Sylvia] came within one foot of Victoria and Christopher. Although [Sylvia]'s face was partially obscured by a hood, Victoria had a clear view of his eyes, and Christopher was able to see his face, and observed that [Sylvia] appeared to have a 'lazy eye.'

"After they passed [Sylvia], Christopher looked back at him and saw him retrieve, with his right hand, a gun from the pocket of his jacket. Christopher then watched [Sylvia], who was about one to two feet away from the victim, aim the gun at the victim's head and fire. [Sylvia] continued firing at the victim, who fell to the ground. Victoria pushed Christopher to the ground, covering him with her body. Once the shots stopped, the Dudleys stood up and quickly walked away. Before doing so, Christopher saw [Sylvia] run around the corner, turning left on Stapleton Street, heading south.

"The victim died at the scene as the result of multiple gunshot wounds. He had been shot six times. Based on the presence of soot and gun powder stippling on the victim's face, the forensic pathologist who conducted the autopsy opined that one of the gunshot wounds to the victim had been inflicted from a distance of between one to three inches from his face. Based on the nature of the victim's wounds, the forensic pathologist testified that the victim would have died within minutes.

"People in the vicinity of the shooting heard shots fired. An employee of the New Bedford police department's division of professional standards, who had just left the building, heard shots and saw a person wearing a dark hooded sweatshirt and dark pants run south on Stapleton Street. She alerted Lieutenant Manuel Ortega and Sergeant August Santos. Sergeant Santos proceeded to chase the person on foot. The person took a right, heading west, on Cove Road, at which point Sergeant Santos lost sight of him. A tow truck operator, Derrick Duarte, working on Stapleton Street, observed that a man who ran past him and who turned right, running west on Cove Road, wore black clothing, including a black hooded jacket made by 'Carhartt.'

"One street over, on Margin Street, a resident who was outside in her driveway saw a person dressed in black rush by her and enter the back yard of 1 Margin Street, which is on the corner of Margin Street and Cove Road. The owner of the home on 1 Margin Street, Joan Martin, had resided there for thirty years and knew [Sylvia]. At various times when [Sylvia] was between the ages of thirteen and seventeen, he had resided at Martin's house.

"Martin was awakened by her security alarm sounding, indicating that the door to her home facing Cove Road had been opened. Soon thereafter, police arrived and asked to enter, which she permitted. In the back yard, around which there was a stockade fence, police found various clothing articles, a bulletproof vest, and a loaded firearm, that Martin claimed did not belong to her or to anyone in her household. Specifically, on the ground by Martin's deck, police found a bulletproof vest and a black hooded jacket made by 'Carhartt.' In addition, police discovered black sweat pants inside a cooler in the yard. Under a 'Burger King' bag and partially inside a drain to the house, police recovered a loaded nine millimeter Glock semiautomatic pistol. Police observed that the basement door to Martin's home, which was not included in her home's alarm system, was ajar.

"Meanwhile, State and local police were looking for the shooter and had begun to set up a perimeter in the area. [Sylvia] emerged near the corner of Margin Street and Cove Road, heading east on Cove Road, and wearing different clothing…[Sylvia] appeared to be out of breath and was perspiring. When asked by Officer Leonard Mota of the New Bedford police department to 'Come here,' [Sylvia] replied, 'What?' and took off running. Officers followed him, but lost sight of him near Shore Street, off Cove Road.

"Officer William Sauve saw [Sylvia] at the intersection of Cove Street and South First Street, heading north on South First Street…[they] eventually caught up with him on Jennings Court...[Sylvia] complied and was taken into custody.

"[Sylvia]'s...hands were tested for the presence of gunshot powder residue...Three particles of gunshot powder residue were detected on the backs of [Sylvia]'s hands. [Sylvia] tested positive for the presence of blood on the palms of both his hands, and on the webbing between the fingers of both his hands.

"Seven discharged cartridge casings were recovered from the sidewalk near the victim's body. A State trooper with the firearms identification unit concluded that, based on his microscopic examination, the discharged cartridge casings recovered near the victim all came from the Glock pistol found at 1 Margin Street.

"Regarding the clothing recovered at 1 Margin Street, inside the black sweatpants (which had been found in the cooler), police discovered an identification card and a letter addressed to [Sylvia]. Inside the pockets of the black Carhartt jacket, another letter relating to [Sylvia], as well as a magazine containing six live cartridges, were found. The magazine could hold a maximum of ten cartridges."

Trial: A jury convicted Kyle Sylvia of murder in the first degree on the theory of deliberate premeditation and unlawful use of a firearm. The jury acquitted Sylvia on using body armor during the commission of a felony.

Afterword: Kyle Sylvia appealed his conviction in 2009 on the grounds that there was an error in the prosecution's opening statement, there was an error in the denial of Sylvia's motion for required findings, there was an error in the admission of certain evidence concerning gunshot powder residue lab test results, that there was an error in the prosecutor's closing argument, and that his convictions of murder in the first degree and unlawful possession of a firearm are inconsistent with his acquittal on the charge of wearing body armor during the commission of a felony.

Kyle Sylvia's appeal was denied.

Further Reading:

"Commonwealth vs. Kyle Sylvia." 456 Mass. 182, December 10, 2009-March 2, 2010. Bristol County. masscases.com/cases/sjc/456/456mass182.html.

"Sentence is Life in Fatal 2005 Shooting." *The Boston Globe* (Boston, Massachusetts), 29 July 2006.

CHRISTOPHER BARROS

Man shot to death in the back yard of 30 Russell Street in New Bedford, Massachusetts, on October 10, 2005.

Victim: Christopher Barros, 25.

Accused: Fagbemi Miranda, 27, Wayne Miranda, 25.

Details: According to Wayne Miranda's appeal in 2010, the facts of the case are as follows:

"Shortly after receiving a dispatch at 8:32 P.M., on October 10, 2005, concerning 'shots fired,' police discovered Christopher Barros lying on the ground by a picket fence in the back yard of 40 Russell Street in New Bedford. The victim had been shot twice and had an 'L' shaped laceration on one of his hands. He was transported to a hospital. He died as a result of one of the gunshot wounds.

"Three witnesses, Kim Deann Reis, John G. Andrade, and Carmen Rodriguez, observed events that immediately preceded the shooting but did not see the shooting itself. Reis did not give a formal statement to police until two years after the event because she was 'scared.' She agreed to testify at trial in exchange for financial assistance in relocating and in exchange for consideration with respect to an unrelated drug charge. Andrade and Rodriguez each spoke with police immediately following the shooting. Subsequently, and before [Wayne Miranda]'s trial, each was paid $3,000 by the New Bedford Area Chamber of Commerce pursuant to a reward program it sponsored. The $3,000 payment was given in return for information Andrade and Rodriguez respectively provided that helped lead to [Wayne Miranda]'s indictment.

"With respect to the events that preceded the shooting, an argument between the victim and [Wayne Miranda]'s older brother, Fagbemi Miranda (Fagbemi), first drew the attention of nearby residents. It took place on Purchase Street, in front of the apartment building in which Reis resided. Reis had known [Wayne Miranda] and Fagbemi, and recently had been introduced to, and spent time with, the victim. On the sidewalk, near Fagbemi and the victim, Reis saw a male standing near a tan automobile.

"Andrade and Rodriguez, who were in Rodriguez's fourth floor apartment on Bedford Street near the corner adjoining Purchase Street, also heard an argument outside. From a window overlooking Purchase Street, they observed Fagbemi, whom they knew, arguing with a man they did not know (the victim). They also observed another man who was on the sidewalk next to a black automobile.

"A few minutes later, [Wayne Miranda] left his house and joined in the argument between Fagbemi and the victim. He then went back inside his house. Soon thereafter, [Wayne Miranda] came back out of his house holding a black gun. His grandmother followed him, attempting to prevent him from leaving and trying to get him to return inside.

"[Wayne Miranda] jumped over the railing on the porch of the house, went over to the victim, and aimed the gun at him.

"Reis heard the victim say, 'Are you serious, Waynie? Are you serious? It's like that? It's like that?' Andrade and Rodriguez observed the victim raise his arms up and Andrade heard the victim say, 'No,' when [Wayne Miranda] pointed the gun at him. Andrade testified that Fagbemi walked over to [Wayne Miranda] saying, 'No, no, no.' The victim took off running up Purchase Street and then turned down Reis's driveway. [Wayne Miranda] ran after the victim, followed by Fagbemi, and next by the man who had been standing near the tan or black automobile. Reis, from a window, yelled to [Wayne Miranda] to think of his daughter.

"The accounts vary on what next took place. Reis, who had a limited view from her position, testified that [Wayne Miranda] stopped running at the end of her driveway where the driveway met the back yard. Fagbemi caught up to [Wayne Miranda] and the two exchanged words. Reis saw [Wayne Miranda] hand the gun to Fagbemi, saw Fagbemi raise his arm and point the gun toward the direction of a fence in her back yard, and then heard two gun shots. She dialed 911.

"Andrade and Rodriguez, who also had a limited view, heard two shots after the men went down Reis's driveway. They did not see [Wayne Miranda] hand the gun over to anyone else. After hearing the shots, Andrade dialed 911.

"Andrade and Rodriguez saw [Wayne Miranda] and Fagbemi leave the driveway. As they were leaving, Andrade saw one of the Miranda brothers pass the gun to the other, but could not say which one passed the gun or which one received the gun. Andrade and Rodriguez watched as [Wayne Miranda] and Fagbemi returned to their house. The other man returned to the automobile that he previously had been standing near and left in it.

"From Reis's driveway, police recovered two nine millimeter discharged cartridge casings that were manufactured by Remington Peters. No weapon was recovered. The Commonwealth's firearms identification expert gave his opinion that, based on his microscopic examinations, the discharged cartridge casings were fired from the same weapon. Particles of gunshot powder residue were detected on Fagbemi's hands. Police found papers belonging to the victim and to Casey DePina inside the victim's automobile.

"[Wayne Miranda] denied any involvement in the shooting. He stated that he had heard shots but had been inside his home working on his computer."

Trial: "[Wayne Miranda] did not testify at trial. His trial counsel attacked the credibility of Reis, Andrade, and Rodriguez in various ways, including bringing out the fact that each received some form of consideration, including monetary consideration, in exchange for their testimony. Also, through the cross-examination of Andrade and several police witnesses, the defense suggested that others may have perpetrated the shooting, and that the prosecution's investigation was faulty for not properly investigating these other possibilities.

"[Wayne Miranda]'s trial counsel called three witnesses: [Wayne Miranda]'s grandmother, who testified that he was home working on the computer at the time of the shooting, and two childhood friends of [Wayne Miranda], who testified that in the hours preceding the shooting, they had installed carpet at [Wayne Miranda]'s home and saw [Wayne Miranda] there. In support of his defense of misidentification, [Wayne Miranda]'s trial counsel called Geoffrey Loftus, a professor of psychology at the University of Washington in Seattle. Dr. Loftus testified concerning the process and quality of memory, and factors that can interfere with the ability to perceive and to recollect.

Wayne Miranda was indicted on a charge of murder in the first degree. In 2008, Wayne Miranda was convicted of murder in the second degree, assault and battery by means of a dangerous weapon (a firearm), and unlawful possession of a firearm.

Fagbemi Miranda was convicted in 2013 by a jury of first degree murder and sentenced to life in prison without the chance of parole.

Afterword: Wayne Miranda appealed his conviction in 2010, but his appeal was denied.

Further Reading:

"Commonwealth vs. Wayne Miranda." 458 Mass. 100, April 6, 2010-September 27, 2010. Bristol County. masscases.com/cases/sjc/458/458mass100.html.

"Commonwealth vs. Wayne Miranda." 474 Mass. 1008, May 12, 2016. Bristol County. masscases.com/cases/sjc/474/474mass1008.html.

"New Bedford Man Convicted of Fist-Degree Murder, Sentenced to Life in Prison." *SouthCoastToday.com*, 6 June 2013. southcoasttoday.com/article/20130606/News/306060352

Vaznis, James. "Man, 30, Arrested on Murder Charges." *The Boston Globe* (Boston, Massachusetts), 25 March 2008.

RUDOLPH SANTOS

Man shot to death on Hillman Street in New Bedford, Massachusetts, on December 24, 2005.

Victim: Rudolph Santos, age unknown.

Accused: Leslie Cole and Vincent Wadlington, ages unknown.

Details: The facts of the case, as detailed in Leslie Cole's appeal, are as follows:

"Shortly before Christmas in 2005, [Leslie Cole] and William Fields, who sold drugs together, discussed the possibility of robbing an unspecified drug dealer in order to resolve a cash flow problem. One day when the two men were visiting the New Bedford home of Fields's friend, Shannon Almeida, they asked her if she knew anyone who had a gun. Almeida responded that she did, and she introduced them to Vincent Wadlington. On the evening of December 24, while at Almeida's house, [Cole], Fields, and Wadlington discussed plans to commit a robbery. They then drove to an apartment in Brockton, where Wadlington retrieved a sawed-off rifle and some ammunition. The three men drove back to New Bedford, stopping at another house so [Cole] could get some dark clothes to wear. At around 10 P.M., [Cole], Fields, and Wadlington returned to Almeida's home, and, approximately ninety minutes later, they decided that they were 'ready to go and do this.' The three men traveled in [Cole]'s motor vehicle to a multifamily home on Hillman Street, parked nearby, put on gloves and masks, walked to the house, and approached the back door. Wadlington was carrying the rifle.

"That night, Christopher Busby was at home in that Hillman Street residence, spending time with his friend, the victim. The two men sold drugs from Busby's apartment, typically to people they already knew. They kept larger quantities of their supply in the cellar, which was always locked. The victim had possession of the key that night.

"Sometime before midnight, Wadlington knocked on the apartment's door. In response to Busby's inquiry about who was there, Wadlington replied that it was 'Eddie,' but neither Busby nor the victim recognized the voice. Busby told 'Eddie' to step near a window so he could see his face. Wadlington complied with the request, and he handed the rifle to [Cole]. Busby did not recognize 'Eddie,' told the man that he would not sell him any drugs, and watched him walk away from the apartment. Several minutes later, Busby started to open the door so he could look outside. [Cole], Wadlington, and Fields kicked the door and rushed into the apartment.

"[Cole] fought with Busby. As Busby tried to defend himself, he felt someone striking him from behind, and he turned to see Fields hitting him with a metal pipe. Wadlington fought with the victim. Shortly after the altercation began, Fields left the apartment, returned to [Cole]'s vehicle, drove to a nearby house, knocked on the front door, and asked the man who answered to call the police because he had heard gunshots. Fields then drove the vehicle back to where the three men originally had parked it, and he fled the scene on foot.

"Meanwhile, back at the apartment, Busby was stabbed multiple times with a knife before collapsing and passing out. When he regained consciousness, he heard men's voices in the kitchen questioning the victim about the location of the drugs and demanding the key to the cellar. Busby quickly grabbed a Samurai sword that was leaning against a wall in the kitchen, swung it at the two assailants, and stabbed one of the men in the leg. After fighting with someone as he made his way down a hallway, Busby managed to reach his bedroom, where he fell onto the bed. He had difficulty breathing and was bleeding. Busby still could hear voices from the kitchen, and he realized that the victim had surrendered the key to the cellar when he heard one of the men running down the cellar stairs and back up again, asking, 'Where are the drug[s]? Where are the drugs, Ru?' Busby then heard the sound of a gunshot and someone saying, 'It's only a .22 rifle.' The next thing Busby remembered was being treated by a paramedic.

"Shortly before 1 A.M. on December 25, New Bedford police Officer Barry Pacheco and Sergeant Francis Rodriques arrived at the Hillman Street residence. After entering the apartment, which was in complete disarray, they observed a man lying on the floor, showing no signs of life. They then heard yelling from another room and discovered Busby lying face down on a bed, covered in blood, saying that he had been stabbed. Paramedics soon arrived and determined that the victim was dead. Busby, who had puncture wounds all over his body, was transported to a hospital and subsequently spent a week in a different hospital recovering from numerous stab wounds. State police criminalists processed the crime scene, including the stairs and walls leading down to the cellar, and collected evidence.

"Following the events at Busby's apartment, Fields eventually returned to Almeida's home where he encountered [Cole], who had a bloody cloth wrapped around his thigh. When Fields asked [Cole] what had happened to his leg, [Cole] replied, 'Well, you know, this is what happened in the house.' [Cole] left Almeida's home at around 6 A.M. on December 25. That same day, an individual named 'Derrick Williams' was treated in the emergency room of Rhode Island Hospital for a laceration to his thigh. A few days later, Fields looked in the trunk of [Cole]'s car and saw what appeared to be a Samurai sword, along with the clothes that [Cole] had worn on the night of the assault. The two men drove to the docks located in the south end of New Bedford and threw the items in the ocean.

"Dr. William Zane, a medical examiner for the Commonwealth, performed the autopsy on the victim. He testified that the victim had a gunshot wound to his right cheek, lacerations to his left upper eyelid and lower lip, contusions to his left cheek and forehead, abrasions on his right cheek and jaw, a gaping cut on the back of his left hand that went to the bone, cuts to his right wrist and forearm, and an eight-inch deep stab wound to his left buttock. Dr. Zane concluded that the victim died from the gunshot wound to his head, which penetrated his brain. He further concluded that a contributing factor in the victim's death was the stab wound to his buttock, which penetrated his lower abdominal cavity."

Trial: Leslie Cole was indicted on March 3, 2006, of murder in the first degree. Cole was convicted of this on theories of deliberate premeditation, extreme atrocity or cruelty, and felony-murder. He was sentenced to life in prison without the possibility of parole.

Vincent Wadlington was convicted of murder in the first degree on theories of deliberate premeditation, extreme atrocity or cruelty, and felony murder. He was sentenced to life in prison without the possibility of parole.

Afterword: Leslie Cole appealed his conviction on multiple grounds. The court affirmed Cole's convictions and declined to grant relief.

Vincent Wadlington appealed his conviction on eight separate issues. The appeals court affirmed Wadlington's conviction and declined to order a new trial or reduce the conviction to a lesser degree of guilt.

Further Reading:

"Commonwealth vs. Leslie Cole." 473 Mass. 317, October 9, 2015-December 18, 2015. Bristol County. masscases.com/cases/sjc/473/473mass317.html.
"Commonwealth vs. Vincent Wadlington." 467 Mass. 192, October 11, 2013-February 14, 2014. Bristol County. law.justia.com/cases/massachusetts/supreme-court/volumes/467/467mass192.html.

KRISTA LUCIANNO

Woman strangled to death with a dog leash on North Main Street in Fall River, Massachusetts, on January 14, 2006.

Victim: Krista Lucianno, 17.

Accused: Christopher Banville, 33.

Details: According to the record of Banville's appeal in 2010, the facts of the crime are as follows:

"The seventeen year old [Lucianno] had made plans for an overnight visit on January 13, 2006, at the home of her maternal grandparents in Fall River. [Banville], her maternal uncle, lived in that home. He was approximately thirty-three years old at the time. The grandparents had two Labrador retrievers that reacted to strangers by barking and baring their teeth.

"During the evening of January 13, [Banville] complained twice to his father that the victim was talking on the telephone to a man he believed was too old for her. His father dismissed [Banville]'s complaints. Around midnight the grandfather went downstairs to check on the victim and [Banville]. The victim was asleep on the couch in the finished basement. He did not see [Banville].

"At around 2 A.M. on January 14 the grandmother was awakened by a sound similar to the alarm on her car, which she had parked in the driveway below her bedroom window. She did not hear the dogs bark, so she went back to sleep. At about 7:30 A.M. the grandfather discovered the victim's body on the floor of the garage, which is located off the finished basement. Her hair was bloodstained, and there was a pool of blood next to her head. She was not breathing and she had no pulse. Her body was cold. She was naked, except for the shirt that had been pulled halfway up her chest. A dog leash was wrapped around her neck, and she had a wound near her right temple. A crowbar was out of place in the garage. The dogs, which regularly slept in the garage, were sitting quietly next to the victim's body. When police and emergency medical technicians arrived, the dogs began barking and baring their teeth at them. It was later determined that the victim died as a result of either a broken neck or a ligature strangulation by the dog leash around her neck.

"In addition to the blood on the victim's hair and the garage floor, there was blood spatter inside the garage, blood on the couch where the victim's grandfather saw her sleeping, and blood on the wall of the stairwell leading to the upper floors of the house.

"[Banville] was nowhere to be found, and the grandmother's car was missing. [Banville] did not have a driver's license, and he had been told he could not use the car. He knew the grandmother kept her car keys in her coat pocket, which she hung in a second-floor closet. Her car keys were missing. Her pocket book, which she kept on the door handle of that closet, was in the basement near the couch. The money she had put inside was gone.

"The missing car was equipped with a 'LoJack' tracking device, which eventually led to its being stopped by a Maryland State police officer on Interstate Route 95 near Baltimore at about 3:15 P.M. on January 14, 2006. [Banville] was the operator and sole occupant at the time. After he was ordered out of the car, the officer noticed what appeared to be bloodstains on the front thighs of his jeans. [Banville] was placed under arrest.

Banville's clothing was secured as evidence and his body was digitally photographed, "allowing the officers to 'zoom in' on the images with the use of a computer; this revealed reddish stains around his cuticles.

A warrant was executed on Banville's person and swabbings of his hands, penis, and genital area were conducted, as well as a combing of his pubic hairs; and collection of his DNA by means of a buccal swab.

"[The police chemist] opined that the victim's DNA was present in the blood swabbed from [Banville]'s fingernails and penis, his shirt collar, the area of the zipper on his jeans, and the crowbar. [Banville]'s DNA was found in swabs of the victim's right hand fingernails, and the saliva swabbed from her breasts…the probability that the DNA was that of someone else was one in 5 quadrillion as to the sample under the victim's fingernails, and one in 410 trillion as to the saliva sample."

Trial: Christopher Banville was convicted of murder in the first degree on theories of deliberate premeditation and extreme atrocity or cruelty. He was additionally convicted of larceny of a motor vehicle.

Afterword: Christopher Banville appealed his conviction in 2010 on the basis of ineffective counsel at trial. The court ruled that after reviewing the briefs, transcripts, entire record, and exhibits, that there was no reason to reduce the degree of guilt or order a new trial.

Further Reading:

"Commonwealth vs. Christopher Banville." 457 Mass. 530, April 8, 2010-August 13, 2010. Bristol County. masscases.com/cases/sjc/457/457mass530.html.

NATHAN HARRIGAN

Man shot at 18 Quequechan Street in Fall River, Massachusetts, on March 18, 2006, with death occurring the next day (March 19, 2006).

Victim: Nathan Harrigan, 22.

Accused: Leonard Gonsalves, 26, Sarath Lon, 23.

Details: Nathan Harrigan was shot about 2 a.m. and died from his wounds the next day at Rhode Island Hospital. He was shot seven times by a .22-caliber pistol. Police recovered 18 spent shell casings but did not locate the murder weapon at the scene, the porch of his apartment at 18 Quequechan Street in Fall River.

It was believed that this shooting was a joint venture, carried out by Leonard Gonsalves and Sarath Lon serving as the getaway driver and accomplice. The district attorney's office said that the motive was gang-related—Harrigan was a reputed member of the Crips and Gonsalves was allegedly a member of the Bloods.

Trial: Sarath Lon was found guilty of second-degree murder and sentenced to life in prison with the possibility of parole in 15 years. In 2008, Leonard Gonsalves was acquitted of the murder at trial.

Further Reading:

Daley, Lauren. "Arrest Made in Fall River Murder." *SouthCoastToday.com*, 21 March 2006.

Holtzman, Michael. "City Man Guilty in Murder." WickedLocal.com, 17 December, 2008. wickedlocal.com/article/20081217/news/312179449.

Richmond, Will. "Gonsalves Acquitted of Murder." *The Herald News* (Fall River, Massachusetts), 20 November 2008.

JUSTIN BARRY-HENDERSON

Man shot to death in the doorway of the City Lights nightclub on Union Street in New Bedford, Massachusetts, on May 21, 2006.

Victim: Justin Barry-Henderson, 20.

Accused: David DePina II, 23.

Details: In a gang-related shooting, Justin Barry-Henderson was shot 10 times and killed by David DePina II. Another victim, John C. Burgos (*see Dana Haywood case*), survived his wounds. Barry-Henderson and Burgos were reputed members of the United Front gang. The father of the victim, Cory Henderson, was sympathetic to the family of Bernadette DePina, the mother of the accused killer, who was shot and killed in her home four days after the death of Barry-Henderson, in a possible revenge murder.

Police identified DePina as a member of the Monte Park gang, a rival of the United Front gang. Two police officers who were on patrol near the shooting saw DePina and another man fire at Barry-Henderson. As DePina fled, they tackled him and recovered the murder weapon. The second shooter escaped and remained unknown.

Trial: After four days of deliberations, a deal was made whereby David DePina would plead guilty to manslaughter, assault and battery with a dangerous weapon, and unlawful carrying of a firearm. In exchange for his plea, DePina was sentenced to 12 years and one day in prison.

Further Reading:

"'Crunchy' DePina Accepts Plea Deal, Sentenced to 12 Years in Prison." *SouthCoastToday.com*, 13 June 2009. southcoasttoday.com/article/20090613/news/906130335

"Father of Murder Victim Speaks." *Seacoastonline.com*, 30 May 2006. seacoastonline.com/article/20060530/News/305309971.

THOMAS REYNOLDS

Young man stabbed to death in his car near a LukOil gas station on Route 6 off of Alden Road in Fairhaven, Massachusetts, on May 28, 2006.

Victim: Thomas Reynolds, 18.

Accused: John Blomgren, 19.

Details: According to reporting in *The Boston Globe*, three teenagers (Thomas Reynolds, John Blomgren, and Mathew Martins) robbed the house of one of their girlfriends and then drove around arguing about whether to return the stolen items. Blomgren, it is said, spilled orange juice in the Jeep Cherokee of Thomas Reynolds, causing an argument which escalated into a fight which evolved into a murder. Thomas Reynolds was stabbed at least seven times and left to die behind the steering wheel in his vehicle.

All three teenagers were students at Fairhaven High School. Blomgren pleaded not guilty and Martens was arraigned on charges of breaking and entering.

Trial: In lieu of a trial, John Blomgren pleaded guilty to manslaughter and was sentenced to serve 15 to 17 years in prison. Blomgren claimed that Reynolds pulled the knife first and Blomgren acted in self-defense.

Further Reading:

Cramer, Maria. "Police Say Break-In Preceded Fatal Stabbing." *The Boston Globe* (Boston, Massachusetts), 31 May 2006.
"Fairhaven Man Pleads Guilty to Killing Friend." *Boston.com*, 27 May 2010. boston.com/news/local/massachusetts/articles/2010/05/27/fairhaven_man_pleads_guilty_to_killing_friend/
Ranalli, Ralph. "Housebreak Probed in Slaying." *The Boston Globe* (Boston, Massachusetts), 30 May 2006.

ANTONIO SEMEDO

Man shot to death as he drove his car on Route 18 in New Bedford, Massachusetts, on June 18, 2006.

Victim: Antonio Semedo, 35.

Accused: Terrell Baptiste, 20, and Reggie Greene, 24.

Details: Antonio Semedo, father of a young child and brother of a New Bedford police officer, was shot and killed in an apparent case of mistaken identity as he drove his car on Route 18 on June 18, 2006, in New Bedford.

The case remained unsolved for four years. In 2010, Terrell Baptiste, a United Front gang member, serving a 15-year federal prison sentence for drug and gun convictions, was charged as the gunman in the crime. Reggie Greene, the driver of the vehicle that was following Semedo, was also charged with murder and accessory to murder before the fact.

Baptiste and Greene were following Semedo thinking he was a rival gang member. "On the night Semedo was killed...Greene, Baptiste and other unidentified members of the United Front street gang left a house party and drove to the South End, when Greene received a telephone call regarding the location of one of the gunmen in his brother's murder. Reggie Greene, Baptiste and their friends allegedly found Semedo's vehicle, followed the car onto Route 18 and tried to verify that the operator was the gang member they were targeting when shots rang out. Semedo's vehicle crashed on the off-ramp to South Second Street. A witness saw the incident and called police."

Trial: After only three hours of deliberation, a jury acquitted Terrell Baptiste of murder, conspiracy to commit murder, assault with intent to commit murder, and assault and battery with a dangerous weapon. There was no published reporting as to the outcome of Reggie Greene's case.

Further Reading:

Fraga, Brian. "Gang Member in Federal Prison Charged with 2006 New Bedford Murder." *SouthCoastToday.com*, 2 June 2010.

JOHN OLIVEIRA JR.

Man shot to death in Swansea, Massachusetts, on July 5, 2006.

Victim: John Oliveira Jr., 35.

Accused: Derek Woollam, 26.

Details: According to Derek Woollam's appeal in 2017, the facts of the case as presented at trial are as follows:

"In 2006, John Oliveira ran a large-scale drug operation out of a studio apartment in a duplex in Swansea. At the time of his death, he had two 'employees': [Woollam], who delivered marijuana to customers and collected the money; and Dylan Hodgate, who broke down the larger quantities of marijuana and repackaged them into smaller bags. Oliveira's girl friend lived in the other apartment in the duplex.

"Oliveira had several rules in connection with his drug business, all designed to protect the operation and minimize detection. For instance, the exterior doors were always to be kept locked, no others could be brought to the house, and one of the four of them was always to be present at the house. Further, [Woollam], the girl friend, and Hodgate were prohibited from being under the influence of drugs.

"In January or February of 2006, Oliveira's girl friend discovered that [Woollam] was using drugs, and began procuring pills from him. [Woollam] and Oliveira's girl friend agreed not to tell Oliveira about their use of pills. Over the course of several months, the relationship between Oliveira and [Woollam] deteriorated. Oliveira complained to his girl friend that [Woollam] was 'never on time,' was 'a slacker,' and 'wasn't doing what he was supposed to do.'

"On July 4, 2006, Oliveira discovered a text message from his girl friend on [Woollam]'s cellular telephone asking [Woollam] for pills. Oliveira was very upset and told [Woollam], 'You broke the rules.' When [Woollam] lied and said that the pills were likely for the girl friend's cousin, Oliveira said that he would speak to the girl friend that night and would 'let [[Woollam]] know' after that. Oliveira sent a text message to his girl friend to let her know that he was 'pissed,' and that he would be coming by the apartment to discuss the matter, warning her 'not [to] lie.'

"At approximately 12:15 a.m., Oliveira received a telephone call and told his girl friend that he was going to pick up Hodgate and would be right back. He never returned.

"The last call made from Oliveira's cellphone was to Hodgate's cellphone at 1:28 a.m. At approximately 1:43 a.m., a Swansea police officer on routine patrol saw a black Mercury Sable (the make, model, and color of [Woollam]'s automobile) pull out of the driveway of the house with two people inside.

"The next morning, Oliveira's girl friend saw Oliveira's automobile in the driveway. The interior door to the studio apartment was locked, and there was no answer when she knocked. This was unusual because Hodgate was normally supposed to be there during the day. She was unable to reach Oliveira, [Woollam], or Hodgate by telephone despite many attempts over the course of the day. When she returned later that afternoon, Oliveira's automobile was in the same spot. When she knocked on the studio apartment door, there was still no answer, and she noticed that the television inside was abnormally loud. Eventually, she discovered that the exterior back door to the studio apartment was unlocked. When she entered, she found Oliveira's body lying in a pool of blood. He had been shot several times and was cold to the touch.

"An autopsy revealed that Oliveira had been shot four times. Two shots to the head were fatal: one bullet entered through the left cheek, and a second entered through the right forehead. The location and path of a third bullet, which entered the lower right side of his torso, was consistent with Oliveira having been shot while lying on his back. The fourth bullet grazed the back of his head.

"Soon after Oliveira's girl friend discovered the body, [Woollam] arrived. Before the police were called, [Woollam] removed marijuana in large duffel bags from the studio apartment and left with them in his black four-door automobile.

"Over the next few days, [Woollam] enlisted help from others to distribute the marijuana that came from the studio apartment, and to clear out a storage locker in his name containing guns and ammunition. He also removed the batteries and subscriber identity module (SIM) cards from his cellphones to avoid being tracked. He admitted to one of the people who assisted him, Michael Pacheco, that he killed the victim because he believed that the victim was going to kill him after learning about the pills, and that Oliveira suspected that [Woollam] was having an affair with Oliveira's girl friend. One to two weeks later, [Woollam] and Pacheco went together to burn a bag containing the sneakers and clothes from the night of the shooting."

Trial: In 2009, a jury convicted Derek Woollam of first degree murder after two hours of deliberations. He was sentenced to life in prison without the possibility of parole.

Afterword: Derek Woollam appealed his conviction in 2017 on the grounds that there was miscarriage of justice on multiple levels. The appeals court disagreed with each charge and denied Woollam's motion for a new trial.

Further Reading:

"Commonwealth vs. Derek Woollam." 478 Mass. 493, October 6, 2017-December 13, 2017. Bristol County. masscases.com/cases/sjc/478/478mass493.html.

"D.A. Convicts Somerset Man of First Degree Murder." *thesunchronicle.com*, 12 February 2009. thesunchronicle.com/taunton/d-a-convicts-somerset-man-of-first-degree-murder/article_ca93f18d-0b4a-5499-8ce7-b6a604994844.html

VALERIE ORANSKY

Woman stabbed to death at Old Country Buffet in Dartmouth, Massachusetts, on July 22, 2006.

Victim: Valerie Oransky, 39.

Accused: Ryan Jones, 28.

Details: According to the appeal of Ryan Jones in 2017, the facts of the case as presented at trial are as follows:

"In July, 2006, [Jones] was working as a dishwasher at a restaurant in Dartmouth. He had been working at the restaurant for more than three years, and his performance was generally satisfactory, but he sometimes had disputes with the manager (victim) over his use of the dishwasher to wash pots and pans...The victim repeatedly told [Jones] not to put the pots and pans in the dishwasher. He often would do so anyway, and undertook various methods to conceal this from the victim.

"At some point, [Jones] began to express his anger about the victim's instructions on dishwashing to other employees. [Jones] told one coworker, 'I'm going to kill that f'ing B.' Another coworker reported that, at least once a week, [Jones] made gestures such as holding up his middle finger behind the victim's back. Another coworker said that [Jones] would 'have a bung[e]e cord in his hand and he would snap it like he was going to choke [the victim] with it.' Approximately two weeks before the stabbing, [Jones] told one of his coworkers that he was going to take the victim to the bathroom early in the morning before the restaurant got busy and stab or strangle her. Several of the restaurant employees reported this statement to the victim, but she interpreted it as a joke.

"On July 22, 2006, [Jones] arrived at work earlier than he did ordinarily. He told the victim that something was wrong with one of the toilets, and they walked toward the women's restroom. Shortly thereafter, [Jones] left the restroom and told a coworker that she should telephone 911 because someone had come through the back door with a knife and had stabbed the victim. By the time paramedics arrived, the victim was not breathing. She had been stabbed multiple times, strangled, and beaten. The medical examiner determined that the cause of death was multiple stab wounds, with injury to the aorta, lung, and kidney, and blunt trauma with brain contusions. A knife, a bungee cord, and a pipe from the dishwasher were found in the bathroom stall where the victim's body was found. A membership card for a wholesale club with the name of someone who did not work for the restaurant also was found on the floor near the victim.

"While many of [Jones]'s coworkers were visibly upset at news of what had happened to the victim, [Jones] was described as being calm…[Jones] had blood spots on his face and glasses and was hiding his left hand. [Jones] told…the investigating officers that the perpetrator was a black man wearing a white shirt, black pants, a dark hooded sweatshirt, white sneakers, leather gloves, and a black mask. He said that the man had come through the back door with a knife and initially tried to stab him, before stabbing the victim and running out the back door.

"Several restaurant employees had seen [Jones] heading toward the bathroom with the victim, and the investigation almost immediately focused on [Jones]…[Jones] had visible cuts on one hand and on his left side, which he said he had sustained when he attempted to defend himself from the victim's assailant. Ultimately…[Jones] told police that he had stabbed the victim; it was a 'mistake,' but he did not know 'what else…he [was] going to do' because she kept 'nagging' him.

"DNA tests on the blood found on [Jones]'s glasses, socks, and watch matched the victim. [Jones] was a potential contributor to blood found on the knife, a handicapped stall in the women's bathroom that had its own sink, and the wholesale club card."

Trial: A jury found Ryan Jones guilty of murder in the first degree on theories of deliberate premeditation and extreme atrocity or cruelty. He was sentenced to life in prison without the possibility of parole.

Afterword: In 2017, Jones appealed his conviction of first degree murder on the grounds that he was a developmentally disabled person and not competent to stand trial. The appeals court disagreed and the verdict and sentencing was upheld.

Further Reading:

Bloomkatz, Ari. "Worker Charged in Slaying at Dartmouth Restaurant." *The Boston Globe* (Boston, Massachusetts), 23 July 2006.

"Commonwealth vs. Ryan Jones." 479 Mass. 1, November 10, 2017-February 20, 2017. Bristol County. masscases.com/cases/sjc/479/479mass1.html.

Ellement, John R. "Suspect in Killing Said to Tell of His Plan." *The Boston Globe* (Boston, Massachusetts), 25 July 2006.

ESTEBAN TUM CHACH

Man stabbed to death on the corner of North Front Street and Bullard Street in New Bedford, Massachusetts, on September 14, 2006.

Victim: Esteban Tum Chach, age unknown.

Accused: Jonathan Ashley, age unknown.

Details: According to the appeal filed by Jonathan Ashley in 2012, the facts of the case as presented at trial are as follows:

"On the evening of September 14, 2006, the victim, Esteban Tum Chach, a Guatemalan male who stood five feet and one inch tall, and two Guatemalan friends, Carlos and Juan, were walking down North Front Street in New Bedford, headed toward 12 Bullard Street, where both Carlos and Juan lived. The victim was wearing a hat, and had a cellular telephone clipped to his right pocket. As the three approached the corner of North Front Street and Bullard Street, they encountered [Ashley], who was standing outside 352 North Front Street. Without apparent provocation, [Ashley] started an altercation with these men with actions that included taking or knocking off the victim's hat; asking for money; saying, 'Give me five dollars for your hat'; and taking his cellular telephone. An argument ensued that evolved into a fistfight. At this point, [Ashley] drew a knife from his pocket and slashed at the victim, fatally stabbing him in his right side. The fight lasted only a couple of minutes; by the time it was finished, the victim was bleeding heavily. After he stabbed the victim, [Ashley] ran inside 352 North Front Street. About four or five people were standing around [Ashley] and the victim during the fight, one of whom was Joanne Renaud. She saw [Ashley] start an altercation with the three men, grab the victim's hat and demand money for it, hit the victim, and then stab him when he tried to fight back; she also saw [Ashley] run into 352 North Front Street.

"Meanwhile, Carlos telephoned the police at the victim's request, and after the fight was finished, Renaud also telephoned 911; Carlos remained at the scene, as did Renaud and her roommate, who both tried to help the victim. Police and paramedics arrived shortly. The victim later died from this injury.

"The next day, parole Officer Robert Mello, who knew [Ashley], was asked to assist in locating him. Between 4:00 and 6:00 P.M., Mello went to 352 North Front Street and entered the building through the rear. He located [Ashley], crouched down in an attic area on the opposite side of the attic from where Mello entered. At that point, police officers assisted in taking [Ashley] into custody...[Ashley] appeared to have a small abrasion on his cheek or near his hairline, and an injury on his leg, which he said that he had sustained a couple of days earlier."

Trial: Jonathan Ashley was convicted of murder in the second degree. He was sentenced to life in prison with the possibility of parole.

Afterword: Jonathan Ashley appealed his conviction in 2012 on several grounds: denial of his motion to suppress, prejudice exhibited by the prosecutor in his cross-examination of Ashley, and the prejudicial remarks made in the prosecutor's closing statements. Ashley's appeal was denied and his conviction was affirmed.

Further Reading:

"Commonwealth vs. Jonathan Ashley." 82 Mass. App. Ct. 748, September 12, 2012-November 15, 2012. Bristol County. masscases.com/cases/app/82/82massappct748.html.

JAMES CADET

Young man shot to death at the Sunset Hill Housing Project in Fall River, Massachusetts, on September 25, 2006.

Victim: James Cadet, 23.

Accused: David Miller, 29.

Details: According to the appeal of David Miller in 2016, the facts of the case as presented at his trial are as follows:

"At approximately 9:30 P.M. on September 25, Fall River police officers arrived at the Sunset Hill housing development to find the victim lying on a walkway. He had been shot numerous times and had succumbed to those wounds.

"Multiple witnesses observed a large person, ostensibly the shooter, wearing a dark, hooded sweatshirt in the vicinity of the crime scene shortly after hearing gunshots. One witness saw the victim fall on the shooter and the shooter kick the victim multiple times before fleeing the scene. As the shooter fled, another witness recognized him as [Miller] based on his gait.

"At the time of the shooting, [Miller] lived in a unit in Sunset Hill that belonged to his girl friend, Christina Helger. The victim, who had been friends with [Miller], was also a resident of Sunset Hill. However, on the day before the murder [Miller] and the victim got into an argument after Helger had allowed the victim to use her bathroom while [Miller] was not home. As a result of this argument, the victim later returned to Helger's apartment brandishing a firearm. The victim pointed the weapon toward her apartment and stated that there would be 'problems' if she and [Miller] did not leave Sunset Hill. The victim then left without further incident.

"On the day of the murder, Helger twice spoke with the some of [Miller]'s friends over the telephone. These telephone calls led her to drive to a nearby fast food restaurant, meet [Miller]'s friends, and direct them to her apartment. Ultimately she and the group of friends entered Sunset Hill, and got as far as the first building, when they heard gunshots and fled the scene.

"Within five minutes of hearing the gunshots, Helger received a telephone call from [Miller], who asked her to pick him up on a street adjacent to Sunset Hill. When Helger picked [Miller] up, he instructed her to drive to Boston.

"On the way there, [Miller] told Helger that '[the victim] got shot, and that [Miller]]did what he had to do.' Additionally, he began to pray, and he instructed Helger that, if asked, she should lie and say that they had left Fall River at 6 P.M. [Miller] also told Helger to put her hands up if they were stopped by the police because the police would think that [Miller] had 'something on him' and he did not want Helger to get shot.

"After arriving in Boston, Helger observed [Miller] wiping blood off his face. [Miller] then purchased new shoes at a store and threw the pair of shoes he had been wearing in a trash barrel. After visiting his brother at his brother's house, [Miller] and Helger spent the night at a hotel in Boston.

"The following day, Helger and [Miller] traveled to his mother's house, where he destroyed the subscriber identity module located in his cellular telephone.

"The police recovered a black, hooded sweatshirt with the victim's blood, along with a pair of gloves that tested positive for gunshot residue, on the sidewalk of a street near Sunset Hill. They also recovered…twelve .223-caliber shell casings from the scene of the crime. It was later determined that the .223-caliber cartridge casings were fired from a Ruger Mini-14 rifle (rifle) recovered from the residence located in the Dorchester section of Boston.

"At trial, Steve Smith, another Sunset Hill resident, identified the rifle recovered from the Dorchester residence as the rifle that he had given to [Miller] approximately two weeks before the shooting, in exchange for 'crack' cocaine. Smith also gave [Miller] multiple rifle magazines and numerous rounds of .223-caliber ammunition during that transaction. Shortly after the shooting, the police executed a search warrant for [Miller]'s apartment and recovered…a rifle case, .223-caliber ammunition, and rifle magazines, which Smith identified at trial as having previously been his."

Trial: In 2009, a jury convicted David Miller of murder in the first degree, on a theory of deliberate premeditation, and of the unlawful possession of a firearm. Miller was sentenced to life in prison without the possibility of parole.

Afterword: David Miller appealed his conviction in 2016 on the grounds that the judge at his trial improperly denied his pretrial motion to suppress evidence seized from the basement of the apartment adjoining his (among other assertions).

The appeals court denied David Miller's motion for a new trial.

Further Reading:

"Commonwealth vs. David T. Miller." 475 Mass. 212, May 6, 2016-August 17, 2016. Bristol County. masscases.com/cases/sjc/475/475mass212.html.

DWAYNE LASSITER

Man stabbed to death in driveway at 96 Washington Street in Fairhaven, Massachusetts, on November 12, 2006.

Victim: Dwayne Lassiter, 40.

Accused: David Ford, 51.

Details: Dwayne Lassiter often parked his sport utility vehicle in his neighbor's driveway. Both he and David Ford worked for the same building contractor and were friends. However, seemingly out of the blue, Ford became angry when he saw Lassiter's car in his driveway and started a fight with him. He then pulled out a knife and stabbed Dwayne Lassiter to death.

"Ford had a history of assault and battery in several states, including Arkansas and Indiana, but had lived peaceably in the apartment he rented from his boss" ("Neighbor is Slain").

Ford was charged with first-degree murder. He appeared at his arraignment, where he pleaded not guilty, in a wheelchair and wearing a hospital gown. Ford had suffered wounds to his left thigh and face during the altercation with Lassiter.

An off-duty firefighter witnessed the entire event and attempted to break up the fight.

Trial: In lieu of a trial, David Ford pleaded guilty to manslaughter in 2011 and was sentenced to ten years in prison. He was awarded time served while he was awaiting trial, meaning he would serve an additional 6 months and 8 years. With this math in mind, Ford has since been released after serving his sentence.

Further Reading:

Brown, Curt. "Ford Pleads Guilty to Manslaughter in 2006 Fairhaven Stabbing. SouthCoastToday.com, 22 March 2011. southcoasttoday.com/article/20110322/news/103220312.

Cramer, Maria. "Neighbor is Slain in Driveway Dispute." *The Boston Globe* (Boston, Massachusetts), 14 November 2006.

WAYNE MENDES

Man stabbed to death in his home at 1061 Wood Street in Swansea, Massachusetts, on December 5, 2006.

Victim: Wayne Mendes, 52.

Accused: Robert Gonsalves, 21.

Details: Wayne Mendes and Robert Gonsalves were friends at the time of the murder and had been drinking wine at Mendes' home the evening before the event. Gonsalves was to spend the night so that the two could get an early start in the morning, both working for Mendes' landscaping business.

"At some point that evening, the defendant attacked the victim with a steak knife he obtained from the victim's kitchen, after rejecting a sexual advances by Mendes. After the killing, the defendant took the keys to the victim's Hummer and fled the scene in the vehicle. He crashed into a telephone pole approximately a quarter mile down the road, incapacitating the vehicle. The defendant then ran on foot to the nearby Swansea Mall, where he summonsed help for the victim" ("City Man").

Trial: In lieu of a trial, Robert Gonsalves pleaded guilty to the reduced charge of second-degree murder and larceny of a vehicle in 2009. He was sentenced to life in prison with the possibility of parole in 15 years. He was also given an additional 5 years in prison for the larceny charge.

Further Reading:

Richmond, Will. "City Man Gets 20 Years for Murdering his Boss." *The Herald News* (Fall River, Massachusetts), 14 October 2009.

TORY MARANDOS, ROBERT CARREIRO, & SCOTT MEDEIROS

Murder/Suicide at the Foxy Lady club on Route 6 in New Bedford, Massachusetts, on December 12, 2006.

Victims: Robert Carreiro, 33, Tory Marandos, 30.

Accused: Scott C. Medeiros, 35.

Details: Wearing a black suit, ski mask, and bulletproof vest, Scott Medeiros entered the Foxy Lady club in New Bedford, after being kicked out earlier for a dispute with the bartender, and hustled the waitresses and dancers, 14 in all, into the dressing room, after telling them he wasn't after them.

Medeiros then began shooting the occupants using a high-powered rifle and a semi-automatic weapon.

Medeiros killed Tory Medeiros and Robert Carreiro, managers of the club. He wounded three other people, including two responding police officers and a man in the bar who was shot in both legs.

Medeiros went outside and shot at a police cruiser, wounding two. One hundred officers surrounded the club in the ensuing standoff. "Medeiros telephoned them from inside and told them he would not surrender. Inside the dressing room, he ripped off his mask and let the women leave the club. At about 5 a.m., three hours after he had stormed the club, police officers carrying automatic weapons swarmed in and found Medeiros dead. He had shot himself" ("Night of Terror").

Further Reading:

Ellement, John R., and Michael Levenson. *The Boston Globe* (Boston, Massachusetts), 13 December 2006.
"Three Die in Club Shooting." *The Central New Jersey Home News* (New Brunswick, New Jersey), 13 December 2006.

SHAKEEM DAVIS

Young man shot to death in an apartment on Amity Street in Fall River, Massachusetts, on January 17, 2007.

Victim: Shakeem Davis, 15.

Accused: Kyron Gorham, 18, Jason Bates, 18.

Details: According to the appeal of Kyron Gorham in 2015, the facts of the case as presented at trial are as follows:

"[Kyron Gorham] was one of ten to fifteen people who attended a party hosted by Kayla Aguiar at her home in Fall River on January 16, 2007. People were drinking alcohol, and it is not clear whether drugs also were used. [Gorham] did not appear intoxicated. [Gorham] left the party to get more beer. While he was gone, Kayla Joseph and Jasmine Dugan started arguing, and then fighting physically, over a young man named Shakeem Davis, who was not at the party. After some partygoers broke up the fight, Joseph telephoned Davis for a ride home. Davis and some friends arrived. Joseph got into their vehicle. At that time, there had been no communication between anyone at the party, other than Joseph, and anyone in the vehicle. They drove to an apartment on Amity Street. When [Gorham] returned to the party, the festive atmosphere had been dampened by the altercation between Joseph and Dugan. Disappointed and annoyed, [Gorham] telephoned Davis, and they argued. Angered by Davis's insults, [Gorham] went to a friend's apartment to get a rifle that [Gorham] kept there.

"[Gorham] and a friend arrived at the Amity Street apartment where Davis and Joseph had gone. Davis and [Gorham] cursed each other. [Gorham] fired his rifle once at Davis, who was sitting on a couch. He fired several more times as Davis ran for cover. Davis sustained a graze wound to his right hand. Bullets penetrated his anterior right and left thighs, his lower left and lower right back, and the left side of his lower torso. [Gorham] ran from the apartment. He hid the rifle in some bushes. Davis died as a result of multiple gunshot wounds.

"After being told that the police were looking for him, [Gorham] left town. He was arrested in Syracuse, New York, on February 13, 2007, after first giving a false name to police. He gave a video-recorded statement to Syracuse police, which was played for the jury. In his statement [Gorham] admitted shooting Davis. He said he only wanted to scare Davis for being disrespectful. When he pointed the rifle at Davis, Davis grabbed the barrel of the rifle and a tug-of-war ensued. [Gorham] said he pulled the trigger a few times. Davis released his grasp on the barrel after being shot in the chest and stomach. [Gorham] fled, and he discarded the rifle in some nearby bushes."

Trial: Kyron Gorham was convicted of first degree murder and sentenced to life in prison. Murder charges were dropped against Jason Bates and he received a 4-5 year sentence as an accessory to murder.

Afterword: Kyron Gorham appealed his conviction in 2015. His motion for a new trial and reconsideration was denied.

Further Reading:

"Commonwealth vs. Kyron A. Gorham." 472 Mass. 112, March 6, 2015-July 8, 2015. Bristol County. masscases.com/cases/sjc/472/472mass112.html.

JASON GLOVER

Man stabbed to death in home at 788 Dwelly Street in Fall River, Massachusetts, on February 27, 2007.

Victim: Jason Glover, 28.

Accused: Christopher Fisher, 21, Derek Carvalho, 18.

Details: Jason Glover was stabbed to death in Fall River, allegedly after Glover received drugs from Christopher Fisher and Derek Carvalho and refused to pay them.

Trial: Derek Carvalho was charged with accessory after the fact in the stabbing death of Jason Glover. He was held in jail until 2009, when he was released after changing his plea to guilty. The maximum sentence for his charges was 20 months, which he had essentially served. He was sentenced to serve 6 months of probation.

Christopher Fisher was charged with murder in the first degree. In 2010, he pleaded guilty to the reduced charge of manslaughter and sentenced to 19 years and one day in state prison.

Further Reading:

Richmond, Will. "Accessory to Fall River Murder, Derek Carvalho Now Serving Probation." *The Herald News* (Fall River, Massachusetts), 9 December 2009.

Richmond, Will. "Fall River Man Pleads Guilty to Reduced Charge of Manslaughter." *The Herald News* (Fall River, Massachusetts), 9 February 2010.

Richmond, Will. "Man Charged in Murder Case Out of Jail." *The Herald News* (Fall River, Massachusetts), 23 May 2009.

WILLIAM DUPRAS

Man beat to death on Hancock Street in Fall River, Massachusetts, on April 13, 2007.

Victim: William Dupras, 32.

Accused: Stephen Barreto, 35.

Details: On April 10, 2007, Stephen Barreto was beaten and robbed in a deal for fake drugs by William Dupras, Michael Sama, and Donald V. Alphonso. It was during this fight that Barreto killed Dupras.

"According to police reports, Sama, Alfonso and a third man, William Dupras, picked up Barreto as part of a prearranged meeting with the intention of selling him 'beat bags' of cocaine. During the incident the three men allegedly attempted to beat Barreto for the $200 to $300 he possessed. Eventually, the car Sama was operating stopped on Hancock Street, where Dupras and Alfonso got out. Barreto told police he attempted to step out of the car and Dupras yelled at him to get back inside.

"He was then told to hand over his cash and, fearing he was going to be robbed, attempted to push Dupras and run away. Dupras then allegedly grabbed Barreto by the neck, throwing him to the pavement, where a fight quickly ensued.

"Barreto said that while lying on the ground being chocked by Dupras, he then felt Alfonso and Sama kicking him. Barreto said he eventually tried to flee, only to be grabbed by the neck again by Dupras, who threw him back to the ground, grinding his face into the pavement while Alfonso and Sama resumed kicking him.

"A short time later, Barreto said he saw Alfonso and Sama go into the car's trunk, emerging with a 3-foot-long metal pipe appearing to be a tire iron. Seeing this, Barreto said he managed to stand up as he continued to fight with Dupras and then grabbed a item he believed to be a knife off the ground.

"Fearing for his life, Barreto said, he blindly swung his arms, ultimately striking Dupras in the back. Seconds later, according to the police report, Dupras released Barreto and yelled 'I've been stabbed.'

"Dupras was transferred to Rhode Island Hospital where he was pronounced dead" ("Two Face Charges").

Aftermath: A Grand Jury declined to indict Stephen Barreto on manslaughter charges, ruling it a justifiable homicide.

Michael P. Sama, 25, and Donald V. Alfonso, 24, were charged with assault to rob, armed assault to rob, assault with a dangerous weapon, two counts of assault and battery with a dangerous weapon, conspiracy to commit assault to rob, conspiracy to commit assault with a dangerous weapon, two counts of conspiracy to commit assault and battery with a dangerous weapon, and assault and battery.

Update: According to a press release issued on September 29, 2011 by the DEA: "Four men have been sentenced to federal prison for distributing oxycodone in the Fall River, Mass., and Tiverton, R.I., areas. The four were arrested following an investigation which began in the summer of 2010 by agents from the DEA Worcester Tactical Diversion Squad, which included numerous undercover purchases of substantial quantities of oxycodone.

"Steven W. Derr, Special Agent in Charge of the New England field division of the Drug Enforcement Administration for New (DEA) and U.S. Attorney Peter F. Neronha announced that **Steve Jason Barreto**, 21, of Fall River has been sentenced to 70 months in federal prison; Aaron Almeida, 30, of Tiverton, has been sentenced to 37 months imprisonment; **Donald Alfonso**, 30, of Fall River, has been sentenced to 96 months imprisonment; and James Patricio, 25, of Fall River has been sentenced to 24 months in federal prison.

"According to court documents and information presented to the Court, between June 2010 and January 2011, agents with the DEA Worcester Tactical Diversion Squad began an investigation into oxycodone distributors operating in the Fall River and Tiverton, R.I., area. As part of the investigation, DEA agents conducted a number of controlled purchases of oxycodone from the targets. As a result of the investigation, Jason Barreto and Donald Alfonso were charged, arrested and pled guilty to conspiring with each other to distribute oxycodone; and Aaron Almeida and James Patricio were charged, arrested and pled guilty to conspiring with each other to distribute oxycodone. Between the two cases, agents seized hundreds of oxycodone pills, over $17,500 in cash, and a 2005 GMC Yukon Denali.

"The defendants have been detained since their arrests in January 2011."

Further Reading:

"Four Sentenced for Distribution of Oxycodone in Rhode Island and Massachusetts." 29 September 2011. dea.gov/press-releases/2011/09/29/four-sentenced-distribution-oxycodone-rhode-island-and-massachusetts

"New England in Brief." *Boston.com*, 2 June 2007. boston.com/news/local/articles/2007/06/02/judge_denies_officers_request_for_bail/.

Richmond, Will. "Two Face Charges After Fatal Fight." *WickedLocal.com*, 21 August 2007. fall-river.wickedlocal.com/article/20070821/NEWS/308219585.

BABY JAMES CERCE

Baby shaken to death in home at 81 Webster Street in Fall River, Massachusetts, on April 17, 2007. The boy died in May of his injuries, after being taken off life support.

Victim: James Cerce, 8 months.

Accused: Christopher Cerce, 32.

Details: Baby James Cerce was taken to St. Anne's Hospital in Fall River. Doctors detected blood on the brain, behind the retina, and in his stool. They determined that it indicated the baby had sustained injuries due to "shaken baby syndrome." Additionally, the brain damage suffered by little James would be permanent if he survived.

The boy's father, Christopher, told police that he had played with his son after changing his diaper in the morning and then put him down for a nap. He said the baby woke up at 3 p.m. and noticed the child was not well.

As police interviewed Cerce, he admitted that he struck the child in the back of the head. Police learned that the extent of the injuries were more than a result of one strike to the head. After this information was relayed to Cerce, he admitted that he had shaken his son three times while holding him in front of him while standing. He also put the baby down to rest forcefully.

In 1999, Cerce was sentenced to 18 months in prison for driving under the influence of liquor and causing a motor vehicle homicide. The man who died was Cerce's friend and was a passenger in the car. When the accident happened, the friend was ejected from the car and pinned underneath it.

Trial: Christopher Cerce pleaded guilty to second-degree murder in 2009 and sentenced to life in prison.

Further Reading:

Richmond, Will. "Cerce Gets Life for Killing Son." *The Herald News* (Fall River, Massachusetts), 4 May 2009.

JEROME WOODARD

Man shot to death in his home on County Street in Fall River, Massachusetts, on May 12, 2007.

Victim: Jerome Woodard, 28.

Accused: Luis Alberto Montalvo-Borgos, 27.

Details: According to Luis Alberto Montalvo-Borgos' appeal in 2012, the facts of the case as presented at trial are as follows:

"On Friday, May 11, 2007, the victim; his girl friend, Sheena Castle; and their daughter, who was four years of age, went to Fall River to visit Castle's mother, Sharon St. Pierre. St. Pierre lived in an apartment on the second floor of a three-story apartment building. Jose Mercado Matos, known as Jolky, and his then girl friend, known as Liz, lived in an apartment above St. Pierre. Jolky's twin brother, Osvaldo Mercado Matos, known as Valdo, and his girl friend, lived across the hall from Jolky. Yanelly Lorenzi and her boy friend, Raymond Cordeiro, lived in an apartment under St. Pierre. Cordeiro, who had a heroin 'problem' and had previously spent time in prison for selling drugs, was friends with the third-floor residents. Jolky and Valdo were known to sell drugs.

"After arriving at St. Pierre's home, the victim, Castle, and their daughter, went out to visit a friend. At about 9 or 10 P.M., St. Pierre went to bed. Meanwhile, in the apartment building next to St. Pierre's, Valdo went to visit Eduardo Rosario, who lived in a third-floor apartment with his wife, Vilmarie. At around 10 P.M., the men started drinking and watched television in the living room. Vilmarie had gone to bed. As the evening progressed, Valdo became increasingly intoxicated.

"Sometime after 1 A.M., now May 12, the victim, Castle, and their daughter, returned to St. Pierre's apartment building. For a while, the couple talked inside the victim's automobile, which was parked in front of St. Pierre's apartment. Eventually, the couple got out of the automobile, and as they did, the victim accidentally set off its alarm.

"Although the victim shut the alarm off within seconds, the noise agitated Valdo, who began shouting out of Rosario's third-floor window. Valdo called the victim racist slurs and said, 'I got something for you.' The argument lasted about fifteen minutes. From a window of her apartment, Liz tried to stop the argument. Hearing the noise, St. Pierre telephoned 911, but hung up. The victim, Castle, and their daughter, went inside.

"Soon thereafter police arrived at St. Pierre's apartment to investigate the aborted 911 telephone call. St. Pierre lied to the officers, telling them that her granddaughter had made the telephone call while she was 'playing with the phone.' The police left and St. Pierre locked the door. Within minutes St. Pierre and Castle saw [Borgos], who they subsequently identified in a photographic array, break through the door, yell at the victim in Spanish, and point a gun at him. As St. Pierre and Castle fled, they heard multiple gunshots. The victim died as a result of gunshot wounds to his torso with perforations to his heart, lung, and pelvic bone.

"The police later learned about [Borgos]'s whereabouts prior to the shooting. [Borgos] had gone out for the evening with Yanelly, her sister Leisa, and Cordeiro, to a nightclub in Providence, Rhode Island. On the way home, [Borgos] received a cellular telephone call and during the conversation stated, 'Nobody mess with my boy,' and 'I'm going to kill him.' [Borgos] had a silver gun in his hands. Yanelly told [Borgos], 'Think about it,' and not to kill anyone.

"Police recovered seven .22-caliber discharged cartridge casings and two live projectiles from St. Pierre's apartment. Two spent .22-caliber rounds were recovered from the medical examiner's office. The Commonwealth's firearms identification expert opined that, based on his examination, all seven of the discharged .22-caliber cartridge casings recovered were fired from the same unknown weapon. There was no forensic evidence connecting [Borgos] to the shooting.

"[Borgos] did not testify or call any witnesses. The defense was misidentification."

Trial: Borgos was convicted by a jury of first-degree murder and sentenced to life in prison.

Afterword: Luis Alberto Montalvo-Borgos appealed his conviction in 2012. His appeal was denied.

Further Reading:

"Commonwealth vs. Luis Alberto Montalvo Borgos." 464 Mass. 23, September 7, 2012-December 21, 2012. Bristol County. masscases.com/cases/sjc/464/464mass23.html.

BABY JOSHUA PACHECO

Baby shaken to death in home in New Bedford, Massachusetts, on August 14, 2007.

Victim: Joshua Pacheco, 10 months.

Accused: Manuel Antonio Lopez, 28.

Details: After a 911 call at 2:12 p.m., police helped revive little Joshua Pacheco who had stopped breathing. EMS transferred Joshua to St. Luke's Hospital, then taken to Hasbro Children's Hospital in Providence, RI, because his injuries were so severe. He was placed on life support and died on August 14, 2007.

Manuel Lopez, the live-in boyfriend to the child's mother, claimed that he had given Joshua a bath and put him to bed. He then noticed that the boy had stopped breathing and called the police.

The baby was diagnosed with diffuse brain edema and bilateral retinal hemorrhaging, both symptoms of shaken baby syndrome. The Department of Social Services had been monitoring the family after the baby's mother had been a victim of domestic violence. Her boyfriend at the time of the violence had moved out and the agency was unaware that she had invited another person to move in. The social workers said they regularly checked in on the family and that they never saw signs that the baby or his 4-year-old half-sister had been abused physically.

Manuel Lopez was charged with murder.

Trial: Manuel Lopez was found guilty of second-degree murder in the death of Joshua Pacheco and sentenced to life in prison, with the possibility of parole in 15 years, or 2024. He has not, to date, appealed his case.

Further Reading:

Abel, David. "New Bedford Baby Boy Dies as Man Arraigned in Assault." *The Boston Globe* (Boston, Massachusetts), 15 August 2007.

Ellement, John R., and Javiar C. Hernandez. "DSS Role in Child's Family Defended." *The Boston Globe* (Boston, Massachusetts), 16 August 2007.

"Man Gets Life in Prison for Infant's Murder." *The Boston Globe* (Boston, Massachusetts), 28 June 2009.

ALBON WILSON

Man shot to death on the corner of Bonney and Thompson Streets in New Bedford, Massachusetts, on September 30, 2007.

Victim: Albon Wilson, 24.

Accused: Michael V. Feliciano, 17.

Details: Albon Wilson was found dead of four gunshot wounds on the corner of Bonney and Thompson Streets in New Bedford. On October 19, during a routine traffic stop, police arrested Michael Feliciano as a suspect in the murder.

Feliciano had been implicated by three young women. "One witness said Feliciano told her two days before the murder that he would shoot Wilson the next time he saw him. The witness said the pair were friends but had a falling out. Another witness testified that Feliciano called her the night of the murder and said he had shot and killed Wilson. A third witness said she was sitting outside a Crapo Street residence, talking on a phone, when she saw Wilson approach two men on the street whom she recognized. Moments later, she said she heard gunshots and saw the victim and the two other men running in opposite directions.

"During the trial, defense lawyer Theodore Barone said the young woman's statement was induced by constant police questioning. Barone also said the two other witnesses falsely accused Feliciano to deflect attention from themselves because they were under suspicion by police" ("New Bedford Man").

Trial: In 2009, Michael Feliciano was acquitted by a jury of the murder of Albon Wilson.

Further Reading:

Fraga, Brian. "New Bedford Man Acquitted of 2007 Murder in South End." SouthCoastToday.com, 3 June 2009. southcoasttoday.com/article/20090603/NEWS/906030337.

"Teenager is Held Without Bail in Slaying." *The Boston Globe* (Boston, Massachusetts), 20 October 2007.

EDWIN MEDINA

Young man shot to death in front of a County Street house at a New Year's Eve party in New Bedford, Massachusetts, on January 1, 2008.

Victim: Edwin Medina, 15.

Accused: George Duarte, 22.

Details: According to George Duarte's appeal, the facts of the case as presented at trial are as follows:

"On December 31, 2007, Jacqueline Correa-Gonzalez and her roommate, Delphina Thomas, hosted a New Year's Eve party in their second-floor apartment at 370 County Street in New Bedford. When the party began, there were approximately twenty to twenty-five people in the two rooms where the party was being held. After midnight, groups of people who had not been invited, but had heard about the party from friends or on the internet site MySpace, started to arrive.

"A commotion arose when two partygoers began 'play fighting.' One of the hosts of the party asked them to stop. The pair stopped for a moment, but then continued to push each other, and they both fell on the floor. At that point, the hosts and a male friend told everyone that the party was over and that they should leave the apartment. Several groups of people tried to leave the apartment at the same time, causing a bottleneck at the main exit. There was pushing, and shoving in the crowd.

"As the hosts ushered partygoers out of the apartment, a man in a dark hoodie (later identified as George Duarte) took out a .45-caliber handgun and fired a single shot into the air. After the first shot, everybody in the apartment 'froze.' The victim, Edwin Medina, rushed at [Duarte] and tried to 'blindside him.' [Duarte] stumbled, turned around, and shot Medina in the stomach from about five feet away.

"Rashad Coleman, a friend of [Duarte]'s who testified under a grant of immunity, identified [Duarte] as the shooter. Coleman testified that moments before the shooting, he saw [Duarte] 'fidgeting around' and 'reaching towards his body.' He told [Duarte], who was wearing a black hoodie, to 'chill out.' After the shooting, [Duarte] then ran out of the apartment. Several shots were fired on South Sixth Street as [Duarte] and others fled from the party. [Duarte] thereafter went to a friend's apartment at 9 Bedford Street in New Bedford, a few blocks away.

"In the immediate aftermath of the shooting of Medina, the police recovered two .45-caliber shell casings manufactured by Remington Peters from inside the apartment where the shooting took place. During the ensuing investigation, police also recovered four .45-caliber discharged shell casings manufactured by Remington Peters, near the intersection of Bedford and South Sixth Street, the direction in which [Duarte] and others went following the shooting. A single .45-caliber jacketed spent projectile was recovered from Medina's body during the autopsy. In a search of 9 Bedford Street conducted on January 3, 2008, the police recovered a live .45-caliber round of ammunition.

"The Commonwealth introduced evidence that on December 21, 2007, ten days prior to the shooting of Medina, [Duarte] shot an individual named Rico Almeida in the foot. Seven .45-caliber discharged cartridge casings and two jacketed spent projectiles were recovered from the Almeida shooting. A ballistics expert testified that the cartridge casings from the Almeida shooting were also manufactured by Remington Peters, the markings on the spent shell casings from the Almeida shooting were consistent with the markings from the casings recovered in the apartment following the shooting of Medina, and the projectiles recovered from Medina's body and the Almeida shooting had similar striations."

Trial: After a 16-day trial, a jury convicted George Duarte of murder in the second degree and was sentenced to life in prison.

Afterword: In 2015, George Duarte appealed his conviction on the grounds that the prosecutor committed a series of errors during his closing argument, that the trial judge erred by admitting evidence of other bad acts involving the use of firearms, and that the motion judge erred in denying his motion to suppress certain statements.

The appeals court affirmed his conviction.

Further Reading:

"Commonwealth vs. Duarte." Mass. App. Ct. March 9, 2015. casetext.com/case/commonwealth-v-duarte-9

Fraga, Brian. "City Man with Lengthy Criminal Record Charged with New Year's Day Homicide." *SouthCoastToday.com*, 20 February 2008. southcoasttoday.com/article/20080220/News/802200326.

"Murder Trial Set in New Year's Shooting." *The Boston Globe* (Boston, Massachusetts), 8 June 2010.

FREDERICK THOMPKINS

Man beaten to death, but found a week later, at 215 Whipple Street in Fall River, Massachusetts, on February 8, 2008.

Victim: Frederick Thompkins, 47.

Accused: Rene Gosselin, 26.

Details: Frederick (Fred) Thompkins' body was found on February 15, 2008, a week after he died. He was beaten to death on February 8th. He had suffered a cracked skull and his brain was injured. He was left to die in a pool of his own blood in his apartment. Police found footprints in the blood from a size 13 Vans MacGyver shoe. Additionally, they found a pair of glasses in Rene Gosselin's prescription in the apartment—one lens under Thompkins and the frame and other lens 6 feet away. Rene Gosselin wears a size 13 shoe and a Vans MacGyver shoe box was found in Gosselin's home.

Oddly, police found Thompkins with his pants pulled down around his ankles and there was hair, belonging to a woman, in his hands—leading Gosselin to assert the crime was committed by a woman.

It was alleged at trial that Thompkins was a drug dealer and Rene Gosselin was a customer, and that they were friends. Thompkins was a construction worker, artist, and father of 3 children. His family admitted that he began selling marijuana and cocaine after losing his job and the death of his mother.

No fingerprints were found at the scene as doorknobs and counters were wiped clean. Telephone records showed that the last call Thompkins received was from Rene Gosselin.

Trial: Rene Gosselin was convicted of first degree murder committed with deliberately premeditated malice aforethought or with atrocity or cruelty in 2012 and sentenced to life in prison without the possibility of parole.

Further Reading:

O'Connor, Kevin P. "Murder Trial Begins for Tiverton Native Rene Gosselin." *WickedLocal.com*, 20 April 2012. wickedlocal.com/article/20120420/news/304209313.
O'Connor, Kevin P. "Rene Gosselin Found Guilty of Murder, Sentenced to Life in Prison." *The Herald News* (Fall River, Massachusetts), 4 May 2012.

VERONICA ROSALES & LUIS MOULDS-TIUL

Murder/suicide on Tinkham Street in New Bedford, Massachusetts, on February 29, 2008.

Victim: Veronica Rosales, 36.

Accused: Luis Enrique Moulds-Tiul, 43.

Details: Veronica Rosales and Luis Enrique Moulds-Tiul had lived together for a year and a month before her death Rosales asked him to leave. Apparently he kept a key and hid in her bedroom on February 29, 2008. They argued and Moulds-Tiul stabbed her 2 times with a steak knife, once in the chest and once in the rib cage.

A couple shared the apartment with Rosales and came to her defense. The woman was stabbed 8 times but survived. The man struggled with Moulds-Tiul, who committed suicide by plunging the knife into his own chest.

Both Rosales and Moulds-Tiul were Guatemalan immigrants.

Further Reading:

"February 29." *The Boston Globe* (Boston, Massachusetts), 31 December 2008.
Naughton, Michael. "Stabbing Death Rattles New Bedford." *The Boston Globe* (Boston, Massachusetts), 2 March 2008.

JOSHUA FITZGERALD

Man stabbed to death in a fight outside a VFW in Fairhaven, Massachusetts, on April 4, 2008.

Victim: Joshua Fitzgerald, 30.

Accused: Brandon Callender, age unknown.

Details: According to Callender's application for further appellate review, the facts of the case as presented at trial were the following:

"In April of 2008, there were eleven adult children in the Fitzgerald family, eight boys and three girls. One of those children, Joshua, died on April 4, 2008 at the age of thirty.

"On April 4, 2008, Joshua and his younger brother Patrick went to the home of their friend Bob Williams in Fairhaven sometime between 11:00 and noon. They hung out for much of the day. They played the guitar and had a couple of beers. Around dinnertime, they went to Naughty Dawgs on Route 6 for hot dogs. Patrick dropped off Joshua and Williams and then went home. They planned to meet up later at the VFW Hall in Fairhaven, along with brothers Ethan and Joseph Fitzgerald. Tim Borges was putting on a hip-hop open mike night, and Ethan planned to perform.

"Patrick drove to the VFW Hall in his pickup truck, arriving at about 9:00 p.m. He parked near the back. Inside the hall, there were two connected rooms. The hip-hop show took place on one side, and there was a bar on the other side. Eventually, Joshua and Williams arrived in Williams' truck. Joseph, Ethan Joseph's friend Robert Sylvia, and a cousin Colton Fitzgerald also showed up. Shortly thereafter, Patrick's girlfriend Ashlee, his sister Meghan, and his cousin Jared arrived. They moved from the bar area to the hip-hop side.

"Patrick saw people he knew, including Thomas Opozda and David LeBlanc. At about 10:00 p.m., Joshua and Williams left. Williams walked to his truck and got in. He assumed that Joshua was behind him, but he was not. Patrick headed for the exit around this time. He had had two to four beers. As he attempted to leave the hall, he saw Joshua standing outside on the handicapped ramp arguing with someone he did not recognize. When he tried to go to assist Joshua, LeBlanc blocked him, saying, 'You ain't going nowhere.' When Patrick said he was getting his family and leaving, LeBlanc responded, 'F your family.' Patrick asked him not to say that. LeBlanc again said, 'F your family.' At that point, Patrick punched him in the face, knocking him to the ground.

"Patrick then joined Joshua on the ramp, and they attempted to leave. However, he then heard LeBlanc yell out, 'Everybody get 'em.' Although his truck was in the back parking lot, Patrick did not want to get cornered. He and Joshua ran the opposite way. As they turned around, they saw five people charging at them. Most of the forty to fifty people in the building then ran outside. Patrick and Joshua fled the parking lot toward Middle and Bridge Streets. Patrick stopped to catch his breath. He then picked up a wooden sawhorse and attempted to fend off his pursuers. Someone behind him said, 'You're gonna need a weapon.' Someone struck him in the upper back on the left side. He stumbled and ended up near a dumpster in the parking lot of Moriarty's Liquors. A group of males, none of whom he recognized, then surrounded him. They punched him repeatedly. As Patrick tried to protect himself, he felt blood running down his back. By then, he had been separated from Joshua.

"At around this time, Williams grabbed a piece of laminate flooring from the back of his truck and tried to help Patrick. He only made it a few steps before a number of people jumped him and began kicking him repeatedly. He was soon surrounded by ten to fifteen people who were kicking him. He eventually broke free and ran across Middle Street. When the crowd dispersed, he ran back toward his truck. He felt wet and realized he had been stabbed in the side and that blood was pouring out of the wound. He entered his truck, drove out of the parking lot and stopped on Bridge Street. He told a police officer he had been stabbed and then lost consciousness. He spent six days in the hospital.

"As Patrick attempted to fight off his attackers in the Moriarty's parking lot, he heard an engine revving. Joseph yelled to him from his green Saturn. Patrick ran to the car and jumped into the rear seat on the driver's side. Bobby Sylvia was in the front passenger seat. No one had seen Joshua. The car pulled forward along Bridge Street, but Patrick insisted that they stop and find Joshua.

"The car stopped. A few minutes earlier, Joshua had been seen shirtless swinging a two by four at some of his attackers, but by the time Patrick found him, he was curled up on the ground in the Moriarty's parking trying lot to protect himself as four or five males kicked and punched him. Many of the males wore baby blue T-shirts, but Patrick did not recognize any of them. He screamed at them to get off Joshua. As the attackers dispersed, he picked up Joshua and walked him to the car. They entered the back seat, with Joshua sitting on the right side, and Patrick sitting on the left. A group of five to six people surrounded the car and tried to keep it from moving forward. They yelled at them to get out of the car. A black male with an Afro and a hair pick then opened the door on Joshua's side and said, 'Everybody's getting poked.' He then swung a knife around, stabbing Joshua in the abdomen. According to Sylvia, the knife never came near Patrick, although Patrick testified that it struck his right wrist. Someone then pulled Joshua out of the car. He ran to the sidewalk onto Middle Street and then to Bridge Street and finally onto Main Street. Joseph pulled up next to him, and Joshua jumped into the car. They left.

"As they turned toward Route 6 and headed for the hospital, Patrick felt some pain and discovered he was bleeding from his stomach, back and wrist. Joshua drifted in and out of consciousness. He said, 'I'm not gonna make it. Take care of my sons. Tell my mother I love her. I love you guys.' He was unconscious by the time they arrived at St. Luke's hospital. Patrick recalled being taken out of the car on a stretcher and next recalled waking up three days later at Rhode Island Hospital.

"Stacey Pettey knew the defendant Brandon Callender and saw him at the VFW Hall on the night of the incident. His hair that night appeared to be similar to the medium length hair depicted in a photograph she viewed. She did not recall anything in his hair. She also described the rap battle that took place on stage. Almost everyone left when a fight broke out outside. Pettey remained in the building. About ten minutes after the fight started, Callender came inside. He said he had gotten into a fight, that his arm was hurting and that he thought he had stabbed someone. He went into the bathroom. Pettey and Callender left and walked to a nearby Dunkin' Donuts. Callender made a phone call, and shortly thereafter, a car with two young women pulled up. The two of them got in. Callender complained that he had been hit by a two by four, that his arm hurt, and that he may have stabbed someone.

"Dr. Mindy Hull, a Medical Examiner for the Office of the Chief Medical Examiner, performed an autopsy on Joshua Fitzgerald on April of 2008. He was 5' 6" tall and weighed 169 pounds. She observed him to be edematous, which means that fluid collected within his body when he went into shock. She also observed evidence of extensive medical treatment. The surgeons cut through the stab wound in the abdomen, so it was incorporated into a larger incision. However, it appeared to be vertical. Although there was an attempt to repair the wound, there is evidence that the stab wound penetrated the liver by about two and a half inches. The liver tends to bleed a lot. Although there is evidence of a number of contusions and abrasions, she concluded that the cause of death was the stab wound to the liver. There was significant blood found in the abdomen. The blood loss would have resulted in Joshua's death within minutes without intervention. He received medical intervention, which prolonged his life by several hours. Ultimately, the medical intervention was not enough."

Brandon Callender was indicted on May 9, 2008, on charges of murder, armed assault with intent to murder, and assault and battery by means of a dangerous weapon.

In 2009, the Commonwealth filed an interlocutory appeal on the grounds that the trial judge should not have granted Callender's motion to suppress statements he made during a police interrogation. The court ruled that Callender's right to cut off questioning was not honored and the motion to suppress was affirmed.

In 2012, Callender filed a motion to suppress evidence and a motion to dismiss. In 2013, Callender filed a motion to suppress recorded statements. The court denied the motion except to exclude recorded telephone calls made to Callender's mother.

Trial: In 2014, Brandon Callender was convicted of the lesser charge of second-degree murder, not guilty of armed assault with intent to murder, and guilty of assault and battery by means of a dangerous weapon. He was sentenced to the mandatory life sentence on the murder count and a 5-8 year sentence to commence on or after the life sentence.

Afterword: In 2015, Callender appealed his conviction. The appeals court affirmed his conviction and denied him a new trial or dismissal of the case.

Further Reading:

"Commonwealth vs. Brandon Callender." Application for Further Appellate Review. .
"Commonwealth vs. Brandon Callender." 81 Mass. App. Ct. 13, September 14, 2011-January 23, 2012. Bristol County. masscases.com/cases/app/81/81massappct153.html.
"Mass. Man Arrested in Multiple Stabbings." *The Burlington Free Press* (Burlington, Vermont), 7 April 2008.

DEREK HOGUE

Man shot to death at 108 Hamlet Street in Fall River, Massachusetts, on June 27, 2008.

Victim: Derek Hogue, 33.

Accused: Jesus Nazareth Gomes, 23.

Details: Derek Hogue was shot to death in his apartment in Fall River. Police arrived after receiving a 911 call at about 1:30 a.m. A neighbor reported hearing from someone that the door to Hogue's second-floor apartment was kicked down before the shooting.

Jesus Gomes was apprehended on an unrelated warrant, charging him with assault and battery with a dangerous weapon, causing substantial injury. He was later charged with obstruction of justice and intimidating a witness. He also misled investigators in connection with the homicide of Derek Hogue.

Gomes was later charged with murder and home invasion. He pleaded guilty on both counts.

Trial: In 2014, after a two-week trial, Jesus N. Gomes was acquitted of the murder of Derek Hogue.

Further Reading:

Fraga, Brian. "Brockton Man Found Not Guilty of Fatal 2008 Shooting in Fall River." *The Herald News* (Fall River, Massachusetts), 29 June 2008.

Moss, John. "Man Accused of Misleading Police in a Murder Probe." *The Herald News* (Fall River, Massachusetts), 29 June 2008.

DAVID WALSH

Man killed in power boat collision in Buzzards Bay, Dartmouth, Massachusetts, on July 18, 2008.

Victim: David Walsh, 64.

Accused: Fred Bevins III, 60.

Details: On a sunny day in Buzzards Bay, David Walsh and a friend, Warren G. Hathaway, 66, were sailing back to South Dartmouth in a 35′ Freedom sailboat, *Priority*. His sailboat was hit unexpectedly from behind by a 63′ express Sea Ray cruiser named *Reasons*, operated by Fred Bevins III. Walsh was knocked overboard and killed. Hathaway was deep in the cabin and was suffered only minor injuries.

Bevins was charged with boat homicide by negligent operation. Bevins claimed he as readjusting his chartplotter/gps and did not see the sailboat in front of him. Bevins was traveling with his wife Ellen north around 1:45 p.m., 4 ½ miles south of Padanaram Harbor in Dartmouth.

Walsh's sailboat had the right of way under international navigation rules as it was fully under sail. At the time of the collision, seas were less than one foot and winds were 5 to 10 knots.

A marine surveyor's report estimated that the speed of *Reasons* was 20 knots at the time of impact. Under full sail, without his motor running, the speed of *Priority* was estimated at 3 knots.

Walsh was a respected yachtsman and was past president of the Buzzards Bay Regatta and a member of the New Bedford Yacht Club. Bevins had multiple road violations in his past, including 9 charges that include speeding and illegal operation and a license revocation for receiving three speeding tickets in 30 days.

In 2009, Bevins pleaded guilty to negligent operation of a vessel and was given a one-year suspended sentence, 10 years supervised probation, surrender of his Coast Guard captain's license for 5 years and his driver's license for 3 months. Additionally, Bevins was prohibited from using, operating, chartering, or being a passenger on any vessel for 3 years.

It was reported that had this been a motor vehicle accident the sentencing would have been similar as Bevins had no criminal felony record and it was not proven that drugs or alcohol was involved.

Further Reading:

"Boat Operator Pleads Guilty in Crash that Killed Dartmouth Sailor." *The Herald News* (Fall River, Massachusetts), 5 November 2009.

"Death by Speed." BoatTest.com, 11 November 2009. boattest.com/view-news/3852_death-by-speed.

Landry, Chris. "Boater Grounded for 3 Years in Fatality." *SoundingsOnline.com*, 31 December 2009. soundingsonline.com/news/boater-grounded-for-3-years-in-fatality

ROBYN MENDES & KATHERINE GOMES

Two women stabbed to death in of New Bedford, Massachusetts, on January 3 and 4, 2009.

Victims: Robyn Mendes, 48, and Katherine Gomes, 61.

Accused: Gary Gomes, 35.

Details: According to *The Boston Globe*, "Gary A. Gomes had twice been convicted of attacking his former girlfriend, at one time even dragging her into the woods and choking her. Six months after being released from the short jail term…he allegedly attacked the woman again… killing her and stabbing his mother to death in a macabre four-day stretch of violence.

"Gomes…allegedly used the blood of this estranged girlfriend, Robyn N. Mendes, to write "I [heart] you' on the wall above the body… found in Gomes's mother's apartment Tuesday…He had put clothes on her body and makeup on her face after killing her on Sunday. The body of Gomes's 61-year-old mother, Katherine A. Gomes, was found in a separate room in the Independence Street apartment. He had killed her Saturday with the same knife.

"In another twist to the gruesome killings, Gomes had allegedly left an unlighted stove on full blast and a space heater turned to high in an apparent attempt to rig an explosion Tuesday in the apartment. He then barricaded himself inside Mendes's home on Phillips Road, on the other side of the city, keeping her 12-year-old daughter hostage with plans to kill Mendes's estranged husband, Victor Mendes."

Gary Gomes was charged with two counts of murder and kidnapping. He pleaded guilty to first-degree murder in the death of Robyn Mendes and manslaughter in the death of his mother…He was sentenced to life in prison without a chance of parole for the murder and 18-20 years for the manslaughter of his mother.

Further Reading:

Brown, Curt. "Gomes Sentenced to Life in Prison, Asks for Forgiveness." *SouthCoastToday.com*, 24 February 2012. southcoasttoday.com/article/20120224/NEWS/202240333.

Ellement, John R., and Milton J. Valencia. "Details Emerge in Grisly Killings." *The Boston Globe* (Boston, Massachusetts), 8 January, 2009.

TROY PINA

Man shot to death in a car on Route 24 in Freetown, Massachusetts, on May 17, 2009.

Victim: Troy Pina, 29.

Accused: Thomas Jeffries, 30, Marcus Mitchell, 20, Jose Fernandes, 23.

Details: The facts as presented at trial are as follows:
"[Marcus Mitchell] and several others, including Thomas Jeffries, were involved in a drug distribution enterprise in Taunton known as 'Team Supreme.' In early 2009, various members of Team Supreme were engaged in a feud of unspecified origin with Francisco Monteiro.

"[Mitchell] told Jeffries that Monteiro was looking for [Mitchell], and Jeffries gave [Mitchell] a firearm for his protection. When Jeffries subsequently met with Monteiro, perhaps in an effort to resolve the feud, Monteiro assaulted Jeffries and took his automobile keys. On April 24, 2009, the cooperating witness, who was a member of 'Team Supreme,' was shot outside a bar; Monteiro was suspected of having committed the shooting.

"On the night of May 16 or in the early morning hours of May 17, after learning that Monteiro had been seen at a bar, Jeffries, [Mitchell], and two others drove to the bar in two vehicles to retaliate against Monteiro. When the group arrived at the bar, they saw Monteiro leave in a vehicle with Troy Pina and two others. They followed Monteiro's vehicle, approached it on the highway, and, using at least three firearms, fired at the vehicle. Pina was struck by one of the bullets and died shortly thereafter.

"On July 14, 2010, the cooperating witness was arrested for the unlawful possession of a firearm found in a vehicle he was driving. [Mitchell] had been a passenger in the vehicle but fled before the police stopped the vehicle. When the cooperating witness was in custody, unable to post bail, he agreed to cooperate in the investigation of Pina's killing and, as part of his cooperation, agreed to record telephone calls with [Mitchell] and others.

"As a result of his cooperation, the cooperating witness was released from custody while awaiting trial on the firearms charge.

"The cooperating witness told the officers that, because [Mitchell] knew that he had been arrested on the firearms charge and had been held in custody on that charge, the firearms arrest would be an 'expected' subject of discussion between the two in their first long conversation following his arrest, and it would arouse [Mitchell]'s suspicion if he failed to mention the firearms case and instead started asking questions about Pina's killing. He also told the officers that he wanted [Mitchell] to 'corroborate his story' that the firearm belonged to [Mitchell] and that [Mitchell] had left it in the automobile when he fled.

"The officers told him to do 'whatever he had to do to get conversation' about the murder.

"In the presence of the officers, the cooperating witness telephoned [Mitchell] and immediately admonished [Mitchell] for leaving the firearm in the vehicle that the cooperating witness had been driving, telling [Mitchell] that he was 'on the verge of losing...everything' he had because [Mitchell] ran without taking the firearm with him. [Mitchell] admitted on several occasions that the firearm was his and apologized to the cooperating witness for leaving it in the vehicle when he fled. The cooperating witness asked [Mitchell] if there were any 'bodies on that gun,' and [Mitchell] said that he did not know. Eventually, '[t]he conversation became heated,' and the cooperating witness ended the telephone call without discussing Pina's killing.

"On May 6, 2011, [Mitchell] was indicted for the murder of Pina and for several other offenses related to the May, 2009, shooting, as well as for the unlawful possession of a firearm on July 14, 2010."

Trial: After a three-week trial in 2014, Thomas Jeffries was convicted of first-degree murder, as well as three counts of armed assault to murder, three counts of assault with a dangerous weapon, and carrying a firearm without a license. He was sentenced to life in prison without the possibility of parole.

In 2013, Jose Fernandes was found guilty of first degree murder and was sentenced to life in prison without the possibility of parole.

According to the Massachusetts prison system, Marcus Mitchell is incarcerated in MCI Shirley (Medium Security), but no information can be found as to the outcome of his trail.

Further Reading:

"Commonwealth vs. Marcus Mitchell." 468 Mass. 417, February 3, 2014-June 18, 2014. Bristol County. masscases.com/cases/sjc/468/468mass417.html.
"Guilty: Taunton Man Convicted of Murder in 2009 Route 24 Slaying." WickedLocal. com, 30 May 2014. wickedlocal.com/article/20140530/news/140539643.

JOHN K. MARTIN

Man shot as he attempted to stop an armed robbery at 171 Coggeshall Street in New Bedford, Massachusetts, on June 20, 2009. He died the following day.

Victim: John K. Martin, 32.

Accused: Corey Princiotta, 20, Mark Goulart, 19.

Details: "On June 20, 2009, [Corey Princiotta] entered the Petro-Mart at approximately 8:33 p.m. He was described as 5' 10" to 6' 2" tall, very skinny and weighing approximately 160 pounds. He appeared to be Hispanic and was speaking in street slang. He was wearing a gray hooded sweatshirt with the hood tied tightly over his head. After he purchased a beverage from the clerk, another customer, John Martin, entered the store. The shooter drew a black firearm from his waistband, pointed it at the store employee and demanded money while declaring that a robbery was occurring. At that time, Martin confronted the shooter and unsuccessfully attempted to grab the firearm. In response, the shooter fired and hit Martin in the right temple, killing him.

"The New Bedford Police and the Massachusetts State Police investigated Martin's death. Investigators concluded that the defendant and Goulart planned to rob the Petro-Mart to repay a drug debt. After consulting photo arrays, several witnesses identified Corey Princiotta, the defendant, as a friend of Mark Goulart. Goulart's residence, twenty-three Bentley Street, is within a few city blocks of the Petro-Mart.

"Witnesses described Goulart leaving his apartment with the defendant on the night of the robbery and shooting. The defendant wore a gray hooded sweatshirt with the hood tied tightly around his face. A witness also reported that Goulart owned a similar hooded sweatshirt, but Goulart had disposed of it around the time of the crimes. The two men were seen leaving the apartment building at the same time but they departed in different directions. After the robbery and shooting, the defendant and Goulart returned to Goulart's apartment, but the defendant was no longer wearing the gray hooded sweatshirt. Approximately ten minutes after the aborted robbery and shooting, both men appeared to be scared and started to argue about the location of the gray sweatshirt. The defendant stated that he took the sweatshirt off, folded the gun inside of it and hid the items under a car on Sawyer Street.

"Eyewitnesses corroborated the Sawyer Street location as consistent with the shooter's path of travel after fleeing the Petro-Mart. They also told investigators that the defendant was concerned about leaving DNA evidence in the sweatshirt, and that Goulart planned to recover the sweatshirt ("Commonwealth vs. Corey Princiotta").

Princiotta were charged with first-degree murder, attempted armed robbery, and carrying an illegal firearm. Under state law, Goulart was also charged with murder. When the police searched Goulart's home, they recovered a large sum of marijuana. He was additionally charged with distribution of marijuana.

There were no further records about this case found.

Further Reading:

"Commonwealth vs. Corey Princiotta." October 9, 2014. Bristol County. ma.findacase.com/research/wfrmDocViewer.aspx/xq/fac.20141009_0001599.MA.htm/qx.

Nicas, Jack. "Two Held in Fatal Shooting at Store." *The Boston Globe* (Boston, Massachusetts), 17 July 2009.

WAYNE RICE

Man shot and killed inside the Andrews-Dahill VFW Post hall in New Bedford, Massachusetts, on June 23, 2009.

Victim: Wayne Rice, 41.

Accused: Adam Pina, age unknown.

Details: A party was being held at the Andrews-Dahill VFW Post hall in memory of Tazmyn "Taz" Soares, an 18-year-old New Bedford man who was killed in a shooting in Boston in December of 2007.

Surveillance video taken from inside the VFW showed Wayne Rice, a known West End gang member, was armed with a gun. Adam Pina told investigators that Rice pulled the gun during a fight that erupted when his companion sat in Rice's chair. A crowd was seen assaulting the man and Pina pulling him away before the shot from Pina was fired. Pina fired a second time as Rice crawled to the main entrance.

Trial: In 2011, Adam Pina was acquitted of murder. Pina's attorney believed that this verdict indicated that Pina had acted in self-defense when he shot Rice.

NOTE: Wayne Rice was a passenger in the car in which Troy Pina was shot to death on Route 24 in Freetown. Troy Pina and Adam Pina are not related.

Further Reading:

Fraga, Brian. "Adam Pina Acquitted of Murder Charges for Shooting Wayne Rice in New Bedford VFW Hall." *SouthCoastToday.com*, 7 April 2011. southcoasttoday.com/article/20110407/news/104070345.

Winokoor, Charles. "Witness to Local Highway Drive-By Shot Dead in New Bedford." *Taunton Daily Gazette* (Taunton, Massachusetts), 26 June 2009.

BIANCO ROSADO

Young woman shot to death outside 22 Collins Street in New Bedford, Massachusetts, on July 1, 2009.

Victim: Bianca Rosado, 18.

Accused: Erick Cournoyer, 17.

Details: Victor Comacho and his girlfriend Bianco Rosado had been harassed by another teen couple, Erick Cournoyer and Kelcie Carter. The girls had decided to fight and arrangements were made to conduct the fight outside 22 Collins Street, Erick Cournoyer's home.

Comacho and Rosado arrived but did not notice that Cournoyer was hiding behind a tree. As they got out of the vehicle, Cournoyer approached them and an argument began. Cournoyer pointed his gun at the couple and fired repeatedly, striking Rosado in the chest and Comacho in the leg. Rosado died about 90 minutes later at St. Luke's Hospital in New Bedford.

Rosado was the mother of a 15-month-old girl and had just graduated from New Bedford High School.

Erick Cournoyer was charged with second-degree murder, assault and battery with a dangerous weapon, illegal possession of ammunition, and two counts of possessing an illegal firearm.

Trial: In 2014, Erick Cournoyer was found guilty of all of the above and sentenced to life in prison with the possibility of parole in 15 years.

Further Reading:

"Local Man Gets Life for 2009 Slaying." *The Boston Globe* (Boston, Massachusetts), 19 September 2014.

Ballou, Brian R. "Youth Arranged in Woman's Fatal Shooting." *The Boston Globe* (Boston, Massachusetts), 4 July 2009.

CHARLES SMITH

Man shot to death on Fifth Street in the Corky Row neighborhood of Fall River, Massachusetts, on July 28, 2009.

Victim: Charles Smith, 23.

Accused: Jessie Eaton, 35.

Details: Charles Smith had known mafia ties and a long criminal history. He was sitting in a car, parked on Fifth Street in the Corky Row neighborhood of Fall River. He was shot in the back of the head with a .45-caliber gun.

Jessie Eaton was charged with manslaughter.

Trial: Jessie Eaton was found guilty of manslaughter and was sentenced to 15-16 years in prison.

NETTIE BECHT & LUIS DIAZ

Man and woman shot to death at Westlawn housing complex in New Bedford, Massachusetts, on August 14, 2009.

Victim: Nettie Becht, 36, Luis Diaz, 43.

Accused: Elvin E. Valentin, 60.

Details: According to the appeal by Elvin Valentin, the facts of the case presented at trial are as follows:

"[Elvin Valentin] and Becht lived in different apartments in the same housing complex in New Bedford. They had been involved in an intermittent relationship that spanned a four-year period; during that period, [Valentin] and Becht occasionally spent the night at each other's apartments and [Valentin] had loaned Becht money. According to [Valentin], Becht had 'cheated' on him and he felt that she was 'using' him. Becht ended the relationship prior to the shootings.

"Becht was treated at a hospital on the night before she was killed. When [Valentin] attempted to visit her there, she told him that she did not want to see him. The next day, August 14, 2009, at approximately 8 P.M., [Valentin] went to the home of a friend of Becht, after Becht failed to return the numerous telephone calls he had made throughout the day. Becht came out of the house and spoke with [Valentin] while they were standing outside the house. She told him that she had started a relationship with someone else and that she was 'done' with him. [Valentin] responded by saying, '[W]e'll see, we'll see,' and told her not to do it 'in [his] face.' He left and returned to his apartment.

"Later that night, at approximately 10 P.M., Becht's friend drove her to a bus station to pick up Luis Diaz, a man Becht had met on a 'chat line.' Becht had spoken with Diaz on the telephone, but the two had not met in person. After picking Diaz up from the bus station, the friend drove Diaz and Becht to Becht's apartment and left. At that time, [Valentin] was in his apartment in the same apartment complex, sitting in his kitchen with the lights turned off. He saw Becht and Diaz from his window as they walked toward her apartment. He armed himself with a loaded nine millimeter semiautomatic pistol, which he subsequently told police that he kept readily accessible for protection because he recently had been the victim of a robbery.

"[Valentin] emerged from his apartment carrying the loaded gun. Becht saw that [Valentin] was armed and screamed, 'No, no.' [Valentin] first pointed the gun at Diaz and fired; he then pointed the gun at Becht and fired several more shots. When Diaz tried to get up after he had been shot, [Valentin] said, 'What? You not ready to die yet?' and again fired the gun at Diaz. In all, [Valentin] fired ten shots. Police and paramedics arrived within minutes of the shootings; Diaz was still breathing but Becht was not. Both victims were taken by ambulance to a nearby hospital where, later that night, they were pronounced dead. Each died of gunshot wounds to the torso.

"[Valentin] returned to his apartment and changed his clothes and shoes. He put the gun in a closet in the living room and left the apartment. Immediately after the shootings, [Valentin] spoke to his son on his cellular telephone, and said, 'Hey, I killed Netti because I find her with another guy and I killed that other guy, too.' Shortly thereafter, a police officer noticed [Valentin] walking away from the crowd of people that had gathered. The officer followed [Valentin], who was still talking on his cellular telephone, and ordered him to stop.

"When the officer approached, [Valentin] said, 'Yes, yes. I'm the one who did it.' The officer read [Valentin] his Miranda rights, in English, and handcuffed him. [Valentin] indicated that he understood his rights. Before the officer had asked any questions, [Valentin] asked, 'Is the lady dead?' When the officer responded that he did not know, [Valentin] asked, 'How about the guy? Is he dead?' [Valentin]'s tone was 'casual' and without emotion.

"As the officer spoke to [Valentin], the crowd of people that had gathered at the scene of the shootings began angrily to approach [Valentin]. The officer placed [Valentin] in his police cruiser for [Valentin]'s safety. As they sat in the cruiser, [Valentin] told the officer that he was concerned the crowd would burn his automobile. When the officer asked why he had that concern, [Valentin] replied that it was because he had shot the victims. The officer asked [Valentin] why he had done so, and [Valentin] responded that he had told Becht not to cheat on him. [Valentin] told another officer that the gun used in the shootings was located in his apartment.

"Police transported [Valentin] to the police station, where he agreed to be interviewed. In a video-recorded interview, conducted in English, [Valentin] explained that he had been in a relationship with Becht for about four years, but that she wanted to date other people. [Valentin] stated that he had been sitting in his kitchen with the lights turned off, drinking whiskey, as he waited for Becht to return to her apartment. He said that he had consumed one-half of a bottle of whiskey in the hours before the shootings, and went 'crazy' when he saw Becht walk by his apartment with Diaz because he had been drinking. When asked whether he had made the decision to shoot Becht and

Diaz when he walked out of the apartment with his gun, [Valentin] said, 'Well, yeah, I think that the alcohol made me do the shooting.'

"The primary defense at trial was that [Valentin]'s intoxication warranted convictions of a lesser offense than murder in the first degree. [Valentin] called a forensic psychiatrist as an expert witness to explain generally the effects of alcohol intoxication. In addition, one police officer testified that he smelled the odor of alcohol emanating from [Valentin] as they sat in the police cruiser immediately after [Valentin] was arrested."

Trial: A jury convicted Elvin Valentin of two counts of first degree murder in the deaths of Nettie Brecht and Luis Diaz, on theories of premeditation and extreme atrocity or cruelty. He was sentenced to life in prison without the possibility of parole.

Afterword: Elvin Valentin appealed his case claiming that the judge and the prosecutor erred in a number of ways. The appeals court affirmed the conviction.

Further Reading:

"Commonwealth vs. Elvin Valentin." 474 Mass. 301, January 12, 2016-May 20, 2016. Bristol County. masscases.com/cases/sjc/474/474mass301.html.

Guilfoil, John M., and Emma Rose Johnson. "New Bedford Man Held in Double Killing." *The Boston Globe* (Boston, Massachusetts), 16 August 2009.

SCOTT MONTEIRO

Man shot to death at house party on Elmwood Street in Wareham, Massachusetts, on September 4, 2009.

Victim: Scott Monteiro, 21.

Accused: Vernon Carter, 20.

Details: According the appeal filed by Vernon Carter in 2016, the facts of the case presented at trial are as follows:

"At approximately 10 P.M. on Friday, September 4, 2009, a group of twenty to thirty people, in their late teens or early twenties and generally from the Wareham area, gathered at a residence in Wareham for a 'house party.' People were socializing and drinking, '[j]ust teenage and adolescent kids having fun.' Monteiro, who had turned twenty-one years of age approximately one month before the party, arrived with three of his friends. [Sheldon] Santos was there wearing a gold chain.

"One of the young women at the party had asked the host if she could invite her friend 'Justin.' Between 11:30 P.M. and midnight, Justin arrived with a group of ten to fifteen people. They introduced themselves to one or more partygoers as being from the 'United Front' in New Bedford. The party became more 'tense' after the group's arrival, and someone in the group started to complain, 'This party is whacked. . . . There's no bitches.' A short time later, the majority of the New Bedford group left the house. Within a few minutes, two to five people reentered and approached Santos. Santos had been sitting on a sofa with his girl friend, and Monteiro was sitting on a nearby chair. Santos stood up when approached, and a few people from the New Bedford group surrounded the sofa area so as to prevent anyone from leaving. [Carter] pulled a gun out of his pants, pointed it at Santos's head, and said, 'Run your chain.' He reached toward Santos, and Santos dropped to the floor. Monteiro then stood up, held his hands out with palms facing up, and calmly said, 'Chill, we are all just chilling.' [Carter] fired three shots, and a single bullet hit Monteiro above his right eye. At some point during this altercation, Santos suffered a face injury that required sutures; he also lost his gold chain.

"One of Monteiro's friends attended to him as the remaining partygoers dispersed. The police and emergency medical services personnel arrived a few minutes after the shooting. Monteiro was lying on the floor, breathing but unresponsive. He was transported by ambulance to a nearby hospital. Monteiro died from a gunshot wound to the head.

"The police recovered a spent shell casing from the ambulance and, during Monteiro's autopsy, recovered three fragments of a shell casing from Monteiro's head. The shell casing from the ambulance was from a .22-caliber firearm, and the fragments were consistent with being from the same firearm.

"The police spoke to witnesses the night of the party, many of whom gathered outside of the house after the incident. At least one of the partygoers knew [Carter] by name and provided that information to police. Using that information, Wareham police compiled two photographic arrays containing [Carter]'s photograph. The following morning, the police showed the first array containing eight photographs to the witness who knew [Carter]. The witness did not identify [Carter]'s photograph in this array. Less than one hour later, the police showed the witness the second array containing six photographs. The witness identified [Carter] in the second array, explaining that he recognized [Carter] in the first array but did not identify him because he was 'nervous.'

"Approximately one and one-half hours after the identification, Wareham police notified police in New Bedford that [Carter] was a suspect in a homicide investigation and requested that they question him. Within one hour of the dispatch, New Bedford police officers observed [Carter] walking and stopped their cruiser to speak to him. [Carter] stopped and agreed to accompany them to the police station for questioning. At the police station, the officers recorded the interview. [Carter] told them that he had been at the party but stayed outside the house. After questioning [Carter] for approximately one hour, the police released him.

"The following morning, [Carter] went to the house of a woman he had known since he was a child and asked if he could stay with her because the police were looking for him in connection with an incident at a party in Wareham. She said, 'no,' because her family was there. As she hugged him goodbye, she felt something 'heavy' and 'hard' in [Carter]'s waist.

"State police arrested [Carter] later that day pursuant to a warrant. He was wearing a black hat displaying the word 'Invincible.' The State police interrogated [Carter] on September 6 and 7, 2009. [Carter] told police that he was at the party, he did not have a gun, but he knew that at least four people in his group were carrying firearms. He said that Santos and his 'squad' had guns and threatened someone in the New Bedford group. He said he saw the shooter 'cock' the firearm and 'pistol whip' Santos, and that he was about five or six feet from the shooter when the gun was fired. [Carter] also told police that one of the people in his group, 'Justin,' hid a gun after the party, and he directed police to the apartment where the gun could be found. The police seized a .38-caliber firearm from the apartment, which did not fire the shell casing obtained from the ambulance and was not consistent with the firearm used as the murder weapon.

"Within forty-eight hours of the shooting, four witnesses identified [Carter] as the shooter in photographic arrays. They and other witnesses described the shooter as between five feet, five inches and five feet, nine inches tall, skinny, 'light skinned,' and wearing a black hat. One of the witnesses testified that the shooter was wearing a hat displaying the word 'Invincible.' The police showed the witnesses an additional photographic array containing other people mentioned by [Carter] as being at the party. Except for one witness who identified a photograph of Justin as being at the party, no other potential suspects were identified."

Trial: In April, 2013, a jury convicted Vernon Carter of first-degree murder on a theory of felony-murder, based on the predicate felony of armed robbery. He was also convicted of armed robbery, assault and battery of Sheldon Santos, possession of a firearm, and possession of ammunition.

Afterword: Vernon Carter appealed his conviction in 2016. The appeals court found that he had no merit to his claim and upheld his conviction.

Further Reading:

"Commonwealth vs. Vernon T. Carter." 475 Mass. 512, April 8, 2016-September 19, 2016. Bristol County. masscases.com/cases/sjc/475/475mass512.html.

ELIZABETH BARROW

Woman suffocated to death in the Brandon Woods Nursing Home in Dartmouth, Massachusetts, on September 24, 2009.

Victim: Elizabeth Barrow, 100.

Accused: Laura Lundquist, 98.

Details: According to *The Boston Globe*, this most unusual story is as follows:

Laura Lundquist, 98, was very upset because she believed that her 100-year-old roommate at the Brandon Woods Nursing Home was conniving to take over their room. At 6:20 a.m., only 20 minutes after staff had seen her returning to her bed from the bathroom, Elizabeth Barrow was found dead with bed sheet pulled over her head a plastic bag tied around her head. The women had been arguing about Lundquist placing a table at the foot of Barrow's bed. Apparently, it made it hard for Barrow to walk to the bathroom. A nurse's aide moved the table so Barrow could have a path to the bathroom, and Lundquist punched her. It was reported that Lundquist vowed that she would get Barrow's window-side bed as she was planning to outlive her.

Lundquist told the investigators that she was in the bathroom when Barrow died and heard her scream. She didn't want to do anything because she was afraid she would get in trouble. She thought that Barrow had committed suicide.

Lundquist was indicted on second-degree murder charges. She was sent to Taunton State Hospital for competency evaluation. It was determined that Lundquist had a long standing diagnosis of dementia. Additionally, she had exhibited erratic behaviors. Previously, she felt that another roommate wanted to strangle her in her bed.

Lundquist was found not competent to stand trial and committed to Taunton State Hospital, living past 102 years in 2014, at last count.

Further Reading:

Abel, David, and Shelley Murphy. "Woman, 98, Indicted on Murder Charges." *The Boston Globe* (Boston, Massachusetts), 12 December 2009.

OSVALDO GONSALEZ MARTINEZ

Man shot to death at 68 Aetna Street, Fall River, Massachusetts, and dumped it in the water off Little Compton, Rhode Island, on December 27, 2009.

Victim: Osvaldo Gonsalez Martinez, 27.

Accused: Arnaldo Flores, 26.

Details: Arnaldo Flores shot Osvaldo Martinez in Fall River and then, with the help of his sister, Neidy Mendez, and her boyfriend, Carlos Rivera, wrapped the dead body in a carpet, drove to Little Compton from, and dumped it into the waters near Taylors Lane.

Flores contended that the death of Martinez was self-defense. Witnesses, however, said that Martinez had planned to rob Flores when he went to the Aetna Street apartment the day he was killed. Flores admitted that he was a drug dealer and Martinez was fronting the drugs (selling them for Flores).

According to *The Herald News*, "When Martinez and Mendez went to Aetna Street, Flores was alone in the apartment. Rivera and Mendez were off to Taunton to complete a drug deal. Flores didn't trust Mendez, so he would not let him in. He let Martinez in. Shortly after that, Martinez was dead from three bullets fired from a .45-caliber pistol Rivera kept in the home."

Trial: Arnaldo Flores was found guilty of second-degree murder and sentenced to life in prison.

Further Reading:

Moss, John. "Fall River Man Wanted in Connection with Murder Surrenders." *WickedLocal.com*, 9 January 2010. wickedlocal.com/article/20100109/News/301099789.
O'Connor, Kevin P. "Fall River's Drug Underworld Revealed in Flores Trial." *The Herald News*, 21 May 2011.

CHAPTER 3

2010-2016
IT'S NOT GETTING ANY BETTER

In 2010, there were an astounding 214 murders in Massachustts, the highest recorded in the years 2000-2016—5 of which were in Fall River and 3 in New Bedford. This figure in both cities was higher than the United States average for cities of the same size. The good news is that by 2015 the murder rate in Massachusetts had dropped from 214 to 131. Fewer murders are often the result of sweeping incarceration of street gang members and violent felons, as well as enforcing federal gun laws and taking unregistered and stolen firearms off the streets. The SouthCoast is certainly not Chicago or Los Angeles, but a single murder is still one too many, especially for the victims and families involved.

In Fall River there have been 13 murders in the first 6 years of the decade starting in 2010 and 21 in New Bedford. While Fall River had a zero murder rate in 2013, New Bedford has not been so lucky. In that same year, there were 6 murders reported in "The Whaling City." Are these numbers still due to what New Bedford mayor Frederick Kalisz (1998-2006) termed a "demographic transition," where newly arrived immigrants clash with longtime residents, leading to violent misunderstandings and mistrust between citizens and city officials?

According to Vox.com, criminologists still debate what caused the decrease in violent crime since the 1990s. Theories range from changes in policing tactics, more incarceration, and reductions in lead exposure as a child. However, no one can definitively say. Experts have developed many theories for the rise of murder rates. Dwindling resources have caused some police forces to pull back on previous tactics and strategies. Some argue that the easy availablity of higher-caliber weapons give rise to higher murder rates.

Studies that examine income inequality and poverty rates show that there is a connection to higher crime and murder rates. There is more likely to be violent murders when that segment of the population feels that an isulting remark, lack of status, and the widening disparity in income can increase the feeling of loss of opportunity—leading to the belief that there are only winners and losers. Desperation sparks violent acts.

In 2016, the poverty rate in Fall River was 22%—almost double the Massachusetts state average of 11.4%. Economic development is not advancing as quickly as other regions in the state. The average per capita income for Fall River was $22,154, lower than the national average of $29,829, and significantly lower than the statewide average of $38,069.

In 2016, the poverty rate in New Bedford was even higher—23.5%. The per capita income was $22,056, even lower than Fall River's.

With both of the SouthCoast's major cities experiencing such conditions, criminolgoists predict that both cities are situated for an explosion of violent crime.

Let's look at the demographics of both cities. Could it be that the diversity of Fall River and New Bedford is a contributing factor to their murder rates?

According to the United States Census of 2010, the population of Fall River was 88,857. The largest racial groups within the city are 83.4% Non-Hispanic White, 3.5% African American, 2.5% Asian, 0.2% Native American, and 7.4% Hispanic or Latino. 49% of residents are Luso-American or have origins somewhere in the former Portuguese Empire (Cape Verde, Medeira, the Azores, and Porgugal)—37% of the population described themselves as being of Portuguese ancestry. The next largest groups by ancestry are French 12.4%, Irish 8.9%, Cape Verdean 8.1%, English 6.0%, French Canadian 5.9%, Puerto Rican 4.5%, and Italian 3.6%.

The 2010 Census for New Bedford counted 95,072 residents. The racial makeup of the city was 66.1% Non-Hispanic White, 9.69% African American, 0.1% Native American, 1% Asian, 0.05% Pacific Islander, 13.51% from other races, and 3.92% from two or more races. Hispanic or Latino of any race were 16.11% of the population. The city is very multi-cultural and diverse; 46.7% of residents are Luso-American. The ethnic makeup of the city is estimated to be 33.8% Portuguese, 10.1% Puerto Rican, 9.1% French, 8.8% Cape Verdean, 6.9% Irish, 5.3% English.

Studies have shown, unexpectely and counter-intuitively, that higher levels of ethnic and linguistic diversity tend to aid in the reduction of crime, leading us to fall back on the idea that poverty can be cited as a precipitating factor, no matter the cultural and racial makeup of a community.

ARTHUR BURTON

Man shot to death in the backyard of a home on Purchase Street in New Bedford, Massachusetts, on January 20, 2010.

Victim: Arthur Burton, age unknown.

Accused: Seth Andrade, 19.

Details: According to the appeal of Seth Andrade, the facts of the case presented at trial are as follows:

"Shortly after 8:30 P.M., on January 20, 2010, [Arthur Burton] was shot and killed in the backyard at 192 Purchase Street in New Bedford. [Burton] died as a result of two gunshot wounds to the head, with injuries to his skull and brain. One bullet entered the right side of [Burton]'s face about one-half inch to midline on his nose and traveled upwards, front to back and lodging underneath the parietal scalp of the right side of his head. The presence of stippling at the site of the entrance to that wound indicated that [Burton] had been shot…from a distance of eighteen to twenty-four inches. The second bullet entered the back of [Burton]'s head on the right side, traveled down through his skull, and exited on the left side of his face, just below his earlobe.

"At the time of the shooting, nearby residents heard loud bangs, sounding like 'pops' or firecrackers. Two young men, appearing to be in their late teens, were seen leaving the area. One was wearing a brown canvas jacket and had a hood over his head; the other was wearing a hooded sweatshirt and a blue 'puffy' down jacket.

"The murder weapon was never found. Police, however, found a .380-caliber discharged cartridge casing and one spent projectile at the scene. A firearms identification expert gave his opinion, based on his microscopic examination of the spent projectile recovered at the scene and the projectile recovered at [Burton]'s autopsy, that the bullets had been fired from the same weapon.

"At approximately 7:45 P.M. on the day of the murder, [Burton] had attempted to purchase marijuana from a family friend and his supplier. [Burton] was accompanied by three men who wore hooded sweatshirts. [Burton] got the money for the drugs from one of these men. The money, however, was not real, and the supplier left with the drugs.

"[Burton] and the men he had been with also left. They were picked up by a taxicab at 8:01 P.M. and were dropped off near the residence of Edwin Jorge. Shortly thereafter, at 8:20 P.M., a taxicab returned to the area near Edwin's home and drove three men, including [Burton], to Acushnet Avenue, which is behind Purchase Street. The telephone call to the taxicab company for this ride was made from [Burton]'s cellular telephone.

"At about midnight, Edwin received a telephone call from his brother, Jordan, and went to the residence of Tyrone Solano. There he picked up Jordan, Solano, and [Andrade], and drove them to his mother's home in Fall River. When Edwin asked what was going on, [Andrade] said, 'Drop it.'

"About one week later, at Edwin's mother's home, Edwin had a conversation with [Andrade] about [Burton]'s death. [Andrade] stated that [Burton] 'did niggers dirty, so he had to go.' [Andrade] told Edwin that, when [Arthur Burton] was looking at his telephone, he had 'popped him,' and then 'popped him again.'...[Andrade] told Edwin that they had disposed of all the evidence with the exception of his jacket, which he had left at Solano's home.

"Police recovered [Andrade]'s brown jacket at Solano's home. Subsequent forensic testing on the jacket revealed gunshot residue on the lower sleeves and cuffs of the jacket, as well as inside the right front jacket pocket.

"[Andrade] initially denied that he was in the backyard of 192 Purchase Street when [Burton] was killed. Later, however, he admitted to being there and to wearing a brown jacket. He recounted that [Burton] had been trying to purchase marijuana from someone at that address when a person came into the yard and shot him. [Andrade] described the second shot as the 'finishing' shot. When confronted with the officers' assertion that gunshot residue had been found on his jacket, [Andrade] stated that he went shooting on occasion at a relative's home in Dartmouth.

"[Andrade] did not testify. The theory of the defense was that someone else had shot [Burton]. He called one witness, a forensic chemist...who testified that the negative control used by the Commonwealth in its gunshot residue testing had been contaminated. The defense also attacked the credibility of Edwin, arguing that the jury should not 'believe a thing [he] says.'"

Trial: In 2012, a jury convicted Seth Andrade of murder in the first degree on the theory of deliberate premeditation, and of unlawful possession of a firearm. He was sentenced to life in prison without the possibility of parole.

Afterword: Seth Andrade appealed his conviction in 2014 but the court ruled that his complaints had no merit and denied the request.

Further Reading:

"Commonwealth vs. Seth Andrade." 468 Mass. 543, May 9, 2014-June 25, 2014. Bristol County. masscases.com/cases/sjc/468/468mass543.html.

ANDREW TAYLOR

Man shot to death at the home of the accused in Tiverton, Rhode Island, on January 30, 2010.

Victim: Andrew Taylor, 25.

Accused: James Lapre, 24.

Details: James Lapre planned to rob Andrew Taylor of Freetown, Massachusetts, after Lapre was told by Taylor that he had an insurance settlement and planned on purchasing a large amount of prescription drugs to sell. Lapre shot Taylor on January 30, 2010, and left is body in the trunk of a rental car on Jones Street in Fall River. The car was towed to Freetown and one week later the body was discovered.

Blood traces were found in James Lapre's home, where authorities believe the murder took place.

Taylor was a college student, studying computer science in Fall River at Bristol Community College.

Trial: James Lapre pleaded no contest to first degree murder and was sentenced to life in prison without the possibility of parole. Lapre also received a 5-year sentence for failing to report a death, to be served consecutively.

Further Reading:

Vital, Derek. "James Lapre Sentenced to Life in Prison for Murder of Freetown Man." *The Herald News*, 30 September 2011.

JONATHAN NIEVES

Man shot to death at the Sunset Hill housing project on Bay Street in Fall River, Massachusetts, on February 26, 2010.

Victim: Jonathan Nieves, 25.

Accused: Erroll Powell, 21.

Details: According to the appeal brought by the Commonwealth, the facts of the case are as follows:

"On February, 26, 2010, or in the early morning hours of the following day, Jonathan Nieves was shot to death in his motor vehicle when he was mistaken for a gang member, 'PZ,' who was suspected of killing a member of the Mafiosa Street gang, to which [Powell] belonged. That night, [Powell] was informed by a female friend that PZ was at a night club in Fall River. The friend, who was accompanied by [Powell]'s girl friend, had mistaken Nieves for PZ. The two women followed Nieves in a motor vehicle when he drove away from the night club and kept [Powell], who was driving a motor vehicle owned by his neighbor, apprised of his location. A short time later, the women heard shots in the area where Nieves had parked. [Powell] returned his neighbor's motor vehicle sometime after 2:30 A.M. on February 27.

"After obtaining more information about what had occurred that evening, the police arrested [Powell] at 1:30 P.M. on June 14, 2010, on the charge of larceny of the neighbor's motor vehicle. Although the police apparently had probable cause to arrest [Powell] for murder, they did not obtain an arrest warrant for that charge, because they had not yet been authorized to do so by the district attorney. [Powell] was placed in a cell at the police station at approximately 2:45 P.M. and was held there until 11:45 P.M., when a State trooper went to retrieve him for an interview and found him partially asleep. The State trooper and a Fall River police officer thereafter interviewed [Powell] for two hours. [Powell] was alert and cooperative but yawned throughout the interview. After providing a Miranda waiver at the beginning of the interview, [Powell] began to talk about the motor vehicle larceny charge. The officers indicated that they were interested in discussing the murder of Nieves and that they believed that [Powell] was the perpetrator. During the course of the interrogation that followed, [Powell] admitted to shooting Nieves and made further inculpatory statements. Two months later, [Powell] was indicted on charges of assault and battery by means of a dangerous weapon, unlawful possession of a firearm, armed assault with intent to murder, and murder in the first degree."

Trial: Erroll Powell pleaded guilty to manslaughter, assault and battery with a dangerous weapon, and carrying an illegal firearm in a plea deal with the District Attorney's office. Powell was sentenced to 20 to 25 years in state prison.

Afterword: In 2014, the Commonwealth appealed the pretrial ruling to suppress statements made by Erroll Powell 9 hours after his arrest on another charge. According to the Rosario rule, any statements made after 6 hours in custody and before being brought to court for arraignment are not allowed into evidence. The court agreed with the previous ruling disallowing those comments to be entered into evidence.

Further Reading:

"Commonwealth vs. Erroll Powell." 468 Mass. 272, February 6, 2014-June 6, 2014. Bristol County. masscases.com/cases/sjc/468/468mass272.html.
"Manslaughter Conviction Leads to Two Decade Sentence for Fall River Man." *The Herald News,* 22 March 2016.

DAVID ARRUDA & ALFRED ARRUDA JR.

Murder at 80 Edmund Street in Fall River and suicide at the Watuppa Boat Club on Beaulieu Avenue in Westport, Massachusetts, on March 1, 2010.

Victim: David Arruda, 42.

Accused: Alfred Arruda Jr., 43.

Details: Within 40 minutes of filing a restraining order against his son Alfred Arruda Jr., Alfred Arruda Sr, his sister Barbara Platt, and Arruda's son David returned to their home at 80 Edmond Street in Fall River. At 12:20 p.m., when David got out of the car and approached the porch, he was shot in the chest. Barbara was getting out of the car when she was shot. She survived her wound.

Alfred Arruda Jr. then drove to Westport in his green Ford Explorer and shot himself at the Watuppa Boat Club at 1:15 p.m.

According to reporting in *The Herald News*, "The restraining order, through March 15 when a hearing was scheduled, ordered that Alfred Arruda Jr. 'immediately surrender' to city police all guns, ammunition, gun licenses and firearms identification cards, and that his license to carry weapons be immediately suspended. A notice was to be issued immediately to city police, the order said. A starting date of recent problems was listed as Feb. 24, when the father wrote that 'Freddie (his son) put me in imminent danger by refusing my caregiver to administer my medication to me. On Feb. 24 Freddie called the police to remove my caregiver from the property against my wishes, causing me to go without appropriate care for the rest of the evening,' he wrote. He also wrote that his son that night was 'aggressive' and 'forceful.'

"Court records reported that the 6-foot, 270-pound Alfred Arruda Jr. had access to three handguns and two rifles. It said he had no history of violence toward police and had a history of alcohol/drug abuse."

Further Reading:

Holtzman, Michael. "Gunman's Father had been Granted Restraining Order Just Prior to Shooting." *The Herald News*, 3 March 2010.

CONRAD BEAULIEU

Man stabbed to death in his home at 31 Woodland Circle in Tiverton, Rhode Island, on September 4, 2010.

Victim: Conrad Beaulieu, 62.

Accused: Joel Beaulieu, 29.

Details: The undisputed facts of the case presented to the Rhode Island Superior Court in Joel Beaulieu's request for a determination of his sanity are as follows:

"At one minute past midnight on September 5, 2010, Corporal Kenneth Cabral, of the Tiverton Police Department, responded to the Beaulieu residence at 31 Woodland Circle after being dispatched for a domestic in progress. Corporal Cabral immediately observed Mrs. Beaulieu, covered in blood, lying outside of the home on a walkway near the driveway. Patrolman Jonathan Cunningham entered the residence with Corporal Cabral and Patrolman Warren Caldwell. They observed Conrad Beaulieu, lying in blood and motionless, in the kitchen. Patrolman Cunningham also observed a knife sheath at the bottom of the stairs. In the Patrolman's presence, Corporal Cabral and Patrolman Caldwell asked Mr. Beaulieu 'who did this to you' and he responded three times 'son.' Simultaneously, Officer William R. Monroe asked Mrs. Beaulieu 'who did this to you' and she twice responded 'he did it' and gestured toward [Joel Beaulieu], who was ordered to lie face down on the walkway.

"[Joel Beaulieu] was then approached by Officer Louis Farias, Jr., who asked him what his name was and why he was injured. [Joel Beaulieu] responded that 'his hand hurt and he [could] feel something on his back.' After inspecting him, Officer Farias informed [Joel Beaulieu] that 'his back was fine and that he had a cut on his hand.' When the Officer asked [Joel Beaulieu] what happened that evening, he uttered that 'he had stabbed his parents with [a] knife.' After Officer Farias read [Joel Beaulieu] his rights, he inquired why [Joel Beaulieu] would want to stab his parents. [Joel Beaulieu] then responded that 'his father sexually abuses him,' 'he was abused by his father last night while his mother watched,' 'he was in bed last night and awoke with his father on top of him from behind abusing him,' 'his mother was watching the act,' 'he started to vomit in bed,' and 'he was in fear he was going to be abused tonight and wanted to stop it before it happened again, so he stabbed his parents.' [Joel Beaulieu] further volunteered that he had purchased a knife in New Hampshire, which he retrieved from the garage. He also admitted that he began stabbing his father in bed and continued to stab him as Mr. Beaulieu ran to the kitchen. [Joel Beaulieu] stated that 'he just wouldn't go down.'

"At nineteen minutes after midnight, Little Compton Firefighter, Fred M. Melnyk, Jr., arrived on the scene and was assigned to transport [Joel Beaulieu] to Newport Hospital. Firefighter Melnyk cut off [Joel Beaulieu]'s blood-soaked tee-shirt and [Joel Beaulieu] told him that 'he thought his penis was cut off,' although Firefighter Melnyk noted that there was 'no indication of injury.'

"Firefighter Melnyk overheard the accompanying officers, Corporal Cabral and Officer Jason Dunlea, question [Joel Beaulieu] about his motives for the stabbings. [Joel Beaulieu] stated that Mr. Beaulieu 'raped him' two nights before. [Joel Beaulieu] explained that Mr. Beaulieu jumped on his back and began kissing his neck and cheek 'while saying 'I love you." [Joel Beaulieu] told Firefighter Melnyk that he stabbed his mother because '[s]he is the one who gives me the meds.' He further added that his parents 'were plotting to kill [his] grandparents tomorrow' and that his grandparents 'wanted [him] to do it.'

"Mrs. Beaulieu recounted the events of the evening prior to the attack, September 4, 2010. On that night, she asked [Joel Beaulieu] if he would like to go to Butler Hospital as he was having trouble sleeping and could be provided medication there that would assist him. When [Joel Beaulieu] expressed a preference to 'try to sleep at home,' Mr. Beaulieu gave him his deceased mother's rosary beads and said: '[p]ut these rosaries under your pillow. She'll help you to sleep.' The Beaulieus retired at approximately 10:30-11:00 PM.

"Later that night, Mrs. Beaulieu was 'shaken awake.' She got out of bed and saw blood coming down her husband's face. She described that [Joel Beaulieu] then 'turned on [her]' and struck her in the head with a knife. She ran downstairs and outside, through the garage to the driveway, where she collapsed. Mrs. Beaulieu believes that [Joel Beaulieu] came out the front door and continued to stab her. She further believes that 'he was out of his mind.' [Joel Beaulieu] told his mother that he could not believe she was still breathing and she said, 'Joel, I love you.' Mrs. Beaulieu also stated that the last words she heard from her husband was '911.'

"Mr. Beaulieu perished at the hands of [Joel Beaulieu], who savagely and relentlessly inflicted over fifty stab wounds to his father's 'face, head, neck, chest, sternum, back, shoulders, arms and hands.' Mrs. Beaulieu suffered a severed ulna nerve in her left arm, as well as numerous lacerations and stab wounds to her head, neck, chest, and face. By her own account it is a 'miracle' that she survived."

Trial: The trial had been held for two days in late November 2011, when the defense requested a ruling about the sanity of Joel Beaulieu.

Afterword: In December of 2011, the Rhode Island Superior Court determined that Joel Beaulieu was not guilty of the murder of his father by reason of insanity.

Further Reading:

"Rhode Island vs. Joel Beaulieu." Filed 15 December 2011. law.justia.com/cases/rhode-island/superior-court/2011/10-0380.html

Sanderson, Matthew. "Superior Court Judge Declares Joel Beaulieu Not Guilty by Reason of Insanity." *Patch.com*, 16 December 2011. patch.com/rhode-island/tiverton/superior-court-declares-joel-beaulieu-not-guilty-by-r397f585ced

OLIVIA CRUZ

Woman neglected by her caregiver son, resulting in her death, on Douglas Street in Fall River, Massachusetts, on September 29, 2010.

Victim: Olivia Cruz, 90.

Accused: Filip M. Cruz, 51.

Details: In the appeal for the conviction of Filip Cruz, the facts of the case were presented as follows:

"In September, 2008, [Filip Cruz] lived with his parents, Olivia and Antonio, in Fall River. Olivia suffered from dementia associated with Alzheimer's disease. She was obese and could not move without assistance. Antonio, who was eighty-nine years old at the time of the events in question, was also in poor health and could not care for Olivia on his own. Thus, [Filip Cruz] assumed responsibility for his mother's care. He claimed to have bathed, dressed, and fed Olivia daily, and had left his job in order to provide her with full-time care.

"On September 28, 2010, paramedics were dispatched to the Cruzes' home in response to a report that Olivia had suffered a stroke. [Filip Cruz] was outside when the paramedics arrived. He was agitated and urged the paramedics to get his mother out of the house. When the paramedics entered the house, they were overwhelmed by the odor of feces, urine, and rotting flesh. They found Olivia slumped over in a recliner. She was lethargic and incoherent. She was also dirty and unkempt, and as the paramedics were moving her in preparation for transport to the hospital, they found a dirty underpad, known as a 'Chux,' stuck to her skin. She was in acute distress: she had a weak pulse and was extremely dehydrated.

"Olivia was taken to the trauma room at St. Anne's Hospital in Fall River and found to be in septic shock. The subsequent examination revealed that Olivia had decubitus ulcers (deep open sores) which had grown to the size of softballs that encompassed her entire buttocks such that her bones were visible. Olivia underwent emergency surgery to remove the infected tissue, which had become gangrenous. However, the surgery was not successful and Olivia died the following morning as a result of sepsis and septic shock caused by the widespread infection. The surgeon opined that the ulcers would have taken six weeks to develop, and according to the medical examiner who conducted the autopsy, Olivia could have been in a state of septic shock for up to a week. The medical examiner also opined that the infection resulting from prolonged immersion in feces could have affected Olivia for over a week and up to six or seven months. Both the surgeon and the emergency room doctor who treated Olivia testified that the sores were preventable and could have been treated, at least initially, by moving Olivia to alleviate the pressure on her buttocks. [Filip Cruz] claimed that he moved his mother from the recliner daily to bathe her, but Antonio contradicted this claim and told the police that [Filip Cruz] did not take Olivia out of the recliner. [Filip Cruz] acknowledged that he noticed a 'reddened area' on her buttocks approximately two weeks prior to Olivia's death, and that she had been confined to the recliner for two or three weeks.

"The Commonwealth presented evidence of the complete squalor in which Olivia and Antonio lived. After Olivia died, the police executed a search warrant at the home and found rotting food in the kitchen and flies everywhere. A commode covered with dried feces was in Antonio's bedroom. The jury also heard evidence of [Filip Cruz]'s unusual behavior, which ranged from being anxious and agitated when the paramedics arrived, to being uncooperative and flippant with medical personnel at the hospital. Upon learning that the police wanted to speak with him about his mother's condition, [Filip Cruz] responded, 'Are they going to arrest me now or later?'"

Trial: Filip Cruz was found guilty of wantonly or recklessly permitting serious bodily injury to his mother, an elder or person with a disability under his care, who died of sepsis caused by an infection, and with having wantonly or recklessly committed or permitted another to commit abuse, neglect, or mistreatment upon the victim. He was sentenced to 9 ½ years in prison, followed by 2-3 years of probation.

Afterword: On appeal, Filip Cruz challenged the sufficiency of the evidence claiming, in particular, that the Commonwealth failed to prove that he acted wantonly or recklessly. He also argues that his convictions are duplicative because one of the convictions was a lesser included offense of the same thing. The appeals court disagreed and affirmed his conviction.

Olivia's husband, Antonio, passed away before the trial began.

Further Reading:

"Commonwealth vs. Filip M. Cruz." 88 Mass. App. Ct. 206, February 27, 2015-September 4, 2015. Bristol County. masscases.com/cases/app/88/88massappct206.html.

O'Connor, Kevin P. "Fall River Man Sentenced to Serve 9-10 Years for Fatal Neglect of his Mother." *The Herald News*, 28 September 2012.

MICHAEL CORREIA

Man stabbed to death outside an AA meeting near the Trinity Church Soup Kitchen on Purchase Street in New Bedford, Massachusetts, on October 20, 2010.

Victim: Michael Correia, 34.

Accused: Jonathan Keith Niemic, 22.

Details: In the appeal for the conviction of Jonathan Niemic, the facts of the case were presented as follows:

"[Jonathan Niemic] was incarcerated on an unrelated matter from about the middle of August, 2010, until October 15, 2010. While he was incarcerated, [Niemic] wrote a letter to a woman named Lisa whom he had started dating in June. In the letter he confessed that he thought she was 'perfect.' During [Niemic]'s incarceration [Michael Correia] took notice of Lisa and began flirting with her. After [Niemic] was released from his incarceration he learned of the developing relationship between [Correia] and Lisa. This angered [Niemic], who told a friend that the next time he saw [Correia] he was going to punch him in the head. On October 19, 2010, [Niemic] and Lisa socialized with another couple until about 11 P.M. At one point [Niemic] and Lisa became involved in a mild argument over [Correia]. The two couples agreed to get together the next day.

"The two couples met at about 2 P.M. on October 20, as planned. At about 7:30 P.M. they went to a soup kitchen in New Bedford because Lisa had forgotten her key to the addiction recovery house for women where she was staying, and other residents of the recovery house were at the soup kitchen attending an Alcoholics Anonymous meeting. She planned to borrow a key from one of the residents who was at the meeting. [Michael Correia] was at the meeting. [Niemic] and Lisa appeared to be having a serious conversation.

"During a break in the meeting [Niemic] walked over to [Correia] and said he had been hearing things that [Correia] was saying about him, and he felt 'disrespected.' [Niemic] then started punching [Correia] in the head. [Correia] tried to deflect the blows and backed away. [Niemic] started chasing and lunging at [Correia]. He stabbed [Correia] six times with a small folding pocket knife, a type of knife [Niemic] owned. The incident lasted no more than thirty seconds. [Niemic] left the scene with the people who had arrived with him. As they were driving, [Niemic] said that he had stabbed [Correia], adding, 'I hope I didn't kill him.' [Correia] died later that night from his wounds, which included two puncture wounds to the heart and one that completely passed through the liver.

"[Niemic] threw the knife into a wooded area. It was later recovered by police. [Niemic]'s friends left him at a supermarket where he telephoned his grandmother. He asked her to give him a ride. [Niemic]'s grandmother drove him to the home of one of his close friends. He told one of the people living there that he had gotten into a fight over a girl with someone at the soup kitchen. He said that he and the other man got into a fist fight, and that the other man got the better of him. [Niemic] said that he went to the vehicle in which he had arrived, retrieved a knife, and then 'slashed' the other man in the chest two or three times. He said that he did not know if the other man was still alive. This person heard him make several telephone calls trying to find out if the other man was alive. [Niemic] seemed very worried.

"Police went to the friend's house looking for [Niemic] at approximately 2 A.M. on October 21, 2010. They found him hiding in a cubby hole in a rear hallway. He was placed under arrest. Police observed a fresh cut on [Niemic]'s right hand between the webbing of his right index finger and his thumb. They also observed three fresh cuts on his left hand, two of which were between the webbing of his index finger and his thumb, and the third was on the pad of this thumb.

"A friend with whom [Niemic] had socialized on October 19 and 20, 2010, testified for the defense. He said that [Michael Correia] threw the first punch. He also testified that about two months before the killing, [Correia] had threatened to stab [Niemic]. [Niemic] testified in his defense. He said that he was fearful of [Correia], who was known as a 'tough guy,' and referred to as 'Big Mike.' [Correia] was 'a lot bigger' and ten years older than [Niemic]. He said that he wanted to resolve their issues by talking when other people were nearby. He testified that [Correia] started punching him and then pulled out a knife. [Niemic] grabbed the blade of the knife and pulled it out of [Correia]'s hand. [Correia] came after him and tried to grab him. [Niemic] swung the knife 'wildly' in order to defend himself. He said that he did not realize that he was stabbing [Correia], or that [Correia] might be seriously hurt, and that he broke down in tears over the incident. He said that he never intended to kill [Correia].

"[Niemic] testified that he once owned a similar knife, but not at that time. He said that the knife that was involved in the stabbing was not his, and that he did not recall telling anyone that the fight was over a girl. He denied going back to the car in which he arrived at the soup kitchen to get the knife, and he said that he had no recollection of telling anyone that he did so. He testified that [Michael Correia] had threatened to stab him about two months before the stabbing."

Trial: In 2012, a jury found Jonathan Niemic guilty of murder in the first degree on a theory of extreme atrocity or cruelty. He was sentenced to life in prison without the possibility of parole.

Afterword: On appeal, Jonathan Niemic asserted errors by trial counsel, by the prosecutor, and by the judge. His judgment was overturned (vacated). The appeals court gave the Commonwealth the option of either retrying Niemic on the murder indictment or accepting a reduction of the verdict to manslaughter.

Retrial: In 2016, Jonathan Niemic was again found guilty of murder in the first degree on a theory of extreme atrocity or cruelty. He was again sentenced to life in prison without the possibility of parole.

Further Reading:

"Commonwealth vs. Jonathan Niemic." 472 Mass. 665, April 9, 2015-September 17, 2015. Bristol County. masscases.com/cases/sjc/472/472mass665.html.

McCready, Dan. "Man Receives Life Sentence in Retrial." *WBSM.com*, 30 September 2016. wbsm.com/man-receives-life-sentence-in-retrial/.

EDWARD PLATTS

Man shot to death while sitting in his car at the Father Diafario Village housing complex on Johnson Street in Fall River, Massachusetts, on November 18, 2010.

Victim: Edward Platts, 31.

Accused: Charles Mendez, 28, Tacuma Massie, 29.

Details: According to the appeal of Charles Mendez, the facts of the case as presented at trial are as follows:

"On the evening of November 18, 2010, just after 6 p.m., [Mendez and Massie] ambushed and robbed Ryan Moitoso in a parking lot. Moitoso thought he was meeting Mendez's girl friend to sell her marijuana. The girl friend drove [Mendez and Massie] near the area where she was to meet Moitoso and let them out of her vehicle. As Moitoso spoke with the girl friend, [Mendez and Massie] approached him from behind. One of them hit him in the head with a hard metal object and told him to empty his pockets. Moitoso turned over some cash and marijuana, and heard a clicking noise that sounded like a gun being cocked, before being allowed to return to his vehicle. [Mendez and Massie] got back into the girl friend's vehicle, and she drove away. When she asked what had happened, one of [Mendez and Massie] replied, 'That's life,' and tossed a bag of marijuana into the front passenger area.

"Next, the girl friend dropped [Mendez and Massie] off at a nearby housing complex where Massie had arranged to meet Platts (victim) on the pretext of wanting to make a marijuana purchase. [Mendez and Massie] intended to rob the victim of the approximately $4,000 that, Massie had learned, he was carrying that day. Prior to the meeting, a witness was parked in the housing complex and, while sitting in his vehicle, observed two men fitting the description of [Mendez and Massie] walk by him. The victim, who had a puppy with him, parked his vehicle behind the witness's vehicle. The witness then observed the same two men walk toward the back of his vehicle. Within seconds, the witness heard a gunshot and a vehicle engine accelerate, and then he felt the victim's vehicle hit the back of his vehicle. The witness telephoned 911 and told the dispatcher that a man had been shot. A resident of the complex looked out of her window at the sound of the gun shot to observe an individual matching Mendez's description get out of the passenger side of the victim's vehicle and quickly leave the scene carrying something clutched to his chest.

"In the meantime, Mendez's girl friend received several telephone calls from Massie between 6:41 and 6:49 p.m. She returned to the complex and picked up both Massie and Mendez, pulling away quickly from the curb where they entered her vehicle. A State trooper who was in the housing complex investigating the 911 call observed the vehicle's hasty departure, and followed it.

"When [Mendez and Massie] were arrested, both were carrying handguns; Massie's was loaded. Massie had more than $4,000 in cash, Mendez's clothes were stained with the victim's blood, and police found the victim's puppy in the vehicle. Police found Mendez's hat in the victim's vehicle.

"The victim was shot at close range behind his right ear as he sat in his vehicle. At trial, Mendez claimed that the victim had drawn a gun on him and, after a struggle, he shot the victim in self-defense. He also claimed that the handgun that he had had in his possession when he was apprehended belonged to the victim."

Charles Mendez and Tacuma Massie, were each indicted on charges of (1) murder in the first degree; (2) carrying a firearm without a license; (3) carrying a loaded firearm without a license; and (4) armed robbery. They additionally were charged with assault and battery by means of a dangerous weapon and armed robbery on separate indictments in connection with a separate incident involving a different individual.

Trial: In September of 2013, both men were convicted of all charges and both sentenced to life in prison without the possibility of parole.

Afterword: Charles Mendez appealed his conviction in 2016. The court affirmed his conviction.

Further Reading:

"Commonwealth vs. Charles Mendez." 476 Mass. 512, October 11, 2016-February 22, 2017. Bristol County. masscases.com/cases/sjc/476/476mass512.html.

MICHAEL DUARTE

Man killed by blunt force trauma to the head with brain injuries at a home on Churchill Street in New Bedford, Massachusetts, on November 5, 2011.

Victim: Michael Duarte, 36.

Accused: Thomas Gardner, 34.

Details: According to the 2017 appeal of Thomas Gardner, the facts of the case are as follows:

"[Michael Duarte] lived in New Bedford with his girl friend and their two daughters. Shortly before 9 a.m. on November 5, 2011, [Michael Duarte] left his home, driving a Honda Civic automobile, after telling his girl friend that he was going to look at a house, located on Churchill Street, that was for sale. He was supposed to return home shortly to take care of his daughters. When [Michael Duarte] failed to return, his girl friend began calling him repeatedly on his cellular telephone beginning at 9:30 a.m., but she was unable to reach him. That afternoon, she drove to the house on Churchill Street that [Michael Duarte] had gone to see, but no one answered when she knocked on the door. Later that evening she contacted the New Bedford police to report that [Michael Duarte] was missing.

"On the morning of November 9, officers with the Fairfield, Connecticut, police department learned that [Michael Duarte]'s Honda Civic was at a rest area off of Interstate Route 95. When the first officer arrived, she observed [Michael Duarte]'s vehicle parked at the far end of the parking lot, and [Gardner] sitting in the driver's seat. When [Gardner] saw the police cruiser, he fled in the vehicle, reaching speeds in excess of one hundred miles per hour and, among other things, struck another vehicle and ran over the foot of a police officer. [Gardner] eventually lost control of the vehicle, abandoning it in a wooded area. He continued on foot until he reached Westport, Connecticut, where he entered a building that was under construction and hid.

"Shortly afterward, police officers arrested [Gardner] as he walked through Westport. [Gardner] initially denied that he was Thomas Gardner and claimed that he was a construction contractor working on the building where he had been hiding.

"[Gardner] was eventually transported to a police station in Fairfield,

Connecticut, where he was questioned by a member of the Massachusetts State police and a detective with the New Bedford police department. The interview was recorded and later shown to the jury at trial…[Gardner] stated that he was traveling with a 'buddy' who was going to Florida and who had agreed to drop [Gardner] off at his mother's house in Pennsylvania on the way. [Gardner] said that he and his friend had left New Bedford late in the evening on November 6 in the friend's Honda Civic. En route, they pulled off at the Fairfield rest stop, where they remained for two days. [Gardner] said that his friend had been inside a restaurant at the rest stop when the police cruiser had appeared, and that [Gardner] fled without him in the Honda Civic. After some prompting, [Gardner] indicated that the person he had been traveling with was [Michael Duarte], who, he suggested, was going to Florida to get away from his girl friend.

"Later that same day, the New Bedford police department contacted [Gardner]'s ex-wife and obtained her permission to search the Churchill Street house. There, the police discovered [Duarte]'s body hidden beneath a staircase in the basement, wrapped in a painter's tarpaulin secured with tape, with a plastic bag placed over his head. A paint can, a white painter's cloth, and other painter's materials had been piled on top of the body. In the kitchen, blood was found on the floor, a ceiling fan, and a wall clock. Police also detected blood on the basement stairs. There was testimony that the blood on the wall clock in the kitchen belonged to [Michael Duarte]. Outside the house, the police discovered a trash bag containing a sweatshirt with both [Michael Duarte]'s and [Gardner]'s blood on a sleeve, a T-shirt with [Duarte]'s blood on the back, and a hammer bearing both [Duarte]'s and [Gardner]'s blood. Subsequent investigation of [Gardner]'s cellular telephone showed that on November 5, 2011, [Gardner] had called [Duarte] at 8:24 a.m. and 10:47 a.m., and that [Duarte] had called [Gardner] at 8:38 a.m. and 9:06 a.m.

"The medical examiner testified that [Duarte]'s death was caused by blunt force trauma to the head and brain injuries. [Duarte] had suffered nineteen lacerations and two abrasions to his head; thirteen of the lacerations went to the bone. There were four distinct skull fractures. All of these injuries were consistent with having been caused by blows from a hammer. All the injuries were inflicted at around the same time and, although any one laceration alone could have been fatal, there was no way to determine the order in which the injuries were sustained, which injury rendered [Duarte] unconscious, or which caused his death. [Duarte] also had lacerations on his face, bleeding around both eyes, and minor abrasions on his right hand. He was missing some teeth that were later discovered in his stomach. The medical examiner opined that [Michael Duarte] had swallowed them prior to his death.

"At trial, [Gardner] admitted that he had killed [Duarte] with the hammer that the police had found, but claimed that he had acted in self-defense. He testified that he was living at the Churchill Street house and that, on the morning of November 5, 2011, he had arranged to meet [Duarte] there to buy heroin from him. When [Gardner] gave [Duarte] money for the heroin purchase, however, [Duarte] became angry because [Gardner] already owed him money and did not have enough cash for the new purchase. According to [Gardner], [Duarte] punched him and a fight ensued, during which [Duarte] tackled him and slammed him to the floor; [Duarte] then got on top of [Gardner], putting his knees on [Gardner]'s chest and his hands around [Gardner]'s throat, choking him. [Gardner] testified that he then grabbed a hammer from a nearby shelf and began 'slapping' [Duarte]'s head with the side of the hammer before finally striking him with the face of the hammer and knocking him out briefly. After [Gardner] stood up and tried to catch his breath, however, [Duarte] regained consciousness, grabbed [Gardner]'s pants leg, and tried to yank [Gardner] back down to the ground. At that point, [Gardner] testified, he struck [Duarte] again with the face of the hammer, killing him. [Gardner] then wrapped [Duarte]'s body in a tarpaulin and put it in the basement; disposed of the hammer and clothes in the trash; took the money from [Duarte]'s wallet; sent a false text message to [Duarte]'s cellular telephone asking him why he had not yet arrived; hid [Duarte]'s wallet and [Duarte]'s cellular telephone; and arranged to meet a friend to sell him [Duarte]'s drugs. The next day [Gardner] fled New Bedford."

Trial: Thomas Gardner was found guilty of murder in the first degree on the theory of extreme atrocity or cruelty. He was sentenced to life in prison without the possibility of parole.

Afterword: Thomas Gardner appealed his conviction in 2017, claiming that (1) the prosecutor's references to [Gardner]'s prearrest silence during cross-examination and in closing argument were improper; (2) the prosecutor mischaracterized evidence during closing argument; and (3) the judge's instructions to the jury concerning lesser included offenses were erroneous. The appeals court affirmed his conviction and refused to grant Thomas Gardner relief.

Further Reading:

"Commonwealth vs. Thomas Gardner." 479 Mass. 764, November 10, 2017-June 18, 2018. Bristol County. masscases.com/cases/sjc/479/479mass764.html.

REKSMEY TIENG

Woman run over and killed in Fall River, Massachusetts, on March 15, 2012.

Victim: Reksmey Tieng, 28.

Accused: Alejandro Delgado, 41.

Details: According to reporting in *The Herald News*, Alejandro Delgado called the Fall River police at 10:32 p.m., saying that Reksmey Tieng was not breathing or responsive. Police arrived to find Tieng on a mattress that was covered with vomit and stained with blood. Delgado was performing CPR and told the officers that Tieng had taken narcotics during the day.

Delgado told police that when he returned to his home at 10:20, shortly after leaving to get cigarettes, he found Tieng unresponsive.

Neighbors had reported hearing Tieng scream at 4:30 p.m. and then seeing Delgado pick her up from beneath his truck and carry her inside.

Delgado claimed that Tieng threatened him with a knife in their home, so he went out to his truck to leave. Tieng then came out, opened the passenger-side door, picked up a box cutter, utility knife, that was inside the cab and swung it at him. Delgado said it was then that he gunned the truck. He didn't mean to hurt her, but the passenger side tire ran over Tieng in her pelvic area.

Delgado said her brought her inside but she refused medical treatment.

Trial: Alejandro Delgado was found guilty of manslaughter and sentenced to 20 years in prison

Further Reading:

O'Connor, Kevin P.. "Fall River Man Charged with Manslaughter in Woman's Death." *The Herald News*, 16 March 2012.

AJA PASCUAL

Woman shot to death on the 800 block of Cherry Street in Fall River, Massachusetts, on September 29, 2012.

Victim: Aja Pascual, 31.

Accused: Brandyn LePage, 20.

Details: Brandyn LePage met Aja Pascual for a drug deal at midday on September 29, 2012. Pascual was a street dealer of cocaine. Instead, LePage shot and robbed her. Her cell phone was found in the car (the murder scene) and showed a series of calls been Pascual and LePage, prior to the shooting.

DNA tests were conducted on blood spots found on clothing worn by LePage. It proved to be Pascual's.

Trial: Brandyn LePage was found guilty of murder in the first degree, armed robbery, and unlicensed possession of a firearm. He was sentenced to life in prison without parole and 4-5 years in prison on the other two counts, to be served concurrently.

Further Reading:

"Brandyn LePage Found Guilty of Murder." *The Herald News*, 24 June 2016.

LISA MELLO

Woman strangled to death in her home at 500 Ocean Grove Avenue in Swansea, Massachusetts, on November 24, 2012.

Victim: Lisa Mello, 51.

Accused: David Sousa, 53.

Details: David Sousa strangled Lisa Mello, his girlfriend at the time, in her home in Swansea on November 24, 2012. When Sousa was indicted in 2013, he was in custody in Rhode Island on a probation violation from a domestic disorderly conduct charge from May 2004. He was originally sentenced to 1 year in prison with 9 years of probation.

Trial: David Sousa pleaded guilty to manslaughter and was sentenced to 14-20 years in prison. There was no trial. Sousa was credited with time served dating back to December 2013.

Further Reading:

Fraga, Brian. "R.I. Man Gets 14-20 Years for Manslaughter in Swansea Woman's Death." *The Herald News*, 8 May 2015.

BABY ARIEL ELUZIARIO

Infant beaten to death and dropped on the floor in an apartment on Adams Street in New Bedford, Massachusetts, on January 23, 2013.

Victim: Ariel Eluziario, 9 months.

Accused: Ethan Harrison, 21.

Details: According to reporting on the *SouthCoastToday.com*, "On Jan. 23, 2013, about two hours after he started babysitting the child in the New Bedford apartment on Adams Street where he and Amanda lived, Harrison arrived at the mother's workplace, insisting on seeing her, according to Gregg Miliote, a spokesman for Bristol County District Attorney Thomas M. Quinn III.

"The child was limp, unresponsive and in need of medical attention, so a manager at her workplace drove them all to St. Luke's Hospital in New Bedford, Miliote said. The child was treated and then airlifted to Hasbro Children's Hospital in Providence and pronounced dead later that evening.

"According to court records, Harrison told police he grew angry when the baby became 'fussy' and dropped her to the floor, causing her to hit her head. He also admitted 'forcefully picking the baby up' off the floor, snapping her head forward.

"He said he threw the child on the bed so hard she bounced off, falling 4 feet to the floor, hitting her head again. He also shook her, slapped her three times around the mouth and two times on the side of the face.

"Bruising was evident on the baby's face, ears, arms and back, according to Miliote. An autopsy found the child was bleeding between the brain and the skull, and she had brain swelling and lacerations to the lining of her mouth."

Trial: Ethan Harrison pleaded guilty in 2016 to second-degree murder of his former girlfriend's infant daughter. He was sentenced to life in prison, eligible for parole in 15 years of his life sentence.

Further Reading:

Brown, Curt. "New Bedford Man Sentenced to Life in Prison for 2013 Baby Death." *SouthCoastToday.com*, 7 January 2016. southcoasttoday.com/article/20160107/NEWS/160109630.

REBECCA FELTEAU

Woman died from having her throat cut in Ashland Place home in New Bedford, Massachusetts, on March 10, 2013.

Victim: Rebecca Felteau, 33.

Accused: Pedro DeSousa, 47.

Details: Rebecca Felteau worked as a prostitute, with Pedro DeSousa as her pimp. However, it was reported by those who knew her that DeSousa was obsessed with Felteau and would follow her in his car, threatening to hurt her. It was reported that Felteau would call DeSousa daily for money and drugs and in return she performed sexual favors for him. De Sousa was accused of cutting Felteau's throat with a box cutter in his home.

DeSousa was charged in January 2010 with assault and battery for slapping Felteau, but the complaint was apparently dismissed.

Afterword: While there are no news reports regarding a conviction in this case, or whether DeSousa pleaded to the crime, it can be confirmed that Pedro DeSousa is in custody in the Massachusetts prison system as of September, 2018.

Further Reading:

Brown, Curt. "A Stormy Relationship Ends in Death." *SouthCoastToday.com*, 23 March 2013. southcoasttoday.com/article/20130323/news/303230332.

TIFFANY ANN DURFEE

Woman stabbed to death in her 68 North Street apartment in New Bedford, Massachusetts, on March 13, 2013.

Victim: Tiffany Ann Durfee, 35.

Accused: Jeremy Amaral, 34.

Details: Tiffany Ann Durfee was stabbed to death in her apartment on North Street in New Bedford on March 13, 2013. Her assailant was Jeremy Amaral, who left her to die after stealing her 55-inch flat screen television. He sold the TV for drug money.

Trial: Jeremy Amaral was convicted of first-degree murder and witness intimidation and sentenced to life in prison without the possibility of parole.

Further Reading:

"Man Convicted in 2013 Fatal Stabbing." *The Boston Globe* (Boston, Massachusetts), 30 October 2015.

MITCHELL STEVENSON & CHRISTIAN WILSON

Murder/Suicide at 375 Stephen French Road in Swansea, Massachusetts, on June 15, 2013.

Victim: Mitchell Stevenson, 37.

Accused: Christian Wilson, 43.

Details: In a dispute over money owed for a car restoration, Mitchell Stevenson was shot three times outside Christian Wilson's home at 275 Stephen French Road in Swansea. Wilson then went inside the house and shot himself, committing suicide.

Stephenson was a mechanic and had helped Wilson restore a 1965 Chevrolet Impala. The deal between them was that Wilson would pay $5000 for his work and had driven to Wilson's home to collect what was due him.

Further Reading:

Gagne, Michael. "DA Identifies People Involved in Swansa Murder-Suicide." *The Herald News* (Fall River, Massachusetts), 17 June 2013.

JOYCE HOWLAND

Woman died after her throat was cut in her home on Hamlet Street in Fairhaven, Massachusetts, on October 14, 2013.

Victim: Joyce Howland, 69.

Accused: Joshua Silva, 36.

Details: Joshua Silva worked as a contractor and had installed attic insulation for Joyce Howland. Three days later, he returned to steal her jewelry and cut her throat, killing her. He pawned the jewelry for $380 to buy drugs. Silvia was a heroin junkie and often scoped out people's houses while working for the homeowner.

The key evidence for charging Silva was a DNA match for Howland's blood on Silva's pants.

Trial: Joshua Silva was found guilty of first-degree murder and sentenced to life in prison without the possibility of parole.

Further Reading:

Brown, Curt. "Silva Found Guilty of Murder of Joyce Howland in Fairhaven, Sentenced to Life without Parole." *SouthCoastToday.com*, 23 September 2015. southcoasttoday.com/article/20150923/NEWS/150929781.
Crandall, Brian. "Contractor was Early Suspect in Woman's Killing." *TurnTo10.com*, 31 October 2013. turnto10.com/archive/contractor-was-early-suspect-in-womans-killing.
"Man Convicted of Killing Retired Teacher." *The Boston Globe* (Boston, Massachusetts), 24 September 2015.

SHARONE STAFFORD

Man shot to death on the street in New Bedford, Massachusetts, on November 23, 2013.

Victim: Sharone Stafford, 31.

Accused: Hailton DaCosta, 25, Antonio Rodrigues Jr, 28.

Details: During a botched robbery attempt, Hailton DaCosta and Antonio Rodrigues shot and killed Sharone Stafford on the street in New Bedford on November 23, 2013.

Trial: Hailton DaCosta and Antonio Rodrigues were found guilty of second-degree murder and carrying illegal firearms. DaCosta was sentenced to 24 years to life in state prison. Rodrigues was sentenced to 18 years to life. The two had made a plea agreement to testify in exchange for reduced sentences.

Further Reading:

"Two Convicted in Fatal 2013 Shooting." *The Herald News* (Fall River, Massachusetts), 26 November 2015.

DAVID RODRIGUEZ

Man shot to death at Ship's Cove apartment complex, 130 Canal Street, in Fall River, Massachusetts, on January 4, 2014.

Victim: David Rodriguez, 26.

Accused: William Tate, 34.

Details: At 12:55 a.m., Fall River police responded to a 911 call about a man being shot outside of Ship's Cove Apartments in Fall River. Emergency crews found David Rodriguez shot near the loading dock at the apartment building. He was taken to St. Anne's Hospital in Fall River and pronounced dead.

William Tate maintained that he thought David Rodriguez had a gun in his hand, when, in fact, it was a cell phone.

Trial: William Tate was convicted by a jury of second-degree murder and sentenced to serve 15 years to life and then begin a sentence of 3-5 years for illegal possession of a firearm. He will then be required to serve a year for unlawful possession of a loaded firearm. Tate was given credit for the 2 years and 4 months he has served while awaiting trial.

Further Reading:

O'Connor, Kevin P. "RI Man will Serve at Least 19 Years for Fatal Fall River Shooting." *Taunton Daily Gazette* (Taunton, Massachusetts), 24 May 2016.

CONRAD ROY

Man committed suicide after being pressured by his girlfriend to do so in the parking lot of a Kmart in Fairhaven, Massachusetts, on July 12, 2014.

Victim: Conrad Roy, 18.

Accused: Michelle Carter, 17.

Details: In a case that shocked the nation, Michelle Carter sent her boyfriend over a thousand messages in which she insisted that he would be better off if he were dead. Conrad Roy had a history of depression and suicide attempts in his past.

Roy used a gas-powered water pump and died of carbon monoxide poisoning in the cab of his pickup. He continued to text with Carter as he was dying.

Carter's defense attorney stated that she was "brainwashed" by Roy into supporting his plan for suicide and he persuaded her to help him end his life.

The facts of the case as presented at Carter's appeal are as follows:

"On the afternoon of July 13, 2014, an officer with the Fairhaven police department located the deceased in his truck, parked in a store parking lot. The medical examiner concluded that the victim had died after inhaling carbon monoxide that was produced by a gasoline powered water pump located in the truck. The manner of death was suicide.

"The victim had been receiving treatment for mental health issues since 2011. In 2013, the victim attempted to commit suicide by overdosing on acetaminophen. A friend saved his life by contacting emergency services.

"During the course of the investigation into the victim's suicide, a police review of his recent electronic communications caused them to further explore his relationship with [Carter]. The victim and [Carter] met in 2011 and had been dating at various times during that period, including at the time of the victim's death. Because they did not live in the same town, the majority of their contact took place through the exchange of voluminous text messages and cellular telephone calls. The grand jury heard testimony and were presented with transcripts concerning the content of those text messages in the minutes, days, weeks, and months leading up to [Carter]'s suicide. The messages revealed that [Carter] was aware of the victim's history of mental illness, and of his previous suicide attempt, and that much of the communication between [Carter] and the victim focused on suicide. Specifically, [Carter] encouraged the victim to kill himself, instructed him as to when and how he should kill himself, assuaged his concerns over killing himself, and chastised him when he delayed doing so. The theme of those text messages can be summed up in the phrase used by [Carter] four times between July 11 and July 12, 2014 (the day on which the victim committed suicide): 'You just [have] to do it.'

"Cellular telephone records that were presented to the grand jury revealed that the victim and defendant also had two cellular telephone conversations at the time during which police believe that the victim was in his truck committing suicide. The content of those cellular telephone conversations is only available as reported by [Carter] to her friend, Samantha Boardman. After the victim's death, [Carter] sent a text message to Boardman explaining that, at one point during the suicide, the victim got out of his truck because he was 'scared,' and [Carter] commanded him to get back in.

"It was apparent that [Carter] understood the repercussions of her role in the victim's death. Prior to his suicide, [Carter] sought (apparently unsuccessfully) to have the victim delete the text messages between the two, and after learning that the police were looking through the victim's cellular telephone, [Carter] sent the following text message to Boardman: 'Sam, [the police] read my messages with him I'm done. His family will hate me and I can go to jail.' During the investigation, and after cross-referencing the text messages in [Carter]'s cellular telephone and those in the victim's cellular telephone, the police discovered that [Carter] had erased certain text messages between her and the victim...[Carter] acknowledged in a text message to Boardman that she could have stopped the victim from committing suicide: 'I helped ease him into it and told him it was okay, I was talking to him on the phone when he did it I could have easily stopped him or called the police but I didn't.'"

Trial: Michelle Carter was charged with involuntary manslaughter. She was sentenced to 2 ½ years in prison but 15 months of her sentence was suspended while she appealed her conviction.

Afterword: Michelle Carter appealed her conviction in 2016 on the basis that the Grand Jury erred in returning this indictment. The appeals court disagreed and her conviction was upheld. A second appeal was filed and adjudicated in October of 2018. The ruling of court has not yet been released.

Further Reading:

"Commonwealth vs. Michelle Carter." 474 Mass. 624, April 7, 2016-July 1, 2016. Bristol County. masscases.com/cases/sjc/474/474mass624.html.
Phillip, Abby. "'It's Now or Never': A Teen's Deadly Texts." *TampaBay.com* (Tampa, Florida), 3 September 2015.

SOPHIE KOSTEK

Woman punched to death at 857 Wilbur Avenue in Somerset, Massachusetts, on August 7, 2014.

Victim: Sophie Kostek, 88.

Accused: Michael Kostek, 63.

Details: Sophie Kostek was found lying topless, her mouth and eyes ringed with bruises, and bruises on her hands and arms on August 7, 2014. Her son, Michael, was in the next room with numerous prescription pill bottles and nine bottles of Jack Daniels whiskey. He had blood on his sheets and on his hands. He claimed his mother, for whom he was sole caretaker, had fallen down the stairs. The evidence supported the theory that he had beat her to death.

Michael Kostek's attorney claimed he had a severe substance abuse problem and suffers from mental health issues as well.

In 2009, Michael Kostek had been charged three times with operating a motor vehicle under the influence.

Kostek pleaded guilty to manslaughter in 2017 and was sentenced to up to 10 years in prison.

Further Reading:

Fraga, Brian. "Somerset Man Pleads Guilty in Death of Disabled Mother." *Providence Journal*, 9 May 2017.

McNeill, Claire. "Man Charged with Punching Mother." *The Boston Globe* (Boston, Massachusetts), 9 August 2014.

MELISSA WHITE

Woman shot to death in Ocean Grove in Swansea, Massachusetts, on August 24, 2014.

Victim: Melissa White, 23.

Accused: Timothy Levesque, 56.

Details: According to reporting in *The Herald News*, "White's shooting occurred after she and two men had gone to Levesque's Coolidge Street home to confront one of Levesque's sons because of an altercation that had occurred about 30 minutes earlier. In that incident, it is alleged that Levesque's son and a friend pulled up alongside two men on the street, then assaulted and 'sucker-punched' them before leaving the scene.

"About a month earlier, on July 16, 2014, one of Levesque's sons was stabbed after being robbed by two young men at Ocean Grove and Bluff avenues, the same corner where White was shot. Levesque's son, then 21, survived the attack." White's associates were known to often walk past Levesque's home, taunting and intimidating his family.

"Levesque worked for more than 20 years as a state correctional officer in Bridgewater, and helped run a family landscaping business before his arrest in 2014.

"According to online court records, White, at the time of her death, had a pending criminal case out of Rhode Island for assault and disorderly conduct charges. *The Providence Journal* reported that police arrested White for allegedly punching a man outside a Providence nightclub in October 2013. The following month, the court issued a warrant after she missed a court hearing, according to online court records.

"According to testimony at Fall River Superior Court, Levesque, a licensed gun owner, grabbed his pistol and followed after White and her two associates when they left his house around 1:30 a.m. on Aug. 24, 2014. Levesque reportedly confronted them near the corner of Ocean Grove and Bluff avenues, smacked one of the men, and shot White in the ensuing confrontation, attorneys said."

Levesque claimed that he shot White after she had struck him with a crowbar. Forensics showed that White was between 2 to 5 feet away from Levesque when she was shot. There was audio surveillance evidence that Levesque warned White to "drop the bar" before the shot was fired.

Trial: Timothy Levesque was acquitted of the charge of manslaughter. His defense attorney claimed this was proof that the jury believed Levesque when he said it was in self-defense.

Further Reading:

Fraga, Brian. "Levesque Found Not Guilty in Swansea Manslaughter Case." *The Herald News*, 22 August 2017.

KYLE BRADY

Man shot to death in the intersection of Albert and Huard Streets in Fall River, Massachusetts, on January 1, 2015.

Victim: Kyle Brady, 28.

Accused: Jeffrey Souza, 24.

Details: According to reporting in *The Herald News*, "Witnesses told police that [Kyle] Brady and [Jeffrey] Souza had been having a 'beef' over the past few months because Brady was dating the mother of Souza's children. The same woman had an active restraining order against Souza, who was arrested and charged with violating that order last August for allegedly sending threatening text messages to the woman's relatives, according to court documents.

"On the night of New Year's Eve, witnesses said Souza was 'bad-mouthing' Brady at a local bar. After being told about Souza's remarks, Brady reportedly agreed to meet him for a fight at Maplewood Park. Brady and two companions left a party at the Venus de Milo and drove back to Fall River. When they arrived at the park, they saw Souza and several other people already there, according to police reports.

"As they pulled into the park, Brady jumped out of the vehicle and approached the crowd. One witness said she confronted Souza after seeing him standing in the street and firing a silver gun into the air. The witness said she then noticed Brady lying on the ground, and went to assist him, according to police reports. Another witness who was with Brady told police that he heard two gunshots, then saw Brady on the ground, with an unknown man on top of him and Souza standing over Brady with a gun in his hand.

"The witness said he went to help Brady, and added that the vehicle that allegedly brought Souza to the crime scene left abruptly, with the driver reportedly saying, 'I'm sorry, Jeffrey, I can't let you in,' according to police reports.

"Other witnesses also reported hearing gunshots.

"One man driving by the scene said he heard a loud pop, then turned around and saw people "scurrying around." The witness got out of his car and saw a man — later identified as Brady — fall to the ground.

"One neighbor described seeing two men walking north on Huard Street, both with blood on their hands. After asking them what happened, the men said, "Some guy got shot, we tried to help him," according to court documents.

"Police officers later recovered a silver .357-caliber revolver with two spent shell casings in the cylinder and a dark-colored handle just a few feet from where Brady fell.

"The firearm appeared to be covered in blood. A pocket knife was also located about a foot from the firearm. According to police records, Souza did not have a license to carry a firearm or a firearm identification card."

Trial: Jeffrey Souza was found guilty of second-degree murder and related firearms charges. He was sentneced to life in prison with the possibility of parole in 15 years.

Further Reading:

Fraga, Brian. "Jury Finds Souza Guilty in Fall River New Year's Day Murder." *The Herald News*, 27 September 2016.

Fraga, Brian. "Witnesses Say Fall River Shooting Victim was in Dispute with Man Over Ex." *The Herald News*, 2 January 2015.

MABILIA MARANHAO & SHARIF GOODE

Murder/Suicide of couple at 598 Brock Avenue in New Bedford, Massachusetts, on January 15, 2015.

Victim: Mabilia Maranhao, 22.

Accused: Sharif Goode, 22.

Details: About three days after the murder/suicide, Mabilia Maranhao and Sharif Goode were discovered in Goode's residence in New Bedford. The couple had been killed with gunshot wounds to the head and were found lying on top of each other in the bathroom.

The two had been dating for a short while before the tragedy.

It is unclear in the reporting who shot who and then committed suicide. In cases such as these, it is often the man who kills the female and then himself.

Further Reading:

Brown, Curt. "New Bedford Murder-Suicide Victims Identified." *SouthCoastToday.com*, 16 January 2014. southcoasttoday.com/article/20140116/News/140119905.

ANTHONY CARVALHO

Man shot to death near Whipple and Osborne Streets in Fall River, Massachusetts, on March 20, 2015.

Victim: Anthony Carvalho, 20.

Accused: Kevin Lara, 19, Mickey Rivera, 19, Tavon Pires, 17.

Details: Anthony Carvalho was found in the middle of the street in Fall River's South End, suffering from multiple gunshot wounds. He had been robbed of the drug money he had collected.

Trial: The trial is pending for Kevin Lara and Tavon Pires. Mickey Rivera was indicted on charges that included armed assault with intent to rob, attempted armed and masked robbery, conspiracy, and witness intimidation.

Afterword: In a horrific turn of events, Mikey Rivera was released from custody on September 19, 2017, after his bail was lowered from $35,000 cash to $1000. While on GPS monitoring and with his case pending, he crashed head-on into a sport utility vehicle in Cotuit, killing Kevin Quinn, 32, of Mashpee. Quinn was a Marine veteran who served two tours in Afghanistan was a new father. In fact, he was traveling home after seeing his newborn for the first time.

Further Reading:

"Fall River Teen Gets 8 to 10 Years in State Prison." *SouthCoastToday.com*, 8 December 2015.

Fraga, Brian. "Man Involved in Fatal Cape Crash was Tied to Fall River Murder." *The Herald News*, 30 July 2018.

BRIAN JONES

Man stabbed to death at 477 Third Street in the Corky Row neighborhood of Fall River, Massachusetts, on May 30, 2015.

Victim: Brian Jones, 53.

Accused: Adrienne Brown, 37.

Details: According to eyewitnesses, Adrienne Brown stabbed Brian Jones three times during an argument outside her residence on May 30, 2015—after she confronted him about an argument he had earlier in the day with Brown's 19-year-old daughter over $50 Brown's daughter owed Jones. It was reported that Jones threatened to slice her daughter's throat and that he held a beer bottle in one hand while arguing with Brown. Brown said she grabbed the knife that Jones had dropped during their confrontation. Brown said that Jones leaned over her, threatened to stab her, and grabbed her by the back of her collar. It was then, she said, she picked up his knife and swung it at Jones in self-defense.

Trial: Adrienne Brown was acquitted of first-degree murder but convicted of the lesser included charge of voluntary manslaughter. She is expected to serve from 8 to 20 years in state prison.

Further Reading:

Fraga, Brian. "Jury Finds Brown Guilty of Manslaughter in Fall River Stabbing Death." *The Herald News*, 10 February 2017.

MARCEL FRANCOIS

Man shot to death in Harrington Park behind the Hathaway School in New Bedford, Massachusetts, on June 11, 2015.

Victim: Marcel Francois, 19.

Accused: Syrelle Grace, 18.

Details: According to reporting, "Francois approached Grace at the park and the two men argued, prosecutors said. Grace was armed with a handgun and fired three shots. Two struck Francois in the abdomen and the heart, which caused his death, and the third landed in the basketball court's pavement. Neighbors heard the gunshots and rushed out to give first aid, but Francois died either in the ambulance on the way to St. Luke's Hospital or at the hospital. Several witnesses identified Grace as the shooter.

"There were two confrontations with friends of the victim that led to the killing, prosecutors said. Grace had 'interactions' with one of Francois' friends on Facebook on May 15, 2015, and toward the end of that month Grace pulled a gun on the man and robbed his marijuana. About 45 minutes before the killing, a second friend approached Grace and the defendant hit him on the side of the head with a handgun.

"Then at 11:45 p.m. on June 11, 2015, Grace was in Harrington Park and Francois and the friend whose marijuana was stolen saw him and Francois approached the defendant. Francois and Grace argued and the defendant shot him, prosecutors said.

"The confrontation between Grace and Francois took three seconds, 'three tragic seconds,' according to prosecutor Robert DiGiantomaso. 'Instead of using his fists, this defendant pulled out his illegal gun and killed him. This is the essence of the needless tragedy.'

"Earlier in the day, Francois was in Harrington Park with one of his sons, DiGiantomaso said. 'There is no justification. This is a meaningless, senseless tragedy. It's heinous and stupid.' After prosecutors read the facts of the case into record, Judge Dupuis asked Grace if the allegations were true and he said they were, admitting he robbed someone of their marijuana, hit someone on the side of the face with a gun and killed Francois."

In 2017, Syrelle Grace pleaded guilty of manslaughter possession of a firearm, possession of a loaded firearm, assault and battery with a dangerous weapon, and armed robbery with a gun. He was sentenced to 13 ½ to 18 ½ years in state prison.

Further Reading:

Brown Curt. "Taunton Man Pleads Guilty to Manslaughter in 2015 New Bedford Killing." *SouthCoastToday.com*, 28 September 2017. southcoasttoday.com/news/20170928/taunton-man-pleads-guilty-to-manslaughter-in-senseless-2015-new-bedford-killing.

DONALD A. DEPINA

Cab driver shot to death in a parking lot outside Brooklawn Park in New Bedford, Massachusetts, on November 28, 2015.

Victim: Donald Depina, 66.

Accused: Alexander Mills, 18, plus a 16-year-old male.

Details: Part-time cab driver Donald Depina was killed in his cab on November 28, 2015, in New Bedford. Prosecutors say that Alexander Mills bragged to his friends that he had shot a cab driver.

Depina had picked up Mills and a 16-year-old around 10:30 p.m. from a gas station on Purchase Street and drove them to the remote location where he was found, as they requested him to do. The fare was $6.50. When they arrived, it was reported, Mills shot Depina in the head from behind, got out of the cab, and shot him again. He then dragged his body from the vehicle and went through Depina's pockets, taking his belongings.

Mills tried to make purchases with Depina's credit card and surveillance footage captured him doing so. In addition, Mills left a round of ammunition that matched those casing found at the crime scene.

Reportedly, Mills suffers from significant mental health issues, hears voices that tell him to hurt people, and suffers from PTSD from an incident that happened to him when he was eleven.

The teens are still awaiting trial at this date.

Further Reading:

Ransom, Jan. "Slaying of Taxi Driver Stuns New Bedford." *The Boston Globe* (Boston, Massachusetts), 1 December 2015.
Ransom, Jan. "Suspects Held in Driver's Killing." *The Boston Globe* (Boston, Massachusetts), 2 December 2015.

MARIA BRANCO

Woman neglected to death in Fall River, Massachusetts, on April 13, 2016.

Victim: Maria Branco, 78.

Accused: Antonio Branco, 56.

Details: Maria Branco was severely neglected and grossly underfed by her caregiver, her son Antonio. She had been starved for several months before he took her to the hospital. She weighed only 80 pounds and was covered in bedsores. She died 4 days later.

Branco's father had been removed from the home several years earlier for domestic abuse and Antonio was not only caring for his mother but for his two sisters, both in their 50s, each with intellectual disabilities.

Branco was additionally charged with assault for abusing his two sisters, who were found locked in the 77 Holden Street family home. One sister was beaten and had black, bloodied, swollen eyes. The other had injuries to her hand.

Trial: In 2017, Antonio Branco was found guilty of manslaughter in the death of his mother. He was sentenced to 5 years in state prison.

Further Reading:

Fraga, Brian. "Fall River Man Found Guilty of Manslaughter in Mother's Death." *The Herald News* (Fall River, Massachusetts), 6 December 2017.

JOHN CLOUD

Man shot to death in Pocasset Hill Cemetery in Tiverton, Rhode Island, on June 13, 2016.

Victim: John Cloud, 81.

Accused: Edward Acquisto, 80.

Details: John Cloud was trying to recover money that had been owed to him for a number of years from Edward Acquisto. The two men met in the Pocasset Cemetery off Main Road in the town. After shooting Cloud three times, Acquisto tried to escape both Fall River and Tiverton Police. After he exited his car and shot at the police, he was fired on by five police officers simultaneously in a residential neighborhood on Ford Farm Road in Tiverton. Acquetino had been previously convicted of manslaughter and was released as a paroled felon in 2003 after serving time for first-degree sexual assault. He had a lengthy criminal record.

Further Reading:

Crimaldi, Laura. "Man Kills Fellow Parishioner in Cemetery Over Unpaid Debt." *The Boston Globe* (Boston, Massachusetts), 2 July 2017.

SABRINA DASILVA

Woman shot to death in the parking lot of her apartment complex in New Bedford, Massachusetts, on July 3, 2016.

Victim: Sabrina DaSilva, 19.

Accused: Walter DaSilva, 45.

Details: Citing prior court documents that outline his history of violent threats against his family for over 10 years, Walter DaSilva was charged with murdering his daughter, Sabrina, in the parking lot of her apartment complex. He was additionally charged with carrying an illegal firearm and the unlawful possession of a loaded firearm.

No motive was shared.

Walter DaSilva was convicted previously of attempted murder of his estranged wife, Lilian Silva, with a knife in 2002. He was sentenced to 8 to 10 years in prison. In February 2012, he was released to immigration officials (he was in the country illegally from Brazil).

At the time of the murder, DaSilva was a fugitive from justice, stemming from probation violations in the 2002 case. The family believed him to be back in Brazil and was surprised that he was still in the United States.

As of this date, Walter DaSilva's trial is pending.

Further Reading:

Otarola, Miguel. "Father Charged in Kill of 19-Year-Old Daughter." *The Boston Globe* (Boston, Massachusetts), 9 August 2016.

JERROD COHEN

Man shot to death at 129 Plain Street in Fall River, Massachusetts, on July 11, 2016.

Victim: Jerrod Cohen, 29.

Accused: Jayden Smith, 16, Joel Lopez 16.

Details: According to reporting, "Just before 9:30 p.m. Monday, Cohen and a friend, saw two young men walking up Plain Street, staring at them and their neighbors who were socializing outside 129 Plain St., witnesses said.

"But when Cohen, who also lived at 129 Plain St., and his friend approached their fence, to see what the suspicious individuals wanted, at least one of the suspects opened fire from across the street, striking Cohen in the chest with a bullet that went through his body and damaged the building's vinyl siding.

"Cohen turned around and ran into his apartment building, but he collapsed on the first floor landing. A neighbor tried to put pressure on the wound, but Cohen seemed to know he was dying, according to the neighbor who captured some of Cohen's last words.

"'My kids,' Cohen said. The neighbor replied, 'Don't worry about your kids.'
"Cohen responded, 'I love you all.'
"Cohen was rushed to Rhode Island Hospital, where he was pronounced dead later that night" ("Teenager Charged").

Witnesses said that two young men, wearing black hooded sweatshirts and jeans, had walked past a group socializing in the parking lot. Cohen and his friend had stepped forward and confronted the teens. The assailants then opened fire and shot Cohen. The attorney for Joel Lopez says that Cohen was armed with a machete and he was a member of the Crips gang. Lopez contends he brought the gun to the scene for self-defense only. The guns were never recovered.

As of this date, the outcome is unknown as the trial has not taken place.

Further Reading:

Fraga, Brian. "Dispute Over Girl Led to Fall River Man's Fatal Shooting, Defense Says." *The Herald News* (Fall River, Massachusetts), 6 September 2017.

Fraga, Brian. "Teenager Charged with Murder as Man Shot on Plain Street in Fall River Remembered." *The Herald News* (Fall River, Massachusetts), 12 July 2016.

UNSOLVED CASES 1800-2016

The unsolved cases on this list reflect those murders that were either never solved or the person accused of the crime was acquitted in a court of law—thereby insuring that the case would remain open.

These individuals are from all three volumes of *Murder, Manslaughter, and Mayhem on the SouthCoast* for the years 1900 to 2016.

A name followed by an asterisk is a case where an acquittal took place.

Cases where the accused were committed to a hospital for the insane are not included on this list.

Victim's Name	Date of Death	Method of Demise	Location of Crime Scene
Sarah Maria Cornell *	Dec. 21, 1832	Hanging	Tiverton, Rhode Island, now Kennedy Park, Fall River
George Thyng *	July 9, 1875	Poisoned	New Bedford
M. Albert Seabury	Dec. 2, 1882	Pitchfork	Little Compton, Rhode Island
John Schofield *	March 22, 1884	Hit in the head	Chace Mill yard, Fall River
Herbert Moxie infant *	Aug. 9, 1885	Drowned	Acushnet River, New Bedford
Andrew and Abby Borden *	Aug. 4, 1892	Hatchet murder	92 Second Street, Fall River
Hattie Carter	April 28, 1909	Unknown	Found in advanced state of putrification at 9 South Water Street, New Bedford
William Bennett	Oct. 14, 1916	Struck from behind	Fairhaven Bridge, Fairhaven
Louis Chounard	Dec. 5, 1925	Shot to death	31 Choate Street, Fall River
Ernest Pelletier *	Aug. 27, 1927	Shot to death	94 E. Main Street, Fall River

Victim's Name	Date of Death	Method of Demise	Location of Crime Scene
Irene Perry	June 29, 1940	Garroted	Dartmouth
Ruth Fuller *	June 30, 1962	Strangled to death	In her home in Fairhaven
Russell Goldstein	Dec. 20, 1969	Shot to death	420 S. Main Street, Fall River
Leonard Ramos	Oct. 21, 1970	Shot to death	1513 Pleasant Street, Fall River
Walter Laberge	Aug. 14, 1971	Stabbed to death	Lafayette Road, Tiverton, Rhode Island
Bruce Calvando *	Nov. 21, 1971	Broken bottle	The Mill bar, 1082 Davol Street, Fall River
Eva Baptiste Timm	June 2, 1972	Shot to death	Surfside Lounge, Cove Street, New Bedford
Kenny Pemberton	Aug. 2, 1972	Shot to death	Fall River
Marvin Morgan *	Aug. 8, 1972	Shot to death	West End Social Club, New Bedford
Thomas McCabe Jr.	Oct. 7, 1972	Shot to death	Camelot Inn, 425 S. Main Street, Fall River
John Walsh	May 13, 1973	Battered with a baseball bat	Outside Pier 14, 263 Bedford Street, Fall River
Walter Henry Cosgrove *	June 29, 1974	Strangled	Ferry Street, Fall River
Abbie Karen Rosofky *	Aug. 31, 1975	Beaten and strangled	North Park, Fall River
Dennis Raimondi	April 1, 1977	Shot to death	In his home in Somerset
Lyla Jean Poitras	June 27, 1977	Shot to death	Tiverton, Rhode Island
Dennis Cardoza *	Dec. 19, 1977	Shot to death	Fall River
Cynthia Machado *	April 11, 1978	Stabbed to death	Our Place Lounge, Rodman Street, Fall River
Sandra Jean Showers *	Aug. 10, 1982	Drowning after blow to head	Cook Pond, Fall River

Victim's Name	Date of Death	Method of Demise	Location of Crime Scene
Robert Blan *	Oct. 7, 1983	Shot to death	41 Harbor Terrace, Fall River
John Gomes	Nov, 21, 1984	Shot to death	Route 195 near Rt. 88, Westport
John Moura	May 30, 1985	Shot to death	Fort Rodman, New Bedford
Deborah Perry	Jan. 1, 1986	Killed and dismembered	Westport
Evelyn Merritt	Sept. 2, 1986	Shot to death	Slade Street, Fall River
Robin L. Rhodes, Highway Murder Victim	Last seen in New Bedford April 1988	Unknown	Body found on Route 140 southbound in Freetown
Rochelle Dopierala, Highway Murder Victim	Last seen in New Bedford late April 1988	Unknown	Body found in gravel pit along Reed Road, 2 miles from I-195
Debroh McConnell, Highway Murder Victim	Last seen in New Bedford May 1988	Unknown	Body found on Rt. 140 northbound in Freetown
Debra Medeiros, Highway Murder Victim	Last seen in New Bedford, May 27, 1988	Unknown	Body found on Rt. 140 northbound in Freetown
Christine Monteiro, Highway Murder Victim	Last seen in New Bedford late May 1988	Unknown	Not yet recovered
Marilyn Roberts, Highway Murder Victim	Last seen in New Bedford, June 1988	Unknown	Not yet recovered
Nancy Paiva, Highway Murder Victim	Last seen in New Bedford on July 7, 1988	Unknown	Body found on 1-195 westbound in Dartmouth
Debra DeMello, Highway Murder Victim	Last seen in New Bedford on July 11, 1988	Unknown	Body found off east-bound Reed Road ramp of I-195

Victim's Name	Date of Death	Method of Demise	Location of Crime Scene
Mary Santos, Highway Murder Victim	Last seen in New Bedford on July 16, 1988	Unknown	Body found along Rt. 88 in Westport
Sandra Botelho, Highway Murder Victim	Last seen in New Bedford on August 11, 1988	Unknown	Body found along I-195 in Marion
Dawn Mendes, Highway Murder Victim	Last seen in New Bedford on Sept. 4, 1988	Unknown	Body found on westbound Reed Road ramp off I-195
Alphonse Gluchacki *	June 12, 1989	Shot to death	His home on Middle Street, Fall River
Carlos Enrique Hernandez	July 19, 1991	Shot to death	Found off Henry Street, Fall River
Howard Ferrini	August 1991	Beaten to death	Killed in Berkley, found in trunk of car at Logan Airport
Brian Tupaj	July 4, 1998	Shot to death	Lexington & Albion Street, Fall River
Brent Davis	Oct. 25, 1991	Shot to death	Behind Yale Street in New Bedford
Arnold Andrews	Dec. 19, 1993	Shot to death	Near his mother's apartment on Acushnet Avenue in New Bedford
Joseph Medeiros	Feb. 25, 1994	Shot to death	Cook Pond, Fall River
Mark A. Pierce	May 20, 1994	Beaten to death	Near the corner of Sawyer and Mount Pleasant Streets in New Bedford
Peter Kenham	July 26, 1995	Stabbed to death	In his living room in New Bedford
Angel Vasquez	Sept. 30, 1995	Stabbed to death	New Bedford
Daryl Duquette	Sept. 25, 1996	Stabbed to death	Westport

Victim's Name	Date of Death	Method of Demise	Location of Crime Scene
Jane Doe	Oct. 30, 1996	Shot to death and beaten	Found in water off Popes Island Marina in New Bedford
Antonio Simoes	Nov. 16, 1998	Beaten to death	In the basement of 857 South First Street in New Bedford
Ismael Martinez	Jan. 20, 1999	Shot to death	Outside 323 North Front Street in New Bedford
Rose Marie Moniz	March 23, 2001	Bludgeoned to death	3448 Acushnet Avenue, New Bedford
Clifford Barrymore	March 26, 2001	Shot to death	In an apartment at The Willows at Tarkin Hill in New Bedford
Oranuch Sousa	June 16, 2001	Bludgeoned to death	Near Globe Four Corners, south end of Fall River
Maria Mendez	Oct. 17, 2001	Not released	Found in bathroom of her apartment at 71 Chancery Street in New Bedford
Ivandro Correia	Dec. 5, 2001	Shot to death	Ruth Street, New Bedford
Elijah Omar Bey *	Feb. 16, 2002	Shot to death	Acushnet Avenue and Wing Street, New Bedford
Thomas Morgado	May 13, 2002	Stabbed to death	104 Dartmouth Street, New Bedford
Devyn Murphy	Oct. 13, 2002	Stabbed to death	House party in Wareham
Alvis Dexter James	March 30, 2003	Shot to death	In mini-van parked outside the Crossroads Apartment complex in Dartmouth
Robert Benard *	May 5, 2003	Shot to death	Third Street, Fall River
Ronald T. Brooks	July 8, 2003	Shot to death	As he sat outside Navajo Court in New Bedford
Leonard Silviera *	July 11, 2003	Beaten to death	18 Homer Street, New Bedford
Patrick Murphy	Aug. 10, 2003	Stabbed to death	89 Purchase Street, New Bedford

Victim's Name	Date of Death	Method of Demise	Location of Crime Scene
Raymond P. Andrade	Jan. 25, 2004	Shot to death	Near Acushnet Avenue and Griffin Court in New Bedford
Robert Greene Jr.	April 24, 2004	Shot to death	On the front porch of mother's home at 111 Smith Street in New Bedford
Frank Perreira Jr. *	June 17, 2004	Shot to death	134 Ashley Blvd., New Bedford
Clinton Dunston	Oct. 5, 2004	Shot to death	While sitting in a car parked outside 5 Morgan Terrace in South Central New Bedford
Cecil M. Lopes III	Oct. 31, 2004	Shot to death	Outside the United Front housing complex, Chancery and Kempton Streets, New Bedford
Jonathan Butler	Jan. 29, 2005	Shot to death	Smith Street in New Bedford
Antonio Frias	Jan. 30, 2005	Shot to death	In Swansea home of Robert Paquette
Ashley Silva	Aug. 28, 2005	Stabbed to death	Near 115 Ruth Street in New Bedford
Suzanna M. Soares *	Sept. 5, 2005	Shot to death	71 S. Sixth Street, New Bedford
Suzanna Alvarado	Oct. 17, 2005	Strangled to death	Body discovered near junction of Rt. 88 and Interstate 195, Westport
Bernadette "Bunny" DePina	May 25, 2006	Shot to death	In her home at 123 Ash Street in New Bedford
Albon Wilson *	Sept. 30, 2007	Shot to death	Bonney and Thompson Streets, New Bedford
William "Buddah" Payne	Feb. 2, 2008	Shot to death	In vehicle at Purchase and Potomska Streets in New Bedford
Derek Hogue *	June 27, 2008	Shot to death	108 Hamlet Street, Fall River
Paul Elias	June 14, 2009	Punched	Outside Regal Beagle Bar & Grille on Acushnet Avenue in New Bedford

Victim's Name	Date of Death	Method of Demise	Location of Crime Scene
Eric Sullivan	Oct. 29, 2009	Shot to death	Across from former Larry's Sports Pub in Corky Row neighborhood of Fall River, hallway of 263 Morgan St.
Angel Robles Rivera	July 9, 2010	Shot to death	His home on County Street, Fall River
Ricardo Encarnacion	Oct. 30, 2010	Shot to death	On the porch of his home near Tallman and North Front Streets in New Bedford
Anthony Jones	Jan. 5, 2011	Shot to death	Grinnell Street in New Bedford
Timothy Cowart	Jan. 28, 2011	Shot to death	Near the intersection of Thompson and Hyacinth Streets in New Bedford
Vincent Wadlington	Feb. 17, 2011	Not released	Found on railroad tracks near Danforth Street, Fall River
Brian Januario *	March 28, 2011	Shot to death	Body found on Wilson Road in Fall River
Tracy Moneiro	Nov. 27, 2011	Shot to death	Outside his home at 120 Locust Street in New Bedford
Michael Pina	Dec. 2, 2011	Shot to death	At the corner of Dartmouth and Matthew Streets in New Bedford
Scott Souza	July 19, 2013	Shot to death	Inside his Weld Square residence in New Bedford
Daniel Smith	May 30, 2014	Shot to death	Outside a home at 125 Collette Street in New Bedford
Javon Brown *	Jan. 22, 2015	Shot to death	Inside and outside a Metro PCS store at 209 Coggshall Street, New Bedford

Further Reading:

"Cold Cases at a Glance." *SouthCoastToday.com*, 28 October 2007. southcoasttoday.com/article/20071028/news/710280360.

Fraga, Brian. "Da Sutter, cold casees, and New Bedford homicides." *SouthCoastToday.com*, 22 December 2011. blogs.southcoasttoday.com/new-bedford-crime/2011/12/22/da-sutter-and-cold-cases-homicides-clearance-rates/.

Fraga, Brian. "Get caught up on Greater Fall River homicide cases." *The Herald News*, 7 February 2017.

"A roundup of existing cold cases." *WickedLocal.com*, 20 October 2013. wickedlocal.com/article/20131020/news/310209650.

"Unsolved Homicides." *SouthCoastToday.com*, 11 November, 2004. southcoasttoday.com/article/20041111/NEWS/311119980.

ACKNOWLEDGMENTS & RESOURCES

As well as those below who have assisted in this effort, special thanks goes to Mary Faria, the librarian at *The Fall River Herald News*. She spent countless hours assisting me in finding news stories and photos to be reprinted from the archives. I would often leave the newsroom and say goodbye but she knew better and would offer a "see you soon." I would return in a few days with an "I'm back!" We communicated in person and frequently by email. I was in the newsroom so often they wanted to give me my own desk. Thanks, Mary, I could not have done it without you.

I also want to extend my appreciation to my new friend, Doreen Allen, a clerk in the Bristol County Superior Court Clerk's Office. Occasionally, news stories would provide me with the final disposition to the case but often they didn't and this necessitated a visit with Doreen in the Justice Center, second floor on South Main Street, in Fall River. Her associates would alert her to my presence with, "Doreen, your man is here."

She would then join me in a conference room and provide me with the trial dockets so that I could discover the results. We engaged in this activity frequently and she educated me to legal lingo and provided me with court documents to search. Doreen, I will miss our exchanges. Thanks for your help and smiles.

My trips to The Peoples University—the Fall River Public Library—were so frequent that the staff and other visitors to the Ryan Reference Room became friends. Special thanks to Dan Sheahan, who not only helped me gather information but supported my efforts with a friendly salutation—and machine operating instructions. Dan, we will see each other often in Westport if not Fall River.

When it came to asking the appropriate person to write the Foreword to this book, Federal Judge Edward F. Harrington was on the top of the list. He has spent a half-century adjudicating criminal and civil cases. The retired judge still travels almost daily to his office in Boston to review and issue findings. Yet, he graciously found time to read over this tome and make remarks. He is true gentleman—the country, and especially this author, are lucky to have him. Thanks, Judge, for this effort—but, more importantly, your friendship.

Always helpful were Fall River historians Michael Martins and Dennis Binette, whose sources of information and fountains of knowledge are seemingly endless. Without these two gents, I could never have even started this investigation. A extra special thanks to Dennis, who after a busy season, also willingly agreed to write a sterling back page blurb for this book.

Special Thanks also to Attorney and Deputy District Attorney in Bristol County, William McCauley. McCauley, like the author, is a graduate of Portsmouth Priory and we both were taught English by the late Dom Damien Kearney, O.S.B. His days have been spent in court, filing charges and serving as the primary trial lawyer against many of those in the volumes of the book. His comments are most appreciated.

Last, but certainly not least, it has been my good fortune to work with Stefani Koorey on a number of projects. This book could not have been possible without the amazing writing and research talents of co-author Stefani Koorey. From the first time a few years ago when I told her of my plans her eyes exploded and her excitement motivated me onward. This book is as much a part of her dedication as it is mine. Her editing and suggestions for changes to the text is par excellance and her creativity is fantastic. I am lucky that she still has time to edit my work (it truly needs it) and pass along needed suggestions and improvements to make the narrative and sequence read smoothly. Stef is another person who is a tremendous inspiration and benefit to our area and its history. Stick around, Stef.

Organizations:

SouthCoast Today
The Fall River Herald News
The Boston Globe
Fall River Historical Society—Michael Martins and Dennis Binette
Fall River Public Library—research staff
Christine Miguel, Senior Records Clerk, Tiverton Police Department
Doreen G. Allen, Clerk, Bristol County Superior Court
Little Compton Police Department
Robin Perry, Bristol County Law Librarian
Hilary Kraus, UMass Dartmouth Librarian
Kathy Maiato, Asst. Somerset Town Clerk
Colin Furze, *Fall River Herald News*
State Library of Massachusetts
New Bedford Public Library
Dartmouth Public Library
Fairhaven Public Library
Rhode Island Historical Society
Rhode Island State Archives
Ancestry.com
Newspapers.com

Individuals:

Kathryn Casey
Debbie Charpentier
Thomas Coughlin
(Ret.) Correctional Officer Russell Curran
Atty. Richard Desjardins
Jonathan Eaker
Barry French
Ransom Griffin
(Ret.) F.B.I. Agent Robert Hargraves
Mrs. Barbara Hayes
(Ret.) Det. Theodore Kaegael
Mary Ellen Kennedy
(Ret.) Judge Joseph I. Macy, Esq.
(Ret.) Deputy Chief of Police Fall River, Cathe Moniz
(Ret.) Fall River Chief of Police Daniel Racine
Cukie Macomber
Atty. Peter Paull
Daniel Sheahan
Dr. Philip Silvia
Thomas Slaight
Somerset Police

INDEX

by Stefani Koorey, PhD

Entries are arranged in letter-by-letter order, using the *Chicago Manual of Style, 16th Edition*. References to page numbers for illustrations are indicated by numerals in bold type.

A

Acquisto, Edward, 290
Acushnet Avenue, New Bedford, MA, 63, 110, 117, 147, 167, 175, 248, 297, 298, 299
Acushnet River, New Bedford, 294
Adams Street, New Bedford, MA, 269
Adamsville Church Cemetery, Little Compton, Rhode Island, 14
Adamsville Road, Little Compton, RI, 40
Aetna Street, Fall River, MA, 242
Aguiar, Kayla, 206
Aguiar, Ryan, 121–122
Albert Street, Fall River, MA, 281
Albion Street, Fall River, MA, 297
Alden Road, Fairhaven, MA, 192
Allinson, Aveling, 59, **60**
Allinson, Dwight, 59, **60**
Allinson, Hope, 59, **60**
Allinson, Wayne, 59, **60**
Almeida, Aaron, 210
Almeida, Attim, 121–122
Almeida, Jason J., 100–102
Almeida, Rico, 174, 217
Almeida, Shannon, 185
Almond Street, Fall River, MA, 30, 31
Almy, Charles E., 11
Almy, Frederick, 11
Almy, John E., 11
Almy, Mrs., 18
Almy, Sylvester, 11
Almy, Valentine S., 11
Almy Cemetery, Little Compton, Rhode Island, 11
Alphonso, Donald V., 209–210
Alvarado, Suzanna, 299
Alves, Jason, 161
Amaral, Jeremy, 271
Andrade, John G., 182
Andrade, Raymond P., 299

Andrade, Seth, 247–248
Andrews, Arnold, 297
Andrews, Russell, 100–102
Andrews-Dahill VFW, New Bedford, MA, 232
Antaya, Alexis, 15
Antone, Lamar, 138
Arruda, Alfred Jr., 252
Arruda, Alfred Sr., 252
Arruda, David, 252
Ashland Place, New Bedford, MA, 270
Ashley, Jonathan, 199–200
Ashley Boulevard, New Bedford, MA, 159, 299
Ashley Street, New Bedford, MA, 83
Ash Street, New Bedford, MA, 299
Assonet Burying Ground, Freetown, MA, 12–13
Atlantic Bar & Grill, Fall River, MA, 118
Aubin, Joanne C., 124
Aubin, Kenneth, 124, **124**
Aumuller, Ann, 50

B

Badillo, Orlando, 108
Banville, Christopher, 188–189
Baptiste, Terrell, 193
Barone, Attorney Theodore, 215
Barreto, Stephen, 209–210
Barros, Christopher, 182–184
Barros, Dana, 150
Barros, Filipe, 86, 87–88
Barros, Mario, 97–99
Barros, Michael, 86
Barrow, Elizabeth, 241
Barrows, Elizabeth C., 7
Barrows, George W., 8
Barrows, Isaac C., 7–8
Barrows, Isaac H., 7
Barrows, Mary Melissa, 7
Barrows, Phebe A., 8

Barrows, Polly, 7–8, **8**
Barry, Justin, 174
Barry-Henderson, Justin, 191
Barrymore, Clifford, 298
Barstow's Wharf, Mattapoisett, MA, 59
Bates, Jason, 206–207
Bay Street, Fall River, MA, 250
Beaudreau, Judge Robert H., 68
Beaulieu, Conrad, 253–255
Beaulieu, Joel, 253–255
Beauregard, Omer, 43
Beauregard's Market (Fall River, MA), 43
Becht, Nettie, 235–237
Bedard, Alma E., 61, **62**
Bedard, Wilfred, 61–62
Bedford Street, Fall River, MA, 9, 295
Bedford Street, New Bedford, MA, 183, 217
Bell Rock Road, Fall River, MA, 112
Bennett, William, 294
Bentley Street, New Bedford, MA, 230
Benton, Captain (of the Wave), 37
Berarde, Bruneau, 15–17
Berkley, Massachusetts,
    Ferrini, Howard
Bernard, Robert, 137, 298
Bertozzi, Donna, 77
Bessey, Mr. and Mrs., 38–39
Bevins, Ellen, 225
Bevins, Fred III, 225–226
Bey, Elijah Omar, 117, 298
Birard (Berarde), Aurelie (Peloqun), 17
Bizzarro, Louis, 125
Blackmer Street, New Bedford, MA, 87
Blais, State Trooper Ronald, 97
Blake, Duane L., 70–74
Blanchard, Cleophas, 54
Blanchard, Delvina Grenier, 54
Blau, Robert, 296
Blomgren, John, 192
Bloods Gang, Fall River, MA, 190
Bluefield Street, New Bedford, MA, 108
Bluff Avenue, Swansea, MA, 279
Boissoneault, Letita, 128, 129, 130
Bolay, Joseph, 64
Bolay, Mrs. Joseph, 64
Bolay, Russell, 64
Bonney Street, New Bedford, MA, 215, 299
Borden, Abby, 294
Borden, Andrew J., 294
Borges, Tim, 220
Botelho, Sandra, 297
Bowden, Laura, 142
Bowen, Dr. Seabury, 32
Bowenville (section of Fall River, MA), 27
Boys and Girls Club, New Bedford, 88
Brady, Kyle, 281–282

Branco, Antonio, 289
Branco, Maria, 289
Brandon Woods Nursing Home, Dartmouth, MA, 241
Branquino, Thomas, 81
Bridge Street, Fairhaven, MA, 221
Bridgewater State Hospital, Bridgewater, MA, 54, 56, 67, 68, 120
Briggs, Charles, 25
Brigham, City Marshall Sewell D., 30
Bristol Community College, Fall River, MA, 249
Brock Avenue, New Bedford, MA, 283
Brooklawn Park, New Bedford, MA, 288
Brooks, Ronald T., 298
Brooks Pharmacy, New Bedford, MA, 148, 149
Brophy, William, 120
Brown, Adrienne, 285
Brown, Javon, 300
Buitrago, Jose, 81
Bullard Street, New Bedford, MA, 138, 153, 199
Bullock Road, Freetown, MA, 66
Burgos, John, 174–176, 191
Burton, Arthur, 247–248
Busby, Christopher, 185–186
Butler, Jonathan, 115, 299
Butts, Gideon, 45
Buzzards Bay, Dartmouth, MA, 225
Buzzards Bay, Mattapoisett, MA, 59–60
Buzzards Bay Regatta, 225

C

Cabral, Police Corporal Kenneth, 253, 254
Cadet, James, 201–202
Calden, Dennis, 30–33
Calden, John, 30–33
Caldwell, Patrolman Warren, 253
Callender, Brandon, 220–223
Calvandro, Burce, 295
Camara, Brendon, 142–145
Camelot Inn, Fall River, MA, 295
Canal Street, Fall River, MA, 160, 275
Canto, Joseph, 100–102
Canuel, Linda, 75, 76
Canuel, Melissa, 75
Carpenter, George, 108–109
Carreiro, Maria, 160
Carreiro, Robert, 205
Carter, Hattie, 49, 294
Carter, Kelcie, 233
Carter, Michelle, 276–277
Carter, Vernon, 238–240
Carvalho, Anthony, 284
Carvalho, Carla, 164–165
Carvalho, Derek, 208
Cass, State Prosecutor Frederick, 73
Cassavant, William, 151

Castle, Sheena, 212–213
Cerce, Christopher, 211
Cerce, Baby James, 211
Chabot, Amedee D., 43–44
Chabot, Angeline, 43–44
Chace, Officer Mark P., 16
Chace Mill, Fall River, MA, 34, 294
Chach, Esteban Tum, 199–200
Chancery Street, New Bedford, MA, 115, 174, 175, 298, 299
Charest, Maurice, 70–74
Charles, Daniel, 3–4, **4**
Charlestown Prison, 46–47, 53
Charlton Memorial Hospital, Fall River, MA, 124, 144
Charon, Charles, 29
Charon, Exilda, 27–29
Charon, Frank, 27–29
Charon, Frank Jr., 29
Charon, Mary, 29
Cherry Street, Fall River, MA, 267
Chiaie, Vincent Delle, 69
Chieppa, Charles, 159
Chin, Judge Richard, 114, 127
Choate Street, Fall River, MA, 294
Chounard, Louis, 294
Churchill Street, New Bedford, MA, 263, 264
City Lights Night Club, New Bedford, MA, 191
Clark, Adaline (Hathaway), 12–13, **13**
Clark, John C., 5–6
Clark, Seth, 12
Cloud, John, 290
The Coachman, Tiverton, RI, 72, 74
Coggeshall Street, New Bedford, MA, 81, 230, 300
Cohen, Jerrod, 292–293
Cole, Leslie, 185
Coleman, Rashad, 216–217
Collette Street, New Bedford, MA, 300
Connelly, Detective, 43–44
Contant, Dr., 15–16
Cook Pond, Fall River, MA, 58, 295, 297
Cordeiro, Karen, 164–165
Cordeiro, Raymond, 212
Corky Row (section of Fall River, MA), 137, 164, 234, 285, 300
Cornell, Peleg, 40–42
Cornell, Sarah Maria, 294
Correa-Gonzalez, Jacqueline, 216
Correia, Daniel, 79–80
Correia, Ivandro, 116, 121, 298
Correia, Michael, 258–260
Cortes, Andre, 77
Corvelo, Jessica, 163
Cosgrove, Walter Henry, 295
Coull, Michael, 79

County Street, Fall River, MA, 212, 300
County Street, New Bedford, MA, 216
Cournoyer, Erick, 233
Cove Street, New Bedford, MA, 128, 129, 179, 180, 295
Cowart, Timothy, 300
Crann, James E., 34–35
Crapo Street, New Bedford, MA, 215
Crips Gang, Fall River, MA, 190
Cromwell, Justin, 116
Crowder, Charles, 116
Crowder, Dwayne, 116
Cruz, Antonio, 256
Cruz, Filip M., 256–257
Cruz, Marcus, 115
Cruz, Olivia, 256–257
Cummings, Attorney John W., 23, 32
Cunha, Alfred II, 110
Cunningham, Patrolman Jonathan, 253

D
DaCosta, Hailton, 274
Daily, Officer, 21–22
Danforth Street, Fall River, MA, 300
DaPina, Casey, 184
Dargis, Chad, 116
Dartmouth, Massachusetts, 19
    Barrow, Elizabeth, 241
    Brandon Woods Nursing Home, 241
    Buzzards Bay, 225
    DeMello, Debra, 296
    Dopierala, Rochelle, 296
    James, Alvis Dexter, 298
    Lincoln Park, 72
    Mendes, Dawn, 297
    Old County Buffet, 197
    Oransky, Valerie, 197–198
    Padanaram Harbor, 225
    Paiva, Nancy, 296
    Perry, Irene, 295
    Reed Road, 296, 297
    Walsh, David, 225–226
Dartmouth Street, New Bedford, MA, 298, 300
DaSilva, Sabrina, 291
DaSilva, Walter, 291
Davila, Rey, 160–162
Davis, Brent, 297
Davis, Dr., 15–16
Davis, Shakeem, 206–207
Davol Street, Fall River, MA, 295
Delgado, Alejandro, 266
DeMello, Debra, 296
demographics, Fall River, MA, 246
demographics, New Bedford, MA, 246
Dennis, Raymond P., 30–33
DePina, Bernadette, 191, 299

Depina, Donald A., 288
DeSousa, Pedro, 270
Dexter, Officer, 34
Diaz, Alberto Jr., 146
Diaz, Luis, 235–237
Diaz, Luiz, 146
DiGiantomaso, Robert, 286
Dillingham, Coroner, 15
Dinis, District Attorney Edmund, 67
Dixon, Fred, 160–162
Doe, Jane, 85, 298
Donley, Sergeant, 71–72
Dopierala, Rochelle, 296
Dorr, Steven, 210
Douglas, Tracey Andre, 157–158
Douglas, Massachusetts Governor William L., 46
Douglas Street, Fall River, MA, 256
Dream Cafe, New Bedford, MA, 147, 149
Duarte, Derrick, 180
Duarte, Frank, 69
Duarte, George, 216–217
Duarte, John, 97–99
Duarte, Michael, 263–265
Dublin's Sports Bar, New Bedford, MA, 167
Dubuque, Judge Hugo A., 57
Dudley, Christopher, 179
Dudley, Victoria, 179
Dugan, Jasmine, 206
Dunkin' Donuts, New Bedford, 77
Dunlea, Police Officer Jason, 254
Dunston, Clinton, 299
Dupras, William, 209–210
Dupris, Judge, 286
Duquette, Daryl, 297
Durand, Eric, 142–145
Durand, Michael, 142
Durfee, Tiffany Ann, 271
Dwelly, Medical Examiner John L., 21–22, 23, 28, 29, 30–32
Dwelly Street, Fall River, MA, 208

E
Eagan's Block, Fall River, MA, 27
East End Gang, Fall River, MA, 232
East End Social Club, New Bedford, MA, 295
East Main Street, Fall River, MA, 58, 107, 294
Eaton, Jessie, 234
Edmund Street, Fall River, MA, 252
Elias, Paul, 299
Elm Street, New Bedford, MA, 55
Elmwood Street, Wareham, MA, 238
Eluziario, Baby Ariel, 269
Encarnacion, Ricardo, 300

F
Fairhaven, Massachusetts
    Alden Road, 192
    Bennett, William, 294
    Bridge Street, 221
    Fairhaven Bridge, 294
    Fairhaven High School, 192
    Fitzgerald, Joshua, 220–223
    Fuller, Ruth, 295
    Hamlet Street, 273
    Howland, Joyce, 273
    Lassiter, Dwayne, 203
    Long Road, 103
    LukOil gas station, 192
    Main Street, 222
    Middle Street, 221
    Moriarty's Liquors, 221
    Naughty Dawgs, 220
    Reynolds, Thomas, 192
    Roy, Conrad, 276–277
    Shonheinz, Nancy, 103–106
    VFW Hall, 220
    Washington Street, 203
Fairhaven High School, Fairhaven, MA, 192
Fall River, Massachusetts
    Aetna Street, 242
    Albert Street, 281
    Albion Street, 297
    Almond Street, 30, 31
    Atlantic Bar & Grill, 118
    Bay Street, 250
    Beauregard's Market, 43
    Bedard, Wilfred, 61–62
    Bedford Street, 9, 295
    Bell Rock Road, 112
    Berarde, Bruneau, 15–17
    Bernard, Robert, 137, 298
    Blau, Robert, 296
    Bloods Gang, 190
    Borden, Abby, 294
    Borden, Andrew J., 294
    Bowenville (section of Fall River), 27
    Brady, Kyle, 281–282
    Branco, Maria, 289
    Bristol Community College, 249
    Cadet, James, 201–202
    Calvando, Bruce, 295
    Camelot Inn, 295
    Canal Street, 160, 275
    Carvalho, Anthony, 284
    Cerce, Baby James, 211
    Chabot, Angeline, 43–44
    Chace Mill, 34
    Charlton Memorial Hospital, 124, 144
    Charon, Exilda, 27–29

Cherry Street, 267
Choate Street, 294
Chounard, Louis, 294
Cohen, Jerrod, 292–293
Cook Pond, 58, 295, 297
Corky Row (section of Fall River), 137, 164, 234, 285, 300
Corvelo, Jessica, 163
Cosgrove, Walter Henry, 295
County Street, 212, 300
Crips Gang, 190
Cruz, Olivia, 256–257
Danforth Street, 300
Davila, Rey, 160–162
Davis, Shakeem, 206–207
Davol Street, 295
demographics, 246
Dennis, Raymond P., 30–33
Douglas Street, 256
Dupras, William, 209–210
Dwelly Street, 208
Eagan's Block, 27
East Main Street, 58, 107, 294
Edmund Street, 252
Farrington, Christopher, 118
Father Diafario Village Housing Development, 261
Ferry Lane, 27
Ferry Street, 295
Fifth Street, 234
Fragoza, Gary, 120
Gasiar, David, 120
Glover, Jason, 208
Gluchacki, Alphonse, 297
Goldstein, Russell, 295
Goulart, Susy, 171–173
Hamlet Street, 224, 299
Hancock Street, 209
Harbor Terrace Housing Development, 296
Harrigan, Nathan, 190
Henry Street, 297
Herbert, Robert Jr., 107
Hernandez, Carlos Enrique, 297
Hogue, Derek, 224, 299
Holden Street, 289
homicide rate, 93
Huard Street, 281, 282
Januario, Brian, 300
Joe's Snack Shack, 107
Johnson Street, 261
John Street, 164
Jones, Brian, 285
Jones Street, 249
Leblanc, Edward, 75–76

Lexington Street, 297
Lowell Street, 61
Lucianno, Krista, 188–189
McCabe, Thomas Jr., 295
Machado, Cynthia, 295
McMullen, Annie, 21–26
Mafiosa Street Gang, 250
Manton Street, 120
Maplewood Park, 281
Martinez, Osvaldo Gonsalez, 242
Matos, Raymond, 107
Mechanicsville (section of Fall River), 16
Medeiros, Joseph, 297
Medina, Lisandro, 112–114
Merritt, Evelyn, 296
Middle Street, 297
The Mill Bar, 295
murder rate, 245
Murphy, Ellen, 9–10
Negron, Edward, 112–114
Nieves, Jonathan, 250–251
North Main Street, 27, 188
North Park, 295
North Watuppa Pond, 43–44
Osborne Street, 284
Our Place Lounge, 295
Pascual, Aja, 267
Pelletier, Ernest, 58, 294
Pemberton, Kenny, 295
People Inc., 124
Pier 14, 295
Plain Street, 292
Platts, Edward, 261–262
Pleasant Street, 43, 295
Pleasant View Apartments, 146, 171
population figures, 94
poverty rate, 246
Quequechan Street, 190
Ramos, Leonard, 295
Rivera, Angel Robles, 300
Rodman Street, 295
Rodriguez, David, 275
Rosofky, Abbie Karen, 295
St. Anne's Hospital, 120, 211, 256
Sau, Courtney, 164–165
Save-A-Lot supermarket, 111
Schofield, John, 34–35
Second Street, 294
Ship's Cove Apartments, 160, 275
Shofield, John, 294
Showers, Sandra Jean, 295
Slade Street, 296
Smith, Charles, 234
Smith Street, 75
Sousa, Oranuch, 111, 298

Southeastern Massachusetts Bioreserve, 112
South Main Street, 295
South Park, 72
Spinner's Association, 34
Stewart Street, 27
Sullivan, Eric, 300
Sullivan Drive, 118
Sunset Hill Housing Project, 201, 250
Third Street, 137, 298
Thompkins, Frederick, 218
Tieng, Reksmey, 266
Torres, Jose, 146
Tupaj, Brian, 297
Union Street, 23
Wadlington, Vincent, 300
Walsh, John, 295
Watuppa Heights, 113
Webster Street, 211
Whipple Street, 218, 284
Wilson Road, 300
Woodward, Jerome, 212–213
Faria, Alice Grace, 53
Faria, Anthony Francisco Jr., 147
Faria, Louis, 53
Faria, Marcellino (aka Charles Faria), 53
Farias, Police Officer Louis Jr., 253
Farrington, Christopher, 118
Father Diafario Villiage Housing Development, Fall River, MA, 261
Feliciano, Michael V., 215
Felteau, Rebecca, 270
Fennicks, Tyrone, 117
Fernandees, Jose, 228–229
Ferreira, Kathleen, 151
Ferrer, Antonio, 77–78
Ferrini, Howard, 297
Ferry Lane, Fall River, MA, 27
Ferry Street, Fall River, MA, 295
Fields, William, 185
Fifth Street, Fall River, MA, 234
Finirnov, Peter J., 55–56
Fisher, Christopher, 208
Fisher Road, North Dartmouth, MA, 126
Fitzgerald, Colton, 220
Fitzgerald, Ethan, 220
Fitzgerald, Joseph, 220
Fitzgerald, Joshua, 220–223
Fitzgerald, Patrick, 220
Flores, Arnaldo, 242
Ford, David, 203
Ford Farm Road, Tiverton, MA, 290
Fortes, New Bedford City Councilor Joseph P., 141
Fort Rodman, New Bedford, MA, 296
Foss, Charles (aka D.T. Sherburne), 36–37

Foster, Ellen, 34
Foxy Lady Club, New Bedford, MA, 205
Fragoza, Gary, 120
Francisco, Antonio, 63
Francois, Marcel, 286–287
Fredericks, Detective Dean, 97
Freetown, Massachusetts
    Assonet Burying Ground, 12–13
    Barrows, Polly, 7–8
    Bullock Road, 66
    Frenette, Raymond G., 66–67, **67**
    Hathaway, David S. Jr., 12
    McConnell, Debroh, 296
    Medeiros, Debra, 296
    Pina, Troy, 228–229
    Rhodes, Robin L., 296
    Rounsevell Cemetery, 6
    Szateck, Judith Ann, 66–67, **67**
    Williams, Silas, 5–6
Freitas, Joseph, 77–78
Frenette, Raymond G., 66–67, **67**
Frias, Antonio, 299
Fuller, Ruth, 295

G

Gaouette, Justin K., 128–131
Gardner, Thomas, 263–265
Garron, Robert, 66–67
Gasiar, David, 120
Gauoette, James, 169–170
Geliga, Ramon, 166–168
Geliga, Robert, 166–168
Genesky, Samuel, 63
Gifford, Coroner, 41
Gifford, Warren, 45
Glover, Jason, 208
Gluchacki, Alphonse, 297
Goldstein, Russell, 73, 295
Gomes, Gary, 227
Gomes, Jao, 97, 98
Gomes, Jesus Nazareth, 224
Gomes, John, 296
Gomes, Katherine, 227
Gonsalves, Brandin, 116
Gonsalves, Leonard, 190
Gonsalves, Robert, 204
Gonzalez, Alberto, 152–156
Gonzalez, Fernanda, 152, 154–155
Gonzalez, Reny, 112
Goode, Sharif, 283
Gooseberry Neck, Westport, MA, 45
Gordon, Sheryl, 119
Gorham, Kyron, 206–207
Gosselin, Rene, 218
Goulart, Mark, 230–231
Grace, David, 100–101

Grace, Syrelle, 286–287
Greene, Reggie, 193
Greene, Robert Jr., 299
Griffin Court, New Bedford, MA, 125
Grinnell, Benjamin H., 18
Grinnell, Moses, 18–20
Grinnell, Philip, 45
Grinnell Street, New Bedford, MA, 300

H
Hafiny, Judge Edward F., 58
Hamlet Street, Fairhaven, MA, 273
Hamlet Street, Fall River, MA, 224, 299
Hancock, Clifford, 70, 71
Hancock Street, Fall River, MA, 209
Harbor Terrace Housing Development, Fall River, MA, 296
Harrigan, Nathan, 190
Harrington Park, New Bedford, MA, 286
Harrison, Ethan, 269
Hartley, Dr., 15–16
Harvey, Athena, 95–96
Harvey, Earl H. Jr., 95–96
Hathaway, Attorney, 23
Hathaway, David S. Jr., 12
Hathaway, N., 18
Hathaway, Warren G., 225
Hathaway Road, New Bedford, MA, 89
Hathaway School, New Bedford, MA, 286
Hatheway, Attorney Nicholas, 23
Haywood, Dana, 174–176, 191
Hazard, Richard, 79–80
Head, F. Burton, 46
Hector, William J., 117
Helger, Christina, 201–202
Henderson, Cory, 191
Henry Street, Fall River, MA, 297
Herbert, Robert Jr., 107
Hernandez, Carlos Enrique, 297
Highlander, New Bedford, MA, 149
Hillman Street, New Bedford, MA, 152, 185
Hitt, Frank, 45
Hodgate, Dylan, 194–195
Hogue, Derek, 224, 299
Holden Street, Fall River, MA, 289
Holley, Jermaine, 171–173
Holly Street, New Bedford, MA, 166
Holy Acre (section of New Bedford, MA), 38
Homer Street, New Bedford, MA, 138, 298
homicide rate, Fall River, MA, 93
homicide rate, New Bedford, MA, 93
Horse Neck, Westport, MA, 45
Howland, Joyce, 273
Howland, Sarah, 3–4
Huard Street, Fall River, MA, 281, 282
Hubbard, Corey, 154

Hull, Dr. Mindy, 222
Hunt, Shawn, 152–156
Hurley, Judge Joseph L., 61
Hyacinth Street, New Bedford, MA, 300

I
Independence Street, New Bedford, MA, 227
Industrial Park, New Bedford, MA, 119

J
Jackmon, Kevin E., 89–90
James, Alvis Dexter, 298
Janurario, Brian, 300
Jeffrey, Diana, 55–56
Jeffries, Thomas, 228–229
Jennings Court, New Bedford, MA, 181
Joe's Snack Shack, Fall River, MA, 107
Johnson, Joseph, 49
Johnson, Louisa, 49
Johnson, Rose, 31
Johnson Street, Fall River, MA, 261
John Street, Fall River, MA, 164
Jones, Anthony, 300
Jones, Brian, 285
Jones, Officer, 33
Jones, Ryan, 197–198
Jones Street, Fall River, MA, 249
Jorge, Edwin, 248
Jorge, Jordan, 248
Joseph, Kayla, 206
Joseph, Officer Peter, 104
Juszynski, Mary, 57
Juszynski, Walenty, 57

K
Kalisz, New Bedford Mayor Frederick, 93, 141, 245
Katzmarick, Walentz, 55
Kelly, Police Chief Arthur J. III, 93, 141
Kempton Street, New Bedford, MA, 174, 299
Kenham, Peter, 297
Kenner, Karrah, 160
Kerrshaw, Officer Christopher, 104
King, Charles Caton Jr., 68
Kingsley, George F., 23
Kirby, Edward A., 45
Kirby, Tillinghast, 42, 45–48
Knowlton, Attorney Hosea, 34
Kostek, Michael, 278
Kostek, Sophie, 278

L
Laberge, Walter, 295
Lafayette Road, Tiverton, RI, 295
Lamere, Timothy, 83–84
Lapointe, Daniel, 75–76

Lapointe, Jamie, 75
Lapointe, Susan, 75
Lapre, James, 249
Lara, Kevin, 284
Lara, Olivia Pires, 100–101
Lassiter, Dwayne, 203
Lawrence, Heather, 108
Lawton, Thomas B., 15
Leblanc, David, 220–221
Leblanc, Edward, 75–76
Lecroy, Bobby Joe, 166–168
Lemuel Shattuck Hospital Correctional
 Unit, Jamaica Plain, 96
LePage, Brandyn, 267
Levesque, Timothy, 279–280
Lewis, Robert O., 70–74
Lexington Street, Fall River, MA, 297
Lincoln Park, Dartmouth, MA, 72
Lindsey Street, Fall River, MA, 15
Lingane, Attorney David F., 23
Little Compton, Rhode Island
 Adamsville Church Cemetery, 14
 Adamsville Road, 40
 Almy, Valentine S., 11
 Almy Cemetery, 11
 Cornell, Peleg, 40–42
 Martinez, Osvaldo Gonsalez, 242
 Seabury, M. Albert, 294
 Simmons Hill, 40
 Taylors Lane, 242
Locust Street, New Bedford, MA, 300
Loflin, John, 123
Loftus, Geoffrey, 184
Lon, Sarath, 190
Long Road, Fairhaven, MA, 103
Lopes, Albert Jr., 125
Lopes, Cecil, 175, 176, 299
Lopes, Joel, 292
Lopez, Manuel Antonio, 214
Lorenzi, Yanelly, 212
Lovejoy, Thomas J., 38–39
Lowell Street, Fall River, MA, 61
Lozada, Miguel, 140
L & P Lounge, New Bedford, MA, 100
Lucianno, Krista, 188–189
LukOil gas station, Fairhaven, MA, 192
Lundquist, Laura, 241
Luso Assembly of God Church,
 New Bedford, MA, 87

M

McCabe, Thomas Jr., 295
McCaonnell, Debroh, 296
McCarty, Daniel, 15
McDonalds, New Bedford, MA, 89

McDonough, Patrick F., 69
Machado, Cynthia, 295
McMullen, Annie, 21–26
McMullen, Emma, 22
McMullen, Thomas, 22
McMullen, Thomas Henry, 21–26
Mafiosa Street Gang, Fall River, MA, 250
Magnet Park, New Bedford, MA, 79
Main Event Club, New Bedford, MA, 140
Main Road, Tiverton, RI, 290
Main Street, Fairhaven, MA, 222
Manchester, Samuel B., 14
Manton Street, Fall River, MA, 120
Maplewood Park, Fall River, MA, 281
Marandos, Tory, 205
Maranhao, Mabilia, 283
Margin Street, New Bedford, MA, 53, 180
Marion, Massachusetts
 Botelho, Sandra, 297
Marrero, Felix, 160–162
Marshall, Ryan, 108–109
Martin, Joan, 180
Martin, John K., 230–231
Martin, Terry, 22
Martinez, Ismael, 298
Martinez, Osvaldo Gonzalez, 242
Martins, Mathew, 192
Massachusetts Correctional Institution,
 Cedar Junction, 76, 114
Massachusetts Correctional Institution,
 Shirley, 229
Massachusetts Reformatory for Women,
 New Bedford, MA, 61
Massachusetts State Prison, Boston, 52
Massie, Tacuma, 261–262
Matos, Jose Mercado, 212
Matos, Osvaldo Mercado, 212–213
Matos, Raymond, 107
Matrony, Anton, 51
Matrony, Captain Charles, 50–52
Mattapoisett, Massachusetts, 59–60
 Allinson, Aveling, 59
 Allinson, Dwight, 59
 Allinson, Hope, 59
 Barstow's Wharf, 59
 Buzzards Bay, 59–60
Matthew Street, New Bedford, MA, 300
Mattos, Steven, 83–84
Maxfield, Ellen, 5
Mechanicsville (section of Fall River, MA), 16
Medeiros, Debra, 296
Medeiros, Donna, 108
Medeiros, Joseph, 297
Medeiros, Scott, 205
Medina, Edwin, 216–217

Medina, Lisandro, 112–114
Megna, Joseph, 107
Mello, Lisa, 268
Mello, Police Officer Robert, 199–200
Melone, Louis D., 73
Melynk, Firefighter Fred M. Jr., 254
Mendes, Dawn, 297
Mendes, Keone, 140
Mendes, Robyn, 227
Mendes, Victor, 227
Mendes, Wayne, 204
Mendez, Charles, 261–262
Mendez, Maria, 298
Mendez, Neidy, 242
Merritt, Evelyn, 296
Middle Street, Fairhaven, MA, 221
Middle Street, Fall River, MA, 297
Miliote, Gregg, 269
The Mill Bar, Fall River, MA, 295
Miller, David, 201–202
Mills, Alexander, 288
Miranda, Fagbemi, 182–184
Miranda, Wayne, 182–184
Mitchell, Marcus, 228–229
Moitoso, Ryan, 261
Molina, Alexander, 169–170
Moneiro, Tracy, 300
Moniz, Rose Marie, 110, 298
Montalva-Borgos, Luis Alberto, 212–213
Monteiro, Allan Anthony, 147
Monteiro, Christine, 296
Monteiro, Francisco, 228
Monteiro, Scott, 238–240
Monte Park (section of New Bedford, MA), 174, 175
Monte Park Gang, New Bedford, MA, 115, 116, 117, 125, 174–175, 191
Moran, Patricia, 171
Morgado, Thomas, 298
Morgan, Marvin, 295
Morgan Terrace, New Bedford, MA, 299
Moriarty's Liquors, Fairhaven, MA, 221
Mota, Police Officer Leonard, 180
Moton, Jerome, 112
Moulds-Tiul, Luis, 219
Mount Pleasant Street, New Bedford, MA, 297
Moura, John, 296
Mowbry, Elizabeth Margaret, 38–39
Mowbry, John A., 38–39
murder rate, Fall River, MA, 245
murder rate, New Bedford, MA, 245
Murphy, Devyn, 298
Murphy, Ellen, 9–10
Murphy, John, 9–10
Murphy, Patrick, 141, 298

Murray, Cheryl, 166
Murray, Tom, 166–168

N

Naughty Dawgs, Fairhaven, MA, 220
Navajo Court, New Bedford, MA, 298
Negron, Edward, 112–114
New Bedford, Massachusetts
    Acushnet Avenue, 63, 110, 117, 147, 167, 175, 248, 297, 298, 299
    Acushnet River, 294
    Adams Street, 269
    Aguiar, Ryan, 121–122
    Andrade, Raymond P., 299
    Andrews, Arnold, 297
    Andrews-Dahill VFW, 232
    Ashland Place, 270
    Ashley Boulevard, 159, 299
    Ashley Street, 83
    Ash Street, 299
    Barros, Christopher, 182–184
    Barros, Filipe, 87–88
    Barros, Michael, 86
    Barry-Henderson, Justin, 191
    Barrymore, Clifford, 298
    Becht, Nettie, 235–237
    Bedford Street, 183, 217
    Bentley Street, 230
    Bey, Elijah Omar, 117, 298
    Blackmer Street, 87
    Blanchard, Delvina Grenier, 54
    Bluefield Street, 108
    Bonney Street, 215, 299
    Boys and Girls Club, 88
    Brock Avenue, 283
    Brooklawn Park, 288
    Brooks, Ronald T., 298
    Brooks Pharmacy, 148, 149
    Brown, Javon, 300
    Bullard Street, 138, 153, 199
    Burton, Arthur, 247–248
    Butler, Jonathan, 299
    Canto, Joseph, 100–102
    Carpenter, George, 108–109
    Carreiro, Robert, 205
    Carter, Hattie, 49, 294
    Casssavant, William, 151
    Chach, Esteban Tum, 199–200
    Chancery Street, 115, 174, 175, 298, 299
    Churchill Street, 263, 264
    City Lights Night Club, 191
    Coggeshall Street, 81, 230, 300
    Collette Street, 300
    Correia, Daniel, 79–80
    Correia, Ivandro, 116, 298

Correia, Michael, 258–260
County Street, 216
Cove Street, 128, 129, 179, 180, 295
Cowart, Timothy, 300
Crapo Street, 215
Cruz, Marcus, 115
Dartmouth Street, 298, 300
DaSilva, Sabrina, 291
Davis, Brent, 297
demographics, 246
DePina, Bernadette, 299
Depina, Donald A., 288
Diaz, Luuis, 235–237
Doe, Jane, 85, 298
Dream Cafe, 147, 149
Duarte, Frank, 69
Duarte, John, 97–99
Duarte, Michael, 263–265
Dublin's Sports Bar, 167
Dunkin' Donuts, 77
Dunston, Clinton, 299
Durfee, Tiffany Ann, 271
East End Gang, 232
East End Social Club, 295
Elias, Paul, 299
Elm Street, 55
Eluziario, Baby Ariel, 269
Encarnacion, Ricardo, 300
Faria, Alice Grace, 53
Felteau, Rebecca, 270
Fort Rodman, 296
Foxy Lady Club, 205
Francois, Marcel, 286–287
Freitas, Joseph, 77–78
Gauoette, James, 169–170
Genesky, Samuel, 63
Gomes, Katherine, 227
Gonzalez, Alberto, 152–156
Goode, Sharif, 283
Gordon, Sheryl, 119
Greene, Robert Jr., 299
Griffin Court, 125
Grinnell Street, 300
Harrington Park, 286
Hathaway Road, 89
Hathaway School, 287
Haywood, Dana, 174–176
Highlander, 149
Hillman Street, 152, 185
Holly Street, 166
Holy Acre (section of New Bedford), 38
Homer Street, 138, 298
homicide rate, 93
Hyacinth Street, 300
Independence Street, 227
Industrial Park, 119

Jeffrey, Diana, 55–56
Jennings Court, 181
Jones, Anthony, 300
Juszynski, Walenty, 57
Kempton Street, 174, 299
Kenham, Peter, 297
King, Charles Caton Jr., 68
Lamere, Timothy, 83–84
Locust Street, 300
Lopes, Albert Jr., 125
Lopes, Cecil, 299
L & P Lounge, 100
Luso Assembly of God Church, 87
McDonalds, 89
Magnet Park, 79
Main Event Club, 140
Marandos, Tory, 205
Maranhao, Mabilia, 283
Margin Street, 53, 180
Martin, John K., 230–231
Martinez, Ismael, 298
Massachusetts Reformatory for Women, 61
Matthew Street, 300
Medeiros, Scott, 205
Medina, Edwin, 216–217
Mendes, Keone, 140
Mendes, Robyn, 227
Mendez, Maria, 298
Moneiro, Tracy, 300
Moniz, Rose Marie, 110, 298
Monte Park (section of New Bedford), 174, 175
Monte Park Gang, 115, 116, 117, 125, 174–175, 191
Montiero, Christine, 296
Morgado, Thomas, 298
Morgan, Marvin, 295
Morgan Terrace, 299
Moulds-Tiul, Luis, 219
Mount Pleasant Street, 297
Moura, John, 296
Mowbry, John A., 38–39
Moxie, Herbert, 294
murder rate, 245
Murphy, Patrick, 141, 298
Murray, Tom, 166–168
Najavo Court, 298
New Bedford Area Chamber of Commerce, 182
New Bedford High School, 233
New Bedford Yacht Club, 225
New Bedford YMCA, 61
New Plainville Road, 117
North Front Street, 199, 200, 298, 300
Nye Street, 65

Oak Grove Cemetery, 48
Pacheco, Baby Joshua, 214
Payne, William, 299
Pereira, Frank Jr., 159
Perreira, Frank Jr., 299
Petro-Mart, 230
Phillips Road, 227
Pierce, Mark A., 297
Pina, Michael, 300
Pleasant Street, 61
Poisson, Napoleon, 65
Popes Island Marina, 85, 298
population figures, 94
poverty rate, 245
Presidential Heights housing project, 149
Purchase Street, 50, 69, 97, 123, 141, 182, 183, 247, 248, 258, 288, 298, 299
Regal Beagle Bar & Grille, 299
Rice, Wayne, 232
Rivet Street, 86
Roberts, Marilyn, 296
Rogers, Helen, 65
Rosa, Anderson, 179-181
Rosado, Bianco, 233
Rosales, Veronica, 219
Rosanina, Jeffrey, 81-82
Rose, Marlene, 123
Russell Street, 175, 182
Ruth Street, 116, 169, 298, 299
Ruth Street Gang, 116, 121
St. Luke's Hospital, 86, 103, 116, 166, 214, 222, 233, 286
St. Martin's Episcopal Church, 121
Salisbury Street, 169
Santos, Joshua, 132-136
Santos, Rudolph, 185-187
Savers Store, 95-96
Sawyer Street, 231, 297
Semedo, Antonio, 193
Shark Club, 81
Shore Street, 180
Silva, Ashley, 299
Silva, David, 128-131
Silviera, Leonard, 138-139, 298
Simoes, Antonio, 298
Slocum, Philip D., 36-37
Smith, Daniel, 300
Smith Street, 299
Soares, Suanna M., 177-178, 299
South First Street, 57, 298
South Second Street, 193
South Water Street, 36, 49, 294
Souza, Scott, 300
Spruce Street, 152
S. Sixth Street, 177, 217, 299
Stafford, Sharone, 274

Stag Hotel, 55-56
Stapleton Street, 179
Surfside Lounge, 295
Tallman Street, 300
Tarkin Hill (secion of New Bedford), 298
Tavares, Laurie, 157-158
Thompson Street, 215, 299, 300
Thyng, George, 294
Timm, Eva Baptiste, 295
Tinkham Street, 219
Traynum, Demarco, 89-90
Trinity Soup Kitchen, 258
Turner Court, 38
Union Street, 140, 191
United Front Gang, 174, 191, 193, 238, 239
United Front Housing Development, 175, 299
Vasquez, Angel, 297
Walsh, Annie, 50-52
Welcome Street, 166
Weld Square, 300
Westlawn Housing Development, 115, 235
White, Michael, 147-150
Wilson, Albon, 215, 299
Wing Street, 117, 298
New Bedford Area Chamber of Commerce, New Bedford, MA, 182
New Bedford High School, New Bedford, MA, 233
New Bedford Yacht Club, New Bedford, MA, 225
New Bedford YMCA, 61
New Plainville Road, New Bedford, MA, 117
Niemic, Jonathan Keith, 258-260
Nieves, Jonathan, 250-251
North Dartmouth, Massachusetts
    Fisher Road, 126
    Tolan, Edward J. Jr., 126-127
North Front Street, New Bedford, MA, 199, 200, 298, 300
North Main Street, Fall River, MA, 27, 188
North Park, Fall River, MA, 295
North Watuppa Pond (Fall River, MA), 43-44
Novo, Rui, 132-136
Nye Street, New Bedford, MA, 65

O

Oak Grove Cemetery, Fall River, MA, 16
Oak Grove Cemetery, New Bedford, MA, 48
Oak Grove Cemetery, Pawtucket, Rhode Island, 8
Ocean Grove, Swansea, MA, 279
Ocean Grove Avenue, Swansea, MA, 279
Old County Buffet, Dartmouth, MA, 197
Oliveira, Eric, 138

Oliveira, John Jr., 194–196
Oliveira, Robert J., 103–106
Oliveira, Teddy, 104
Opozda, Thomas, 220
Oransky, Valerie, 197–198
Ortega, Police Lieutenant Manuel, 180
Osborne Street, Fall River, MA, 284
Our Place Lounge, Fall River, MA, 295

P

Pacheco, Police Officer Barry, 186
Pacheco, Baby Joshua, 214
Padanaram Harbor, Dartmouth, MA, 225
Paiva, Nancy, 296
Palmer, Loring, 14
Paquette, Patricia, 142–144
Paquette, Paul, 142
Paquette, Priscilla, 142
Pascual, Aja, 267
Patricio, James, 210
Payne, William, 175–176, 299
Peckham, Reuben, 16
Pelletier, Ernest, 58, 294
Pelletier, Napoleon, 58
Pemberton, Kenny, 295
People, Inc., Fall River, MA, 124
Pereira, Frank Jr., 159
Perez, Jarin, 112–114
Perreira, Frank Jr., 299
Perry, Detective Charles, 97
Perry, Deborah, 296
Perry, Irene, 295
Petro-Mart, New Bedford, MA, 230
Pettey, Stacey, 222
Phillips Road, New Bedford, MA, 227
Pier 14, Fall River, MA, 295
Pierce, Coroner Ebenezer W., 7
Pierce, Mark A., 297
Pina, Adam, 232
Pina, Lydell, 141
Pina, Michael, 300
Pina, Myron, 141
Pina, Troy, 228–229
Pires, Tavon, 284
Pittman, Michael, 152–156
Plain Street, Fall River, MA, 292
Platt, Barbara, 252
Platts, Edward, 261–262
Pleasant Street, Fall River, MA, 43, 295
Pleasant Street, New Bedford, MA, 61
Pleasant View Apartments, Fall River, MA, 146, 171
Pocasset Hill Cemetery, Tiverton, MA, 290
Poitras, Lyla Jean, 295
Popes Island Marina, New Bedford, MA, 85, 298
population figures, Fall River, MA, 94
population figures, New Bedford, MA, 94
Potter, Thomas, 55
poverty rate, Fall River, MA, 246
poverty rate, New Bedford, MA, 245
Powell, Erroll, 250–251
Presidential Heights housing project, New Bedford, MA, 149
Princiotta, Corey, 230–231
Priority (sailboat), 225
Purchase Street, New Bedford, MA, 50, 69, 97, 123, 141, 182, 183, 247–248, 258, 288, 298, 299

Q

Quequechan Street, Fall River, MA, 190
Quinn, Kevin, 284
Quinn, District Attorney Thomas, 94, 269

R

Raimondi, Dennis, 295
Ramiriz, Eliseo, 167
Ramos, Leonard, 295
Reasons (power boat), 225
Reaves, Timothy, 79
Reed, Attorney Milton, 32–33
Reed Road, Dartmouth, RI, 296, 297
Regal Beagle Bar & Grille, New Bedford, MA, 299
Reis, Kim Deann, 182
Renaud, Joanne, 199
Reynolds, Thomas, 192
Rhode Island Historical Society, 3
Rhode Island State Archives, 3
Rhodes, Robin L., 296
Ricard, Delpha D., 68
Rice, Wayne, 232
Richard, Carol, 70–73, 74
Richardson, Hope Ann (Mrs. Calivin Thomas Jr.), 5
Riley, John, 15–17
Rivera, Andres, 163
Rivera, Angel Robles, 300
Rivera, Carlos, 242
Rivera, Mickey, 284
Rivet Street, New Bedford, MA, 86
Roberts, Marilyn, 296
Robinson, George, 34
Rodman Street, Fall River, MA, 295
Rodrigues, Antonio Jr., 274
Rodriguez, Carmen, 182
Rodriguez, David, 275
Rodriguez, Lionel, 108–109
Rodriguez, Nelson, 87–88
Rodriques, Police Sergeant Francis, 186
Rogers, Wayne, 137

Rollins, Frederick, 69
Rosa, Anderson, 179–181
Rosado, Bianco, 233
Rosales, Veronica, 219
Rosanina, Jeffrey, 81–82
Rosario, Eduardo, 212
Rose, Marlene, 123
Rose, Scott, 79
Rosofky, Abbie Karen, 295
Roy, Conrad, 276–277
Rubois, Roger, 138
Ruby, Peter, 147
Russell, Massachusetts Governor William E., 24
Russell Street, New Bedford, MA, 175, 182
Ruth Street, New Bedford, MA, 116, 169, 298, 299
Ruth Street Gang, New Bedford, MA, 116, 121
Rutkowski, Jeffrey, 112–113

S

St. Anne's Hospital, Fall River, MA, 120, 211, 256
St. Luke's Hospital, New Bedford, MA, 86, 103, 116, 166, 214, 222, 233, 269, 286
St. Martin's Episcopal Church, New Bedford MA, 121
St. Pierre, Sharon, 212–213
Salisbury Street, New Bedford, MA, 169
Sama, Michael, 209–210
Sanchez, Darlene, 166
Santiago, Patricio Oscar, 147–150
Santos, Police Sergeant August, 180
Santos, Christopher, 132–136
Santos, Joseph, 147
Santos, Joshua, 132–136
Santos, Mary, 297
Santos, Melissa, 132
Santos, Rudolph, 185–187
Santos, Sheldon, 238–240
Sau, Courtney, 164–165
Sauve, Police Officer William, 180
Savage, Constable Sylvester, 59
Save-A-Lot supermarket, Fall River, MA, 111
Savers Store, New Bedford, MA, 95–96
Sawyer Street, New Bedford, MA, 231, 297
Scarlata, Barbara, 167
Schmidt, Hans, 50
Schofield, John, 34–35
Seabury, M. Albert, 295
Sea Fox (barkentine schooner), 37
Seaver, Officer, 34
Second Street, Fall River, MA, 294
Seilgman, Attorney James, 73
Semedo, Antonio, 193
Shanks, Dr., 57

Shark Club, New Bedford, MA, 81
Sharkey, Michael, 30–33
Shea, Detective, 43–44
Sherburne, D.T. (aka Charles Foss), 36–37
Sherman, Mrs. Sarah, 46
Ship's Cove Apartments, Fall River, MA, 160, 275
Shonheinz, Nancy, 103–106
Shore Street, New Bedford, MA, 180
Showers, Sandra Jean, 295
Silva, Ashley, 299
Silva, David, 128–131
Silva, Joshua, 273
Silva, Lilian, 291
Silva, Manuel, 116
Silva, Matthew, 128–131
Silva, Nicholas, 129–130
Silvia, Manuel, 121–122
Silviera, Leonard, 138–139, 298
Simmons Hill, Little Compton, RI, 40
Simoes, Antonio, 298
Slade Street, Fall River, MA, 296
Slanson, Charles, 25
Slocum, Philip D., 36–37
Smith, Charles, 234
Smith, Danile, 300
Smith, Dennis, 108
Smith, Dr., 15–16
Smith, Jayden, 292
Smith, Steve, 202
Smith Street, Fall River, MA, 75–76
Smith Street, New Bedford, MA, 299
Snell, Angles, 1, 42, 45–48, **48**
Snipe (coal barge), 50, 51
Soares, Suzanna M., 177–178, 299
Soares, Tazmyn, 232
Solano, Tyrone, 248
Solomonsen, Paul E., 81–82
Somerset, Massachusetts, 27, 29
    Bolay, Joseph, 64
    Camara, Brendon, 142–145
    Kostek, Sophie, 278
    Raimondi, Dennis, 295
    Wilbur Avenue, 278
Sousa, David, 268
Sousa, Joseph, 111
Sousa, Oranuch, 111, 298
Southeastern Massachusetts Bioreserve, Fall River, MA, 112
South First Street, New Bedford, MA, 57, 298
South Main Street, Fall River, MA, 295
South Park, Fall River, MA, 72
South Second Street, New Bedford, MA, 193
South Water Street, New Bedford, MA, 36, 49, 294
Souza, Scott, 300

Spencer, State Trooper Anthony, 174
Spinner's Association, Fall River, MA, 34
Spruce Street, New Bedford, MA, 152
S. Sixth Street, New Bedford, MA, 177, 217, 299
Stafford, Sharone, 274
Stag Hotel, New Bedford, MA, 55-56
Staples, Judge Hamilton B., 35
Stapleton Street, New Bedford, MA, 179
Steele, Levicy, 5
Stephen French Road, Swansea, MA, 272
Stevenson, Mitchell, 272
Stewart, Annie, 49
Stewart Street, Fall River, MA, 27
Sullivan, Eric, 300
Sullivan, John, 30, 32-33
Sullivan, Matilda, 55
Sullivan Drive, Fall River, MA, 118
Sunset Hill Housing Project, Fall River, MA, 201, 250
Surfside Lounge, New Bedford, MA, 295
Sutter, District Attorney Samuel, 94
Swansea, Massachusetts
    Aubin, Kenneth, 124, **124**
    Bluff Avenue, 279
    Frias, Antonio, 299
    Mello, Lisa, 268
    Mendes, Wayne, 204
    Ocean Grove, 279
    Ocean Grove Avenue, 279
    Oliveira, John Jr., 194-196
    Stephen French Road, 272
    Stevenson, Mitchell, 272
    Thomas, Elizabeth, 124
    Venus de Milo, 281
    White, Melissa, 279-280
    Wilson, Christian, 272
Sylvester, William, 45
Sylvia, Bobby, 221
Sylvia, John D. Jr., 177
Sylvia, Kyle, 179-181
Sylvia, Robert, 220
Szatek, Judith Ann, 66-67, **67**

T

Tallman Street, New Bedford, MA, 300
Tangherlini, Peter, 119
Tarkin Hill (section of New Bedford, MA), 298
Tate, William, 275
Taunton State Hospital, Taunton, MA, 241
Tavares, Laurie, 157-158
Taylor, Andrew, 249
Taylors Lane, Little Compton, RI, 242
Tejaeda, Luis, 146
Terry, Dr., 23
Therrien, Flora, 51-52
Therrien, Louis, 50-51

Third Street, Fall River, MA, 137, 298
Thomas, Calvin Jr., 5-6
Thomas, Charles H., 18-20
Thomas, Charley, 19
Thomas, Delphina, 216
Thomas, Elizabeth, 124
Thomas, Frank L., 5
Thompkins, Frederick, 218
Thompson Street, New Bedford, MA, 215, 299, 300
Thyng, George, 294
Tieng, Reksmey, 266
Timm, Eva Baptiste, 295
Tinkham Street, New Bedford, MA, 219
Tirado, Robert, 108-109
Tiverton, Rhode Island
    Beaulieu, Conrad, 253-255
    Blake, Duane L., 70-74
    Charles, Daniel, 3-4
    Cloud, John, 290
    The Coachman, 72, 74
    Cornell, Sarah Maria, 294
    Ford Farm Road, 290
    Laberge, Walter, 295
    Lafayette Road, 295
    Main Road, 290
    Pocasset Hill Cemetery, 290
    Poitras, Lyla Jean, 295
    Taylor, Andrew, 249
    Thomas, Charles H., 18-20
    Tiverton Zoning Board of Review, 111
    Tosca, Anthony, 70-74
    Town Cemetery, Common Burial Ground and Memorial Garden, 4
    Woodland Circle, 253
Tiverton Zoning Board of Review, 111
Todman, John, 100-101
Tolan, Edward J. Jr., 126-127
Tolan, Peggy Ann, 126-127
Torres, Jonathan, 108
Torres, Jose, 146, 172
Tosca, Anthony, 70-74
Travers, Danielle, 128, 129
Traynum, Demarco, 89-90
Trinity Soup Kitchen, New Bedford, MA, 258
Tupaj, Brian, 297
Turner Court, New Bedford, MA, 38

U

Union Street, Fall River, MA, 23
Union Street, New Bedford, MA, 140, 191
United Front Gang, New Bedford, MA, 174, 191, 193, 238
United Front Housing Development, New Bedford, MA, 175, 299

V

Valentin, Elvin E., 235–237
Vasquez, Angel, 297
Velez, Raymond, 140
Venus de Milor, Swansea, MA, 281
VFW Hall, Fairhaven, MA, 220
Viger, Christopher, 138–139

W

Wadlington, Vincent, 185–187, 300
Wallace, Rakeem, 154
Walsh, Annie, 50–52
Walsh, David, 225–226
Walsh, John, 295
Wareham, Massachusetts
    Elmwood Street, 238
    Harvey, Athena, 95–96
    Monteiro, Scott, 238–240
    Murphy, Devyn, 298
    Wareham Council on Aging, 95
Washington Street, Fairhaven, MA, 203
Watuppa Boat Club, Westport, MA, 252
Watuppa Heights, Fall River, MA, 113
Wave (barkentine schooner), 36–37
Webster Street, Fall River, MA, 211
Weetamoe Mill, Fall River, MA, 15
Welcome Street, New Bedford, MA, 166
Weld Square, New Bedford, MA, 300
Westgate, Charles, 66
Westlawn Housing Development, New Bedford, MA, 115, 235
Westport, Massachusetts
    Alvarado, Suzanna, 299
    Arruda, Alfred Jr., 252
    Arruda, David, 252
    Duquette, Daryl, 297
    Gomes, John, 296
    Gooseberry Neck, 45
    Horse Neck, 45
    Kirby, Tillinghast, 45–48
    Manchester, Sanuel B., 14
    Perry, Deborah, 296
    Santos, Mary, 297
    Watuppa Boat Club, 252
    Westport Point, 45
Wetmore, Rhode Island Governor George, 20
Whally, Alice, 34
Whipple Street, Fall River, MA, 218, 284
White, Jerome Jaime, 118
White, Melissa, 279–280
White, Michael, 147–150
Wiffin, Dianne, 167
Wilbour, Chief Justice, 3
Wilbur Avenue, Somerset, MA, 278
Williams, Bob, 220
Williams, Mehetible, 5
Williams, Silas, 5–6, **6**
Wilson, Albon, 215, 299
Wilson, Christian, 272
Wilson Road, Fall River, MA, 300
Wing Street, New Bedford, MA, 117, 298
Winslow, Attorney B.F., 10
Woodland Circle, Tiverton, Ri, 253
Woodward, Jerome, 212–213
Woollam, Derek, 194–196

Z

Zane, Dr. William, 187

NOTES

NOTES

ABOUT THE AUTHOR

John B. Cummings, Jr. is a life-long resident of Greater Fall River. His roots go deep, as his grandfather was a Fall River Mayor and his father a practicing attorney in the area for over fifty years.

The author spent his early career years as a bank vice president in the marketing department. He was recognized with advertising copy writing awards for many years. He than became the chief professional officer of the United Way of Greater Fall River where, among other tasks, he authored press releases, wrote promotional material, and annual reports. He retired from the United Way as Endowment Director and was recognized nationally for the program's success. In 2005, he wrote his first historical book for private consumption about the history of the Greater Fall River Development Corporation: *From Little Acorns to Giant Oaks*.

In 2011, the author continued writing local historical books; *The Last Fling-Hurricane Carol 1954*; *Cream of the Crop: Fall River's Best and Brightest*; and *Lobstah Tales: the history of the Moby Dick/Back Eddy Restaurant in Westport, Massachusetts*. He also produced a *Last Fling* DVD with actual hurricane footage and survivor interviews. All books and the DVD are available through the publisher's web site: HillsideMedia.net

This current venture took two years to research and write and includes well over 399 solved and still mysterious murders, manslaughters, and mayhem in the eight SouthCoast cities and towns around Greater Fall River. His extensive research was conducted in the Fall River Public Library, The *Fall River Herald News* Library, and the clerk's office of the Bristol County Superior Court, as well as on the Internet.

His next project is the *Centennial History of the Acoaxet Club* in Westport, which is due out in the summer of 2019.

ABOUT THE AUTHOR

Dr. Stefani Koorey is the author of several books about Fall River history (*Historic Fires of Fall River* and *Images of America: Fall River Revisited*), Lizzie Borden, storytelling in the library, and a seminal work of Arthur Miller scholarship, *Arthur Miller's Life and Literature: An Annotated and Comprehensive Guide*.

She is the co-author, with John B. Cummings, Jr. of *Murder, Manslaughter, and Mayhem on the SouthCoast, Volume One*.

Dr. Koorey owns PearTree Press, an indy book publishing business that produces work related to Fall River History, True Crime, the Borden Murders of 1892, poetry, and topics of regional interest. While her PhD is in theatre history, she is very involved writing and speaking about the history of the region in which she now resides: New England. peartrees-press.com.

[*advertisement*]

The Last Fling

by John B. "Red" Cummings, Jr.

Hurricane Carol 1954, Stories from Westport, Massachusetts

The Last Fling is a fascinating tale of a life-altering event of courage, terror and survival. There are first hand stories from more than 60 individuals and families and what they experienced as their homes and town were torn apart during Hurricane Carol in 1954. The book speaks of the spirit of the times and the people as wind and waves crashed without warning into a Massachusetts coastal town making Carol one of the most destructive natural disasters the area ever endured. The narrative is complemented by more than 40 illustrations. It is an absolutely vivid and charming depiction of life at another time, in a specific place. Most importantly, it is a story about a community, its people and the human spirit and how we all manage to survive in times of disaster as we experience these events together.

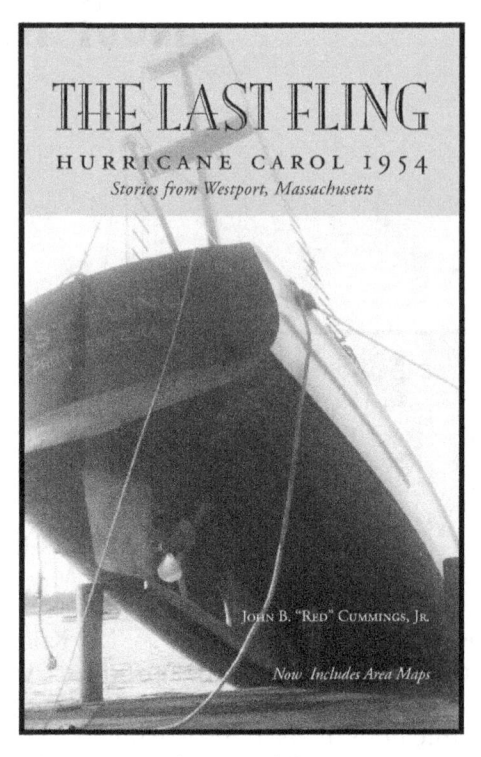

Available ***NOW*** through HillsideMedia.net
$24.95

FOR INQUIRIES, PLEASE CONTACT:
Hillside Media
245 Old Harbor Road
Westport, MA 02790
Tel: 508.636.2831
or John@hillsidemedia.net

[advertisement]

Cream of the Crop

by John B. "Red" Cummings, Jr.

Fall River's Best and Brightest

Cream of the Crop is a fascinating collection of more than 260 intimate mini biographies of not just locally successful individuals but many others who went on to influence their occupations nationally and internationally. Written by a local award-winning author it provides lists of mayors, fire and police chiefs, judges, school superintendents, undefeated and state championship sports teams, and military heroes who died in various wars. It demonstrates how the sons and daughters of one of New England's great cities can touch and influence the world. Beside being an interesting and entertaining read, it is also a valuable historic document and motivational tool for success for current and future generations, not solely from Fall River or Massachusetts but across the nation.

Available **NOW** through
HillsideMedia.net
$27.95

FOR INQUIRIES, PLEASE CONTACT:
Hillside Media
245 Old Harbor Road
Westport, MA 02790
Tel: 508.636.2831
or John@hillsidemedia.net

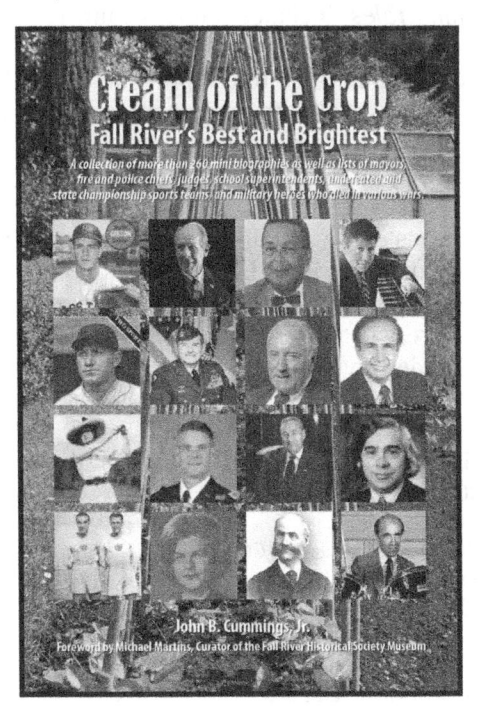

[*advertisement*]

Lobstah Tales

by John B. "Red" Cummings, Jr.

A History of the Moby Dick/Back Eddy Restaurant in Westport, Massachusetts

Lobstah Tales includes stories during different ownership phases of the restaurant since 1953 to the present. The book is illustrated with many photos over the years as well as interviews with owners over time. The book makes a perfect gift for a loved one that has experienced the uniqueness of the restaurant over looking the river over the years. Life-long Westport resident, Richard "Dick" "Hoot" Squire wrote the foreword to the book and blurbs are written by Harbormaster Richie Earle and lobstahmen Capt. John Borden and Everett Mills.

Available **NOW** through HillsideMedia.net
$12.00

FOR INQUIRIES, PLEASE CONTACT:
Hillside Media
245 Old Harbor Road
Westport, MA 02790
Tel: 508.636.2831
or John@hillsidemedia.net

[advertisement]

Historic Fires of Fall River

by Stefani Koorey, PhD

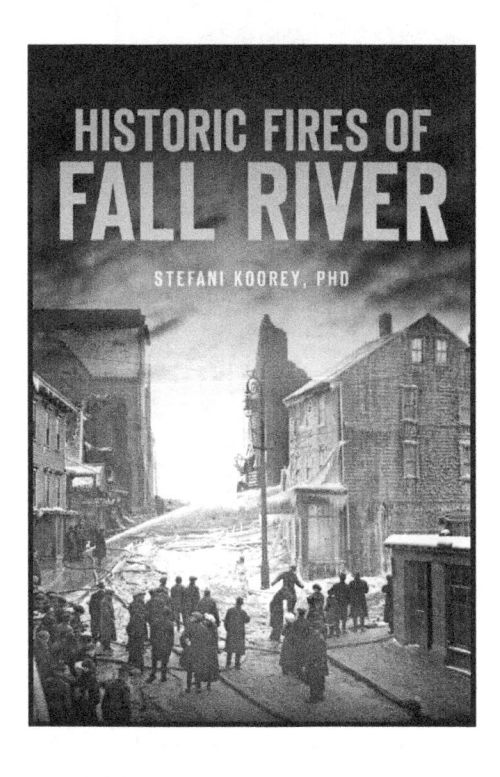

Fall River's textile boom in the nineteenth century brought with it a series of fiery disasters. The Big Fire of 1843 left more than one thousand people homeless and destroyed two hundred buildings, as well as twenty-some acres of land. After the Steiger Store Fire of 1916, mill owners pushed the city to replace horse-drawn brigades with fire engines. The intense heat from the Kerr Mill Thread Fire of 1987 melted hoses as first responders battled the blaze. Author Stefani Koorey chronicles the historic infernos of the Spindle City and celebrates the community's resilience in the face of adversity.

Available *NOW* through amazon.com / $18.96

[*advertisement*]

Fall River Revisited

by Stefani Koorey and the Fall River History Club

Founded in 1803, Fall River changed its name the following year to Troy, after a resident visiting Troy, New York, enjoyed the city. In 1834, the name was officially changed back to Fall River.

The city's motto, "We'll Try," originates from the determination of its residents to rebuild the city following a devastating fire in 1843. The fire resulted in 20 acres in the center of the village being destroyed, including 196 buildings, and 1,334 people were displaced from their homes.

Once the capital of cotton textile manufacturing in the United States, by 1910, Fall River boasted 43 corporations, 222 mills, and 3.8 million spindles, producing two miles of cloth every minute of every working day in the year. The workforce was comprised of immigrants from Ireland, England, Scotland, Canada, the Azores, and, to a lesser extent, Poland, Italy, Greece, Russia, and Lebanon.

Available **NOW**
$22.00

Made in the USA
Middletown, DE
17 September 2024